Jacob Straub

The Consolations of Science

Or Contributions from Science to the Hope of Immortality, and Kindred Themes

Jacob Straub

The Consolations of Science
Or Contributions from Science to the Hope of Immortality, and Kindred Themes

ISBN/EAN: 9783337035556

Printed in Europe, USA, Canada, Australia, Japan

Cover: Foto ©Thomas Meinert / pixelio.de

More available books at **www.hansebooks.com**

THE
CONSOLATIONS OF SCIENCE

—OR—

Contributions of Science to the Hope of Immortality
and Kindred Themes.

—BY—

JACOB STRAUB, A. M.

AUTHOR OF "PROPHECY AND PROPHETS," ETC., ETC.

WITH AN INTRODUCTION BY

HIRAM W. THOMAS, D. D.

PASTOR OF THE PEOPLE'S CHURCH, CHICAGO, ILL.

It is I, myself.—JESUS.

FOURTH EDITION.

CHICAGO:
S. W. STRAUB & CO.
1888.

GEO. DANIELS, Printer,
79 & 81 Randolph St., Chicago.

DEDICATION.

TO THE DYING AND THE BEREAVED; TO THE MINISTERS OF CONSOLATION; AND TO A SAINTLY MOTHER WHO WAS DEEPLY INTERESTED IN THESE PAGES, BUT COULD NOT TARRY FOR THEIR COMPLETION, THIS WORK IS DEDICATED BY

THE AUTHOR.

PREFACE.

A WORD with the reader is asked before he enters on the perusal of the following pages. While I have no apologies to offer for imperfections that may be found in the work, I am desirous that the benefits intended in my labors shall be realized. None will dispute that the subject treated is of the very greatest magnitude and interest,—the most difficult to properly treat, and one in respect to which there is the most intense solicitude.

My calling in life has supplied me a many-years' intimacy with the newly bereaved and the dying not alone, but with the thoughtful people not intimately in the presence of death. And it was from the voices of minds in those conditions that I was prompted to set about these labors.

It was also seen that many times where there exists the most serene confidence that *all is well*, there remain yearnings for still more definite light,—particularly from the facts of nature—from the established truths of science. In the present time, when the more capable minds are so strongly impressed with the results of science, and the necessity that every theory should be solvable by the facts of nature, while still *choosing to believe*, entire contentment in the claim of a future life would, generally, require that some form of proof from nature should sustain it. It is also to be seen that the believer, as well as the unbeliever, is represented in the demand for light from this source.

Such a disposition is, however, not to be rated as really unbelieving. Nor, in the full light of the facts, is it to be deplored. It is characterized by a happy indication. It indicates an expectance, if not of a stronger abstract belief, still of a stronger assurance, by foreseeing the added means of belief from nature's own evidence. The power of abstract belief is in many ways of great value, when not abused; and should be well cultivated. But in its import of good to man, it is not the equal of this much needed assurance of life's continuance in another and superior world.

Besides, this, also, has been a motive to the undertaking of the work: that, if successful, it would not only effect great relief and happiness to many, but would add new stimuli to moral and spiritual enterprises generally.

In setting about the work, it was foreseen, at once, that, to meet the ends in view, there were certain difficulties to be encountered; provided it should be treated affirmatively and *aggressively*, as the facts were warranting and as it required to be done. First, the facts to be employed were mainly in the biological and psychological field. And though they were familiar to readers of that class of literature, it was literature little familiar to the average reader; while to a very large class who were had in mind, the facts and their principles would be altogether new. And without procuring from them a considerable application of thought in reading, the import would, at times, fail to be apprehended.

Also, in making the application of these facts, without this previous qualification, at times effort would be required to follow the lines of evidence, on the part of those not readily inclined to the labor of close reasoning. Then, too, though the facts might be sufficiently familiar, and so, also, the processes of reasoning employed, their new application might, for a time, be to some extent confusing. But mainly in the *new application* of old facts, lies the achievement of the work.

These difficulties were constantly in mind in its execution. Language was sought with reference to its simplicity. Figures were, for the most part, left unused. And so, too, as far as practicable, of technicalities. Facts were defined and applied in the barest forms of language possible. And it is confidently believed that by the painstaking of which the subject will, by most people, be deemed worthy, the most abstruse parts of the work will be satisfactorily mastered, by quite nearly every one of ordinary education.

It is, however, impossible to make light reading of such a subject. Hence, it is not claimed for the book. None should be encouraged to find it of such a character. Only when one is willing to bestow a worthy amount of labor on a subject which involves so great an interest, should he be encouraged to set out upon the task of reading it.

Besides, it is not expected to run on as smoothly as

would a book of equal profundity which consists largely of but the repetition of often exhibited and familiar thoughts. It would be more proper to consider it as a text-book on the subject matter on which it treats, and to be frequently reviewed and referred to, than that a casual reading of it should suffice.

Preparatory to the main part of the work, there are placed several chapters on subjects not intimately relating thereto, by the following of which it was hoped the reader, not conversant with its line of thought, might be led in some measure to anticipate the principles employed and the manner of their employment; thus the more readily to follow the courses of the arguments to their proper conclusions. Also, for the sake of simplicity, but few authorities are brought in. They are such, however, as are quite universally established, and which could be conveniently referred to in any place; or, with little trouble, be procured from publishers. Many tempting references from equally good, but more obscure, authors were from this consideration set aside.

Though indirectly, in the main, the subject of a future life has been quite extensively written upon. The possibilities and probabilities as to such a state, have in this way been searched over with much care and learning; though with quite opposite results. Generally, too, little has been attempted beyond what is merely speculation. Hence, it is to be expected that, by many, the appearance of this work will be regarded with a negative interest—as but still another on the list of unsuccessful attempts to scientifically ground the hope of man's future life and immortality. It is, however, to be hoped that in such cases, in the prospect of a new method of treating the subject, there may be encouragement sufficient to cause an examination of the claims here submitted.

I am unconscious of having treated the subject in any place negatively or tentatively; but in all places positively and conclusively; from a sense of entire assurance that with an adequate exposition of the facts, their evidence of a future life not alone, but of a proper immortality, could not be disputed. Only where I have made due mention of it, have I varied from this rule. And these instances were not where the main question was under consideration; but only where the probable conditions incident to the established fact, were canvassed.

Hence, what failures may be found in making the conclusions attained legitimate, are attributable to oversight in the clear rendering of the arguments employed, and not to a want of a requisite tendency of the facts themselves. But at no stage of an investigation is all said that can and will be said. And what has in this work been imperfectly accomplished, the future, at some hands, will make more clear and strong.

The work was originally designed in two volumes. And in changing the plan, with a view to harmony with plans concerning other forthcoming works, to bring the essential matter into the limits of one, required abridging, in some places, more than I felt sure was best. It would have satisfied me better to have expanded more under some heads. But the limits were fixed over which I could not consistently pass.

In a word to friends who have, for years, been urging me to hasten its publication, I would say that it seemed to me best to make haste slowly, and to mature thoroughly a system of evidence, which, from its being so largely new to the popular mind, might be extensively misunderstood and excite much hostile criticism. I have hastened, but not at the cost of thoroughness. All needed time I freely gave to it. On the literature I bestowed less thought than on the subject matter. If in that respect I have been successful enough to leave my positions well understood, I am content.

J. STRAUB.

Chicago, Ill., 1884.

TABLE OF CONTENTS.

	PAGE
INTRODUCTION	15

CHAPTER I.
THE PURPOSE INDICATED - - - - 25

CHAPTER II.
IMMORTALITY IN HISTORY.—EVIDENCE THAT THE BELIEF IN THE EXISTENCE OF SELF IN A RATIONAL STATE BEYOND DEATH, IS AN ELEVATING INFLUENCE ON THE RACE   40

CHAPTER III.
AN IMPORTANT NEED OF THE CHURCH IS THE ABILITY TO PLACE MORE EMPHASIS ON THE FUTURE LIFE - 60

CHAPTER IV.
IMPORTANCE OF REALIZING POWERS, ESPECIALLY IN APPREHENDING THE EVIDENCES IN RELATION TO THE DOCTRINE OF IMMORTALITY - - - - - 72

CHAPTER V.
TENDENCY OF SCIENCE TO CONFIRM THE THEORY OF A STATE OF IMMORTALITY - - - - 82

CHAPTER VI.

Location of the Spiritual State.—Insensible Worlds that we Know of.—A Universal Mineral Ether   92

CHAPTER VII.

Insensible Worlds that We Know of, Continued.—The Vegetable Realm.—A Vegetable Ether Universal   108

CHAPTER VIII.

Insensible Worlds that we Know of, Continued.—The Animal Element in Nature.—Its Position Interior of the Vegetable.—Its Special Superior Forces and Prerogatives.—The Animal Ether, Etc.   127

CHAPTER IX.

Insensible Substances, Continued.—Intellect Further Considered   144

CHAPTER X.

The Moral Element and State   159

CHAPTER XI.

The Religious Element and State   180

CHAPTER XII.

Man in His Essential Self Continues Beyond the Limits of Physical Existence.—The Objections Reviewed   188

CHAPTER XIII.

MAN IN HIS ESSENTIAL SELF CONTINUES BEYOND THE LIMITS OF PHYSICAL EXISTENCE, CONTINUED.—THE ARGUMENT FOR THE AFFIRMATIVE - - - - - 228

CHAPTER XIV.

MAN'S PROPER IMMORTALITY AFFIRMED BY THE ORGANIC LAW OF HIS BEING - - - - - - 267

CHAPTER XV.

QUESTIONS RESPECTING THE RELATION OF THE TWO WORLDS.—THE LAWS AND MODES OF MENTAL INTERCOURSE, OR THE TRANSMISSION OF THOUGHT - 292

CHAPTER XVI.

QUESTIONS CONCERNING THE RELATION OF THE TWO WORLDS, CONTINUED.—DIFFICULTIES NECESSARILY ATTENDING THE TRANSMISSION OF THOUGHT.—THEY BECOME MORE FORMIDABLE BETWEEN RESIDENTS OF THE TWO WORLDS 817

CHAPTER XVII.

QUESTIONS RESPECTING THE RELATIONS OF THE TWO WORLDS, CONTINUED.—FACTS ESTABLISHING THE POSSIBILITY OF INTERCOURSE BETWEEN MINDS IN THE FLESH AND THOSE BEYOND.—CONDITIONS OF LUCID INTERCOURSE EXTREMELY RARE.—SPECIAL DEVICES FOR THE ATTAINMENT OF INTERCOURSE IMPRACTICABLE AND DANGEROUS TO MIND AND MORALS - - - - - 839

CHAPTER XVIII.

CONSIDERATIONS OF THE CLAIMS OF INTERCOURSE BETWEEN THE TWO WORLDS.—THE PROBABLE AND THE IMPROBABLE.—ITS APPEARANCE IN THE BIBLE, ETC. - - - 368

CHAPTER XIX.

APPROXIMATE ANALYSIS OF REAL LIFE IN THE LAND IMMORTAL.- CHANGES THAT ARE POSSIBLE; THAT ARE PROBABLE; THAT ARE IMPROBABLE; THAT ARE IMPOSSIBLE.—BODILY STATE AND ADVANTAGES.—DEATH AND "OLD AGE" ABOLISHED.—PALPABLE SURROUNDINGS.—RECOGNITIONS, REUNIONS AND COMPANIONSHIPS.—EDUCATION AND WORSHIP - 392

CHAPTER XX.

CONCLUDING REFLECTIONS AND PARTING WORDS - 428

INTRODUCTION.

THERE have been periods when the world held more of the angry spirit of controversy—when the war of words was more common; but there was, perhaps, never a time when so much deep and honest thought was given to the great questions of religion, and when the people were so willing, and even anxious to know the truth, as now. And it may be noted that, as the love of truth is coming to possess the public mind, and as mankind are studying these questions with a broader intelligence and a clearer realization of their relative place and importance, the lines of debate are narrowing down to a few vital points. It is no longer possible in any intelligent community to awaken much interest over such questions as the cut of a gown, or the mode of baptism, or the use of instrumental music in a church. Such debates can have only a local or party interest. Nor does the public mind care much about many of the non-essential isms that divide the Protestant churches, nor those even that are peculiar to the Catholic church.

And why these changes? It is because men of broader minds are coming to see that in the practical work of religion we are all aiming at the same thing; and that whilst some methods may be more efficient than others, the important thing is that the work be done. And in the domain of thought, or looking at religion as a system of doctrines, it is seen that the whole issue turns upon a few vital points, and that if these be clearly established, the foundations are secure; but if these be lost, or be not accepted by faith and reason, then all is lost and there is nothing left about which serious thinkers care to argue.

First among these vital questions—first in the order of reason, and fundamental to the others, is that of Theism—Is there a God? Is there such a thing as Spirit? Does Spirit, Intelligence, Reason, lie back of matter, informing and controlling its phenomena, or is what we call intelligence or reason a result of physical laws? Is mind as it appears in man but the last product of physical organism, or is the mind a something in itself; an entity that gathers about itself a living body? And second, and closely related to the question of Theism, is that of man's continued life beyond what we call death. Does he live on beyond this change in which the body goes back to dust? And it will be seen that the one question depends very largely upon the other. If mind and reason begin in matter, and result from it and this matter that has evolved mind, itself die, and go back to its inorganic state, why should not mind also be dissolved? But if mind be first, if spirit have in itself a life of its own, and have simply dwelt in matter as a house, then why may it not survive? And if it be accepted and proved that there is this finer world of spirit, and that man's real being is cast and conditioned in that world and that both man and his world shall last forever, then arises the question of final cause, or for what is such an existence intended, and how should such a life be lived? And here come in the great questions of righteousness, of duty, and related to these are questions of the ethical character of God, and as to what help through inspiration and the vicariousness of love is offered to man in such a life as this, and what is to be the final destiny of the race.

And thus we can see the real questions of thought centering at last about a few vital points. And it may be noted again, that certain modifying influences have come in to change both the spirit and the ground of the debates.

The earlier and the middle ages, or the ages of faith, affirmed largely and without any hesitancy or misgiving as to the certainty of what they taught. They could define the Trinity, and map out the exact location and limits of heaven and hell. But it came to be known after while that these teachers knew very little of the present nature of man and of the world in which he lived, and as this ignorance of things near at hand became more and more apparent, there arose a suspicion and a distrust of what had been taught about God, and the soul, and the future. And it was only natural that under these circumstances men should begin the work of actual investigation in the study of themselves and of their present world; and as a result of these studies the nature and the mystery of man himself, and to himself, have so widened and deepened, and the world and the universe have so enlarged that mankind now stand amazed and almost overpowered before the revelations of their own discoveries. This, together with the natural reaction from a once too large and easy faith, has brought about a state of thought where many do not care to either affirm nor yet to deny, but say, "We do not know." And men who are not agnostics are so influenced by this larger vision of themselves and the universe that there is more of the true modesty of faith and less of that offensive dogmatism that was once intolerant even of a question, and looked upon honest doubt as a sin; and there seems also to be more of the teachable spirit, and the desire to learn.

The attention of mankind having been called to the material side of things, and their studies of nature having led to such marvelous results, it was not strange that the great questions of religion that had before been largely metaphysical should come over to the material. When chemistry had traced nature back to simple elements, and astronomy had resolved planets and suns into a great order and bound all worlds fast in the law of gravity, it was natural that men should ask, What evidence of God have we found here? What evidence of a spiritual nature in man? In other words, it was natural that they should try to make a science of religion, as well as of nature. And it is just here that the struggle is going on now; and here it is likely to continue for years to come. And it is just at this point that Mr. Straub enters the field with his able and timely work on "The Consolations of Science."

INTRODUCTION.   12

Many have feared that the results of science would be, not only to unsettle the public mind, but to leave the world with less faith in the great central doctrines of religion. As we have seen, as mankind began to look at the larger facts and questions of the universe, the lesser questions—the little side issues of party, began to drop out of sight. But the great questions remain. They will not drop out of sight, nor can thoughtful minds lightly turn from them. Nor can they be taken out of the hands of science and passed back again to the church where they once were. Religion has become a matter of the people; the scientific men of our time are the thinking men. Science having done so much to clear up other mysteries and to lighten the burdens of labor, naturally has the ear and the sympathy of the people. Moreover, it is felt that all truth should be in harmony—that God's two great revelations, the Bible and nature, should teach the same things.

Men of large thought and faith and who have really believed in the truths of revelation, have at no time doubted that all of this sublime study of the natural—this apparent going into bondage to the material, and for the time seeing nothing else, would at the last bring the mind to a clearer realization of the divine. They have believed that this everywhere presence of law, that at first seemed to push back the thought and the necessity of a God—to account for the phenomena of the universe without God, would at last reveal the immanency of his presence, not outside of nature and law, but inside; and thus the fact of the divine be felt and confessed by all. And minds thus illumined have felt all the time that as another result, man himself, instead of dwindling almost into nothingness in comparison to the immensity of things about him, would rise to the higher conception of himself, not as a handful of vitalized dust, but as a life, a spirit, dwelling now in the flesh, but having his real being in the unseen world of truths and principles and moral affections, and hence related to the divine and the imperishable; in his real self, or in the essence of his being, immortal.

So deeply is our author imbued with this faith and feeling that he maintains that all the deeper lines of scientific thought, and of the discoveries made, point in this direction, and are even now far on the way to make the conclusion, if not irresistible, at least so reasonable as not to be doubted; and he predicts a near time when the fact of a continued life beyond death shall be so realized that all shall walk in the light and ecstasy of an assured immortality, and of personal identity, and the sweet companionship of dear ones forever.

The patiently arranged facts, and the careful inductions by which these conclusions are reached, must be found in Mr. Straub's own words; but we may say that the appearance of such a work is just now most opportune. Many minds are doubting; many are asking for more than the words of the Bible; many are fearing that science is working the destruction of faith. At such a time this patient thinker and scholar comes along to tell us of "The Consolations of Science;" that real science is not the enemy of real Christian faith, but the friend;

and is opening wider the doors that lead into the "Holy of Holies," to Spirit and God; that there is an "unseen universe" lying over against and within that which is visible and apparent to the senses. The outer, the visible, is in a state of constant whirl and change; it may be resolved back into its original elements, or dissipated in inpalpable gases; but the universe of life and principles in which man finds his consciousness, his freedom, his real self-hood, is not and cannot be affected by any of these outer changes. Man may sum up in himself all there is of nature below him; but this is not his full measure; he is more; he is a spirit; he has a moral nature; he has the "free-will" that Mr. Darwin admits is "a mystery insoluble to the naturalist." And thus man, though a part of nature, and with a body conditioned in natural laws, has a something beyond this, and hence he may give back his body to the earth and yet himself live on in his finer, his real world of spirit.

And thus, in the light of evolution, the argument for immortality seems to gather strength; for somehow in the long way man has picked up, or come to possess, and to be, a something more than matter. He has attained to liberty, to self-hood, to a moral nature; to a life conditioned in truths and principles that are necessarily imperishable; and having reached this, why not from this deeper rooting in the very essence of things, continue to live on forever?

There is one phase or postulate, however, of the doctrine of evolution, that in the present form of the doctrine, seems to conflict with the Christian idea of immortality, and that is the doctrine of the "survival of the strongest." There is a school of theologians who teach a "conditional immortality;" or that man is not immortal in the essence of his being, but may attain immortality through virtue; and that failing of this, he naturally falls back into non-existence; and with this view the "survival of the strongest" seems to be in perfect accord. But this is not Christianity. Christianity is essentially beneficent. Its very genius places it on the side of the weak, and carries it over into the land of shadows and death to save the perishing. It gathers, not the strong and the well who "need not a physician," but goes to the sick and the dying. It is a gospel to the blind, and the deaf, and the imprisoned; and under its gentle touch even the "bruised reed shall not be broken." Christianity teaches that man is a child of God; that in his very essence he is the "offspring" of God; and that God's greatest care and love go out for the lowest, the worst, the lost, the dead.

But, admitting the theory of a Theistic evolution as a method or process in the great order of things, it may favor, and even illustrate the fact that only goodness can survive, that evil is a passing phase in the experience and training of souls whilst in the body, and that the spirit in its onward march shall cast off these earthly conditions and rise into the higher perfection of the life celestial. This view holds to all that is tenderest and dearest in the genius of Christianity in saving the weakest and the most imperfect; but it saves and develops only the good, and transcends and casts off the bad; and hence looks to the ultimate perfection and the final harmony of the moral universe, and not to the old and offensive doctrine of the permanence and perpetuity of evil and suffering forever. The moral judgment of mankind is not offended at the presence of evil and suffering in the process of development, or in the experience of men, and in the evolution of the good, but any theory that makes evil and suffering appear not only in the process, but in the last result, makes a Theodicy impossible; it leaves the works of God not only unfinished, but unfinishable. It leaves the moral order not only imperfect, but deformed; and hence it leaves to faith but an imperfect God—a God that is not the best; and hence is not God at all. But this view, notwithstanding the powerful and persistent efforts that are made to force it upon the unwilling faith of the age, is fast loosing its hold as a vital belief. Indeed, it has ceased to have much weight with the great mass of thinkers.

It seems then that science is to add her testimony to the Bible in affirming the great truth of the immortality of the race; not only of the individual but of all; and hence the immortality of society; the conscious pursuit and joy of friendship, of truth, of love, forever. And this, with the thought that evil shall end and suffering cease, opens up a future that should give mankind strength and resignation and hope amidst the trials and sorrows of "this present evil world."

It is evident that if immortality be not a fact, the fact can never be proved; nor can it ever be known. We cannot stand on this side of death and certainly affirm that the soul does not live on; and if each one at death should cease to be, no voice can ever reach us from the land of nothingness to tell us there is no future; nor shall we know that we ever had a past; that we ever were. The argument then, and the facts, so far as argument and facts can go, must be on one side; and that is the side of life. Life is. Why should it cease to be? Life is a fact—a persistent energy, making possible and holding all there is in thought, in beauty, in love, in joy. Death is a nonentity, a nothing; or only a passing phase, or an appearance. Death has no God, for " God is not the God of the dead, but of the living "—of life, and hence, in the world of the real there is no death.

H. W. Thomas.

CHAPTER I.

THE PURPOSE INDICATED.

A THOROUGH realization of the continuance of the self of man with all the essential parts of his being beyond death, could hardly fail to produce a beneficial change in the habit of human thought, and consequently in human conduct. Hence, to establish such a realization in the minds of the people is one of the most pressing needs of the age. Especially were such a sentiment beneficial if it included the facts that the social dependencies of mankind are not changed in the change of worlds, and that the consequences of right and wrong doing in this life are necessarily met with in the life beyond.

The prevailing realization as to life is such as to limit it wholly to this visible state. All that there is for man to do and to be, is, practically, with reference to temporal life only. Hence, in a general way, life is little influenced by any of the strong and generous impulses which the consciousness of a responsible after-death existence would call forth. Notwithstanding that there is commonly some impression that something of self continues in the great hereafter—a common expectance and hope of immortality—the impression lacks realness; and hence the impulses derived from it are in the main weak and ineffectual. And, on the other hand, the overwhelming sense of this world—the unqualified realization of these visible surroundings, tending with the average mind to impress this as the whole of human existence—chiefly influences the plannings and policies of action among mankind, who are so largely predisposed to overreaching selfishness.

Looking about upon the world we are living in, and seeing its large adaptation to human happiness, with abundance to supply every need, we may well be astonished to see so much suffering, even in communities of superior intelligence—so much solicitous hard straining, on the part of many good people, to make the ends meet in the matter of an adequate living. And this suggests the questions: Is human effort rightly directed? Is there not an oversight of some greatly important principle of action to which this suffering and this all-absorbing solicitude may be due? Instead of co-operative effort, is there not a conflict of interest, leading to mutual aggression? Is it not too common that the success of one is dependent on the corresponding failure of another? Are the struggles for subsistence not more struggles one with another, than with the resources of nature?

It will be conceded that the means of subsistence and of enjoyment are too little sought in the resources of nature or in the equitable development of a common interest, and too much by appropriating from the rightful possessions of fellow beings. The exchange of commodities from hand to hand, as in the commercial world, is itself one means of producing from nature, and is indispensable to the common good. It serves to convey substance to all the parts and members of the common body of the race, as by the nutritive circulation of the animal body all its functions are ministered to. And also by it there is conveyed some of the needed fraternal feeling throughout the great brotherhood. But too commonly by a short-sighted disregard for the rights of others, the beautiful equity of this system is impaired by diverting what belongs to one, to the title and uses of another, breeding discord and distress to the extent the wrong is indulged.

There is no injustice in according a larger return to the one who achieves more, either by muscle or by brain; it is rightfully due to him. But this must not be from the possessions of others, without an equivalent. Enterprise and genius must not enlarge themselves in this way, or beware of penalties to be paid somewhere!

But so common is the disposition to this kind of sharp bargaining—this "shrewd-business-man" kind of operation—that little objection is raised to it. What the rich autocrat thus is doing, the penniless underling would do. The want of recognizing this injustice is not the mistake of a few nor a class. It is rather a characteristic error of the age, and to be corrected by the introduction of new principles concerning life,—by a reform in popular thought that will bring people from even selfish motives to seek the good of others.

And what thought, brought into common favor, would be better calculated to abolish this oppression in the social body than that which would take in the life beyond the grave as a reality, and that generally one is followed there by the companions of this life, and that the deserts of this life will continue in some measure to affect the soul's happiness in the next?

Then, again, in times of general business depression, accompanied by more than the usual business disasters, there is complaining of want of integrity among men in business relations. And among the diversity of opinions as to the cause, there seems to be one theory quite commonly accepted, which is, this same selfishness. And this might solve the whole problem concerning the evil, if we were content with the immediate cause only, and cared not to understand the remoter cause, which must be remedied before we cease to have trouble of this kind. From a general relaxation of the too rigid intolerance toward the liberties of the people an extreme is attained. Instead of holding restraint upon others too tightly, it has come to be the disposition to let go too much—to care too little for the deportment of others. From a too narrow view to conserve but the interest of self, too little has been the disposition to care for the proper growth of the moral sense in others.

A large part of the world has been affected by a formative period of this kind; partly as the result of certain humane reforms that were persistently urged on by a school of strong agitators. And so great is this change, that whereas a quarter of a century ago, in this country, slavery was commonly approved, now even former slaveholders express themselves opposed to it.

And in respect to religious tolerance the change is quite as great. A quarter of a century ago, to be out of the line of established orthodoxy was to peril one's soul; now, where there is enough religion to admit of belief that one has a soul, it is considered of trifling importance whether he worships by orthodoxy or heterodoxy, or even worships at all.

The growth of liberality has been surprising; but, outside of special friendships, the attainment made has been more to an indifference than to a proper liberality. The large tolerance of our times is to a great extent merely an indifference toward others. And if there is little ill will in it there is likewise little positive good will. Practically, it is that there is little choice at all in the fare of the unaffiliated neighbor. Much of this liberality takes the bad shape of a mere willingness that others may do quite as they please, so long as one himself is undisturbed and thriving in his own inclinations; largely ignoring that invaluable spirit of mutual help among mankind, pertaining to all classes of necessities and uses. Such is not to be confounded with true liberality which consists in sacrificing for the good of others—contributing aid to them in achieving success in all the interests of life.

This formative period will, however, not pass without leaving many good results—substantial gains over the past. Yet the reaction which is to be feared, and which is even now expressing itself in these laments of bad faith in business and social relations, is likely to chill this large tolerance and carry a large part of popular sentiment back again far toward the extreme from whence it was wrested. Only the timely acceptance of a sentiment of liberality on a basis of universal co-operation of the members of the race to elevate each other's lives, and so the common life of society, can avail to reap any very large gain from the crisis.

The love of possession is not wrong. The gratification of self, the establishment of self interest, the acquisition of estates and pleasant surroundings, the subjugation and culture of wild nature, rendering it more beautiful and useful, are in harmony with the highest sense of right. And when one pursues these ends in the spirit of a common interest with his fellows, he brings himself into happy accord with the Deity, and achieves for himself an essential good. Only the tendency to overreach, and trespass on the rights of another, to divert from his possessions to his own, to refuse him co-operative sympathy, can convert the disposition to acquire into wrong.

Whatever other conditions may be found essential to man's real happiness, the well-being of his fellow man, the inspiring influence of his love, gratitude and appreciation, as well as temporal aid from him, is positively indispensable in all places and states of his being. God's chief blessing to man is his fellow man. In him he has the essential external help in the development and utilization of his possessions. Sharing the world with an innumerable family of brothers and sisters—making it to be the common estate of the Great Father for his earthly household, makes the few acres that fall to his lot infinitely more valuable to him than were the title of continents and seas outstretched over the whole face of nature, without the companionship and co-operation of his fellows. The sense of value in it at all would be expelled from it by the expulsion of those by whose appreciation of it, mainly, he gathers the idea of its worth.

TEMPORAL AID NOT ALL THAT IS NEEDED.

Yet the smallest part of the value of this companionship consists in the manifold material aid that is realized thereby. Man lives not by bread alone. He has a nature with wonderful endowments of thought and feeling, requiring appropriate supplies. And these unsupplied would presently leave him an object of misery and imbecility. These supplies are to a large extent the result of reciprocity between the beings who possess these attributes of life in common. There is an influence from the thought and feeling of a fellow being upon which one who has thought and feeling of his own depends for the increase and enjoyment of these parts of his nature. They yield satisfaction only by exchanging with others. What does a fountain yield into which nothing flows,—that has no receptacle into which to flow? The waters themselves would stagnate and die. And what were thoughts and affections to us without intelligent and affectionate objects unto whom to transfer them? It is readily recalled that the mind that is shut up, having to retain its ideas in itself for want of a companion unto whom to impart them, presently becomes unproductive; and, in like manner, the loving sensibilities. And the same results follow when not thus ministered to by others.

The intelligent and refined at once feel the loss keenly when placed in social surroundings that neither receive nor impart upon the grade of their own attainments; and to be permitted to resume proper relations, a festivity of soul takes place which is as gratifying and refreshing to its nature as is physical nourishment to the hungry body.

From every point of view the law is verified that an individual life, abstracted from all associations of its kind, is greatly impoverished and incapable of rising, or even of continued subsistence; and that to himself no less than to others man owes it to seek the competence and accomplishment of his fellow man. Man is ever the chief factor of man's happiness, and to bless his own existence rightly and fully, every transaction, commercially and socially, he must make with consideration of its effect on the welfare of others as well as on his own. Even from the lowest type he may not withhold, with impunity, the aid that would augment happiness and usefulness. Every character of his association has a weight, the influence of which, however remotely, affects his own condition.

But as in the relation of human lives to each other lies the chief interest to human existence, and, under the Deity, the main power of human elevation, to the abuses of that relation must also be charged the bulk of human misery. And in fact there it is found. The disturbing cause of the major part of human distress is not in the Creator, nor in the world man lives in, but principally in the blindness or infirmity by which, in the eagerness to supply his wants, he is misled into trespassing on the domain of others. The light of a true life and of a true immortality has not yet risen upon his understanding, and in this most disastrous ignorance, he has too commonly made the prey upon others the field of his enterprise, and sought his advancement in the depression, instead of the elevation, of his neighbor.

The evil has, in general terms, been pointed out, and by a large number recognized, and the Christianization of the world has been uniformly indicated as the only remedy. And truly the Christian life is the point to be attained. But in Christianizing, special motives are commonly appealed to. The bare word of duty to the sleeping or the dead is insufficient. The history of mankind uniformly teaches that the reforms of life come about by first introducing reforms in the mode of thought; directing the aspirations to the objects corresponding with the change contemplated.

One prominent adjunct to reform has been civil legislation put into the hands of a judiciary and executive. There has not been much lack of good laws; especially when they have come from the representatives of the people; but, however intelligently devised, equal genius has usually foiled them, by the evil disposed. Good people have little need of legal restraints, while the bad usually manage to live in disregard of them. The needed reform is not given into the hands of the legislator, nor the executive, but to him who is able to institute the requisite new order of thought. He is the first to elevate the lives of the people who will first elevate their thoughts and direct their aspirations toward ends that come within the provisions of that universal equity born of the consideration of man's immortal unity with man and with God.

It may also be questioned whether the Christian Church of to-day is bringing to bear all the motives in its Christianizing work that were employed by the Apostolic Church. Man is not fully appealed to when his endless existence, with a never-ceasing responsibility for the deeds of life, is not also appealed to. He is not fully appealed to when the great outlying future of his life beyond death is not made to duly appear, wherein his brother is his companion still, bearing witness of the right and the wrong received at his hands. Being appealed to in the wholeness of his appointed duration and responsibilities, the restricted, selfish policies of this life may soon become too mean for his taste. And his energetic ambition may be set to achieving the greater ends of life—the enriching of mankind in intelligence, and the love of purity and equity. His positive interest to have them so, would be a power to overcome his disinclination to work in the vineyard of souls, to which ordinary entreaties are without avail.

By this view of life, in which the good of the whole is seen to be a necessity to self, while it may not be out of a brother's love for a brother, yet a brother's behavior toward a brother will be attained. And more: would it not be the disposition, under the realization of this state of social unity, presently to look about for the means to realize also that bond of love which is the chief basis of this unity of life and interest of man in man? Assured of its existence and of the superior happiness its realization would confer, would not even the selfish seek to realize it? Would not the masses be largely influenced to that end—accepting gladly the hand that would lead the way to this great good? What but this same Gospel principle of a fellow love, brought to a realization, was it that so strongly attached the poor to Jesus, to follow him and partake of his words of soothing friendship with gladness?

During late years much has been said of the universal brotherhood, and the largest part of our progress is due to the efficiency with which many pulpits, rostrums, books and journals have forced this sentiment upon public notice. But its intellectual recognition is far more extensive than its realization. As a philosophy, it is very commonly accepted, while as a rule of life it extends to but few. And the question is: Why? The answer may be implied in another question: Is the term "brotherhood" rightly understood? Brothers by a common human blood are sometimes aliens at heart, and as readily sacrificed on the altar of greed as is an ox on the shambles.

We have not the full meaning of the brotherhood of man, when we limit life's duration to this visible world, and its sphere of mutual interest to commercial business transactions, however large a good may be realized under these conditions. The life and the brotherhood must be seen to continue independently of the death of the body, and the mutual obligation to include all spiritual aids.

If man's existence is seen to terminate at death, it is not bad reasoning—certainly not improbable reasoning, from the basis of the average attainment in human nature, to conclude that he who will have had the advantage till then, will have had a real gain—will have best served his own interest. Such might well plead: What could it matter to one that he had wronged his brother, if he should have no existence before the time should come at which he would be sensible of the injury that the wrong had been to himself? All the past is dropped into absolute oblivion at the end of conscious existence; and to the one that has passed that point there is no past and has not been. What once was, to him who is not, was not. Only to such as have adequate conscious existence is there a past—has anything transpired. That these conclusions should follow, then, from an unbelief in a proper hereafter, determining man's state to be so indistinguishable from that considered of the common brute, and thus justifying him in a conduct so much like that of the brute, might not appear strange or surprising to such as have prepared themselves therefor by suitable consideration of what such unbelief, if common and natural to mankind, would result in, or would have resulted in.

That the native humanities in man are under all conditions of humanizing tendencies, is plain enough; but these, it will be remembered, always await proper mental stimuli, and what large generosities are to be found among unbelievers must owe their origin to mental stimuli of requisite insight or belief at sometime having occurred to ancestry. But, always unknown to himself, in its fullness, man is measurably conscious of his immortality, and the great ideas and generous impulses incident to its awakening power and tendency, to some extent, have followed and determined the better sentiments of his heart. And is it then not apparent that the spirit of injury and overreaching has more of its own way by whatever measure of unbelief in a common, mutually-responsible life hereafter, exists?

The thoughts of such an immense future, characterized in that way, are necessarily deterring to the evil, as well as elevating to the good, sentiments of life.

It is not too much to say, then, that the change in the habit of thought most needed at the present time, is that to which the dissemination of right views of immortality would lead,—that as true as the coming tomorrow in which are the consequences of to-day, comes the day beyond the nightfall of death to find us still there and in the society and life claims of our neighbors, however different from this in material and aspect that state may be.

To see himself identified with a life extending independently of the flesh into the state or states beyond, there to recognize his full self-hood and to some extent, at least, the sensitive companionship of those who were on earth associated with him in society, is what no one can do and continue his interest in an exclusive selfishness or in any callings that work disadvantageously to present society. Setting aside the just apprehension of a deeper consciousness of the equitable awards of his Maker, and the remembrance that others may have of the good and the bad of his previous life, the ever-present thought of that great outspreading life beyond the grave, with its inflowings into the soul from those new and near spiritual surroundings of enchanting sceneries, holy lives, and divine instructors, also would tend to speedily expel from him all low desires,—separating the pure, generous humanity from the base elements of rudimental existence.

And to the achievement of this much needed mental reform, it is important that science make the great contribution that with an insuppressible tendency at every point it seems ready to make. Never was there more conceded from science to immortality than now. Every law in physical nature, relating thereto, that has been unraveled, is found to be a clue leading beyond the threshold of the spiritual. And the time may well be considered as quite near at hand when the lines of established science, by the conceded rules of knowledge, will be so fully and plainly carried out as that the immortal land will be as confidently regarded as is a neighboring continent by the one not having personally resided thereon. The event of this realization is justly to be regarded as the main great crisis in the mundane great history of the race; not because it shall be the period of the greatest mental maturity but because of its being the accession of the most directly elevating motives to life,—the occasion when the social body of life will be put in the most direct pursuit of its highest ends—to make of this world and all worlds the very best for all.

CHAPTER II.

IMMORTALITY IN HISTORY. EVIDENCE THAT THE BELIEF IN THE EXISTENCE OF SELF IN A RATIONAL STATE BEYOND DEATH, IS AN ELEVATING INFLUENCE ON THE RACE.

THE influence of the doctrine of the proper future life of man, on the progress of mankind, has but few, though important, illustrations in history. Prior to the enunciation of Christianity, there were very few clear ideas on the subject popularly entertained. While a few of the most gifted, spiritually and intellectually, apprehended somewhat clearly the true nature of the state, the masses had not attained to the maturity in which alone the appreciation of it becomes possible. In view of the law of growth that applies to the aggregate race of man the same as it does to the individual, it is not reasonable to expect to find in the early history thereof, commonly pervading it, the high order of thought properly belonging to a later period, and which is better suited to subjects of such a character.

In the natural history of man, more than in the records he has written of himself, is to be seen the grade of thought and the class of ideas which were evolved from his primitive life. Although this theory will hardly provide for the extraordinary individuals that at times are seen to have risen in life and thought far above the surrounding level, by whose capacities the Superintending Life above erected standards of principles for the lives below to ascend upon as fast as mental and moral vitality were attainable.

Only in instances of exceptionally early maturity, does the sentiment of immortality manifest itself as strongly in youth as in middle life; and there not as strongly as in well-preserved old age, where, with a good physical condition, the higher order of faculties begin to rise into supremacy, and the more far-reaching conceptions gather in the principles of faith and philosophy that extend beyond the restrictions of this life into the life beyond. So, likewise, in the earlier and more physical states of the race, we would expect to find generally a smaller development of spiritual sense, and to see it both weaker in its impression upon life and less perfectly apprehending principles of such a nature.

In the great antiquity, back of historic times, it is difficult to find what were the particular thoughts of the people on the great problem of the future state. That our remote ancestry of those times thought upon it, is plain enough every way, but what form their speculations took in detail, we have not the means to determine. The intellectual world is seen to have been quite stationary during many centuries from the time history was first written, and it is but reasonable to suppose that during as many centuries next preceding, the doctrines of future life were quite the same as at the time they began to be put on record; and we would expect to find them all the time growing less defined while following the course of time backward.

ERAS OF SPECIAL ATTAINMENTS.

However, evidences are being noted of there being periodicity in the course of the development of the race,—that there are intellectual and inspirational eras, —that with a sort of tidal action, at times intelligence, or some form of it, fluctuates above its natural level; so that we have come to speak of an age of historians, an age of poets, an age of science, and so on. And that inspirational periods are of like occurrence would naturally follow. And from this, taken with the fact that a basic sameness in the original religions is from nearly all standpoints now being seen, belief is obtaining with some of the best philologists (who are best qualified to determine), that all present forms of religion originated in one inspirational era, in a time perhaps deeply buried in the unknown past. However, investigation has not gone far enough to do away with a difference of opinion as to this.

But while there is no uniformity of conclusion in detail as to how the future life was regarded by the adherents of the great religions in the limits of the historic period, setting aside extremists, whose special claims may not be considered in the limits of this brief chapter, the teachings may be classified into immortality proper, apotheosis and metempsychosis. But neither, purely so. They were more or less confounded with each other; showing unsettled thought on the subject.

In the great divisions of Egypt and India, metempsychosis—the transmigration of the soul—was the universally accepted belief. In Chaldea, the sentiment of future life was weak, but there is no clear proof of transmigration having found favor with them, beyond a few slight innovations. The Chaldean mind fluctuated between a proper immortality and a deification of at least mortals of note.

The worship of the heavenly bodies as the abode of spirits, which also is seen to have been originally practiced in Egypt and India, prevailed to the last with the Chaldeans. These spirits were graded as the heavenly bodies themselves were—from omnipotence, as typified by the sun, down to capacities little above the grade of mortals, as typified by diminutive stars. Out of this doctrine grew the doctrine of apotheosis (the translation of mortals into demigods and gods), probably near the time that the doctrine of transmigration took its origin. Both doctrines became enlarged into disgusting details, in later years. About the time that it began to be believed that Bel, or Baal, the spirit of the sun, was an earthly prince translated into the heavens to become the spirit of the monarch of the day, gods, heroes and men began to be identified with the forms of the lower animals.

Believing that a human soul, distinguished among his kind, might rise to the eminence of the gods in the heavens, would be a natural starting point for the inquiry, What, then, becomes of the souls of the rest of mankind? And it is among this class of believers that we find the first approach toward proper conceptions of immortality.

Among the Chaldeans, in the Hebrew branch, we find the first account of spiritual beings,—angels,—seen in human form. As to where was their place and what was their form, when disappearing from human view, they seem to have had nothing more definite than the viewless air in its upper regions—toward or among the stars, in ethereal abodes, perhaps well enough suited to continue the general human shape. That these angels were believed to be the souls of ordinary mortals, is not probable, though their relation with mortals, and perhaps also their mortal origin, was fully believed. But that the souls of common mankind remained in more humble locations, near the earth or in some mystical region under the earth, would be in harmony with the opinion of the average Hebrew, from the time of Abraham to the carrying away in the Chaldean captivity.

The writer of Genesis represents the patriarchs as being at death gathered to their people (xxv: 8; xxxv: 29; xlix: 33), though the burial place of Abraham was far from that of his fathers. The writer of the First Book of Kings, with a change in the form of language, represents essentially the same thought in reference to the death of David and Solomon, many years later. They slept with their fathers (ii: 10; xi: 43), though David's burial was not with his fathers. This return to their people, which was a hope with them for centuries at least, extending back to the days of Abraham, who probably in faith differed little from his fathers, was more than the commingling of bodily dust. It was a union of the self of one with the selves of the others, whatever the bodily appointments might have been expected to be. Jacob expected to go down to the grave (*sheol*—state of the departed) unto his son (Gen. xxxvii: 35), whom he believed to have been devoured by wild beasts. David, in like faith, dried his tears in the expectation of some day going to his dearly beloved child (II Sam. xii: 23).

While little specific reference to a future life is made in the Old Testament Scriptures, the omission may be quite easily accounted for on the supposition that their view of it, such as it was, was so well known as not to need rehearsing. In our thoughtful day, who, in writing a history of the State or of the Church, would think to insert, extensively, our speculations of future life? It is only in the history of a dogma that systematic statements thereof are likely to occur.

While, as already observed, in ancient Chaldea, the mother of Jewry, the sentiment of the future life was weak, yet in Jewry it had gained strength,—whether much more of clearness or not. Where we find abundant references to the angel of the Lord, and the angels of the Lord, in places where spiritual beings alone could be referred to, and where necromancy, all about, was sufficiently credited as a reality to warrant Saul, by means of it, to evoke the spirit of Samuel (I Samuel xxviii: 10), the sentiment of a future existence was evidently strong enough to materially modify the habits of the people.

The most perfect form of the doctrine, then, at the time extant, we find to have been in the minds of this people. Though the doctrine of transmigration was strong in Egypt, and they were in close contact with that people for a score of centuries, and until a short time before our era, they imbibed little of it.

They may not have believed in the endless continuance of the human soul, but so long as it existed it was its own human self, and was never transformed into a brute, nor reinvolved in flesh of any kind, after its departure from the present embodiment. And, upon the whole, their belief in respect to future life was a stimulant to the higher part of their nature, a fact comporting well with their general superiority as a people.

RELATIVE VALUE OF THE SEVERAL VIEWS OF FUTURE LIFE.

To expect a continuance of life in a state beyond death, though with many distortions of ignorance and perverted passion characterizing the thought, is a strong incentive to the mind, and probably in all cases some advantage to life. To live at all, is a thought of grave influence; but to what extent beyond the moderation of passion affected by it, the doctrine of transmigration may stimulate to any good, is not plain. What one's sensibilities would be when transferred into an ox, crocodile, serpent or insect, could not be very definitely imagined, but there is little doubt that the prospect would be depressing to all that self appreciation so necessary to progress.

One might have the assurance of being personally

exempt from such a fate, but, while believing in it, would necessarily be affected by contemplating it in his surroundings. The melancholy state of the unfortunates moving about him in lower animal forms, would impress him correspondingly. These horrid tombs of gross flesh, incarcerating loved ones, would imprison his own life in overpowering gloom under which no aspirations toward proper attainments could form. For fear of like consequences he would hardly dare to descend into what he would regard as vice, but with the incubus of that spectacle of misery ever bearing down on him, he could not well rise to the use of the finer sentiments that characterize the greater and happier people of the world. History corroborates this view of the case. Where those religious principles have held sway, the cloud of mental night has hung. And ages of time have wrought no perceptible improvement. They have long years ago attained to all that their religion can do for man. The soul of a people cannot rise above the provisions of its religion.

Greece is supposed to have been the oldest of European nations of civilized attainments, and for wealth of intellect, from the time of Homer to Aristotle, was unsurpassed by any nation in the world. The religion of that great people was a wonderful mixture from Asia, Egypt, and primitive European tribes. In the main they were very tolerant; and by the intellectual center they constituted, readily drew to themselves the more rational types of the several great religions. But their fine poetic nature expanded their religious thought into an indefinable tissue of myth. They believed in transmigration, with some modification by the doctrine of apotheosis, which was prevalent with the native barbarian Greeks, and added to by colonization from Asia, perhaps Phœnicia. The element of transmigration, together with their mystic ceremonies, was brought from Egypt. These two main doctrines of immortality, apotheosis and transmigration, brought together in the great mind of the Greek, resulted in something far different from, and superior to, either, as previously known.

The early superiority of the Greeks, however, may have been as much due to a favorable mixture of races as to anything that their yet incomplete religion could have done for them. But proper sentiments of religion can lead to high attainments beyond all other motives. It is, then, the most exalted, and therefore the most exalting, sentiment of life, and the subsequent temporary greatness of that people must have largely depended on their superior attainments in this direction.

The Greeks were lovers of mystery, but at the same time eagerly sought to verify everything by the senses. Hence, to them, the disembodied soul was still material. "It is exhaled with the dying breath, or issues through the warrior's wounds. The sword passes through its uninjured form as through the air. It is to the body what a dream is to waking action. Retaining the shape, lineaments and motion the man had in life, it is immediately recognized upon appearing" (The Doctrine of Future Life.—Alger, p. 175). As bodily substance was of physical atoms, the soul was of divine atoms. Being itself material, though divine, it often was materially affected by other bodily conditions, and even after death, by perhaps no choice of its own, might become entangled with the living body of another soul and thus be re-admitted to this world by supervention of the native occupant and usurping the senses of that body. This might be of a man or of a lower animal.

This was essentially the demonology of the Greeks. Their transmigration was, however, more of the nature of a succession of human bodily existences than what is properly known as transmigration—an indiscriminate transfer into the bodies of all orders of animal life—and was quite commonly looked upon as a favor. Pythagoras, born five hundred and eighty years B. C., the first of the great sages of Greece, was quite of the Egyptian order of transmigrationists. He not only pretended to recollect his adventures in previous lives, even to the name and the shield he bore at the siege of Troy, but to recognize, in the piteous howls of a dog whom his master was beating, the cries of a dear friend who had died years before. He was, however, more of an agitator of a philosophy than a systematic philosopher, and has transmitted his views only by the reports that contemporaries have made of him. The statements referred to sufficiently indicate the visionary character of the man.

Plato, who was less influential with his contemporaries than Pythagoras with his, yet incomparably the better philosopher, frequently made use of language which, if used prosaically, would necessarily commit him to the same doctrine in essentials. Yet, while being a well understood believer in immortality, his position in respect to transmigration of the soul is not taken with sufficient clearness to obviate doubt. Though it is claimed that " the conception of the metempsychosis is so closely interwoven both with his physical system and with his ethical as to justify the conviction that Plato looked upon it as legitimate and valid, and not as merely a figurative exposition of the soul's life after death" (The Doctrine of a Future Life, p. 190).

In brief, then, we note the Greek doctrine of a future life to have had this advantage over that of the Asiatic and African transmigrationists: It regarded the substance of the soul as being divine and deific, not in the fact that it originated from, and was re-absorbed into, the Supreme Spirit, but it was this in its separate individuality. Added to the repeated bodily existences through which the soul might be called to traverse, its normal destiny, by its deific nature, was a seat among the gods.

The principles which were lacking in the Greek doctrine of a future life, in making it a permanently elevating power to mankind, are to be seen in the following facts: By the nature of their theology, the life of the soul might not be endless; the gods themselves were subject to mutilations and transformations, both of body and of estate, and in none of these respects had they necessarily endless life; the individual soul, in rising toward the region or state of the gods, was subject to such eccentric transformations as to destroy, in thoughtful people, all certainty as to the desirableness of future existence; the bond of fraternal sympathy between souls was not universal, nor necessarily enduring. These negatives one needs but to read to realize the depressing influence they necessarily would exert on human ambition after the poetry in them had ceased its effect. Such conceptions of the future—ultimate failure of life's loftiest aim of incessantly advancing toward higher attainments, and the possible separation of the bond of interest that holds in affectionate consideration every man as being a brother—are unfitting to intelligent life, for the rugged labor necessary to even sustain a high order of attainments; while to further climbing they remove the main incentive.

It is not here assumed that there were no principles at fault besides their doctrine of future life, which contributed to the failure of Greek civilization. They were numerous, but mainly in this feature of their religion. It is difficult to see how, with proper conceptions of Deity, human fraternity and immortality, a people could retrograde in civilization! Right conceptions of these must be abandoned before the soul can return to lower levels. In them are provided all virtues requisite for its ceaseless progress. That there is to be seen higher civilization consequent upon the introduction of higher ideas of immortality, is illustrated in this instance of Greece, whose theology differed little from that of Egypt, and was little superior to that of India, but whose theory of future life was above them both, in the full measure that it excelled them in intelligence and in moral refinement. That the higher view of future life occasioned the superior civilization, rather than contrariwise, may be inferred from the fact that, as with all peoples of their time, their instruction was chiefly derived from their religious institutions, philosophy and religion being essentially one; that the civil forms of government of the two blended nations were quite similar and would have required little alteration by the union. Hence, necessarily, the change that first occurred must have been in their religion, wherein the only change of importance was in their doctrine of future life; resulting in essentially that form of it which prevailed with them through the entire period of their history from Socrates down. The doctrine of future life changed but little in that time, while the civilization ceased not to grow in conformity thereto. And it were not incredible that their civilization might have been prolonged and still further developed, if their religious standard had been of the requisite higher order, and embraced the more perfect views of the future state. Unlike the Christian standard, there was little of it which was above the easy conformity of the average Greek citizen of their best age; while the outlook of the future had little to stimulate enterprise. At the summit there was an end of climbing, and the next movement was necessarily a descent.

INFLUENCE OF THE CHRISTIAN VIEW.

Of the influence of the Christian doctrine of future life, we may judge in part by the peoples who have received it in its purity, and so retained it for at least some generations. And here it is unsafe, as many have done, to include under Christianity all who have set claim to its name. The large order of people, headed by the pope in Rome, is the result of a compromise action on the part of the early Christian emperors, with heathenism, by which was left out much that was Christian and incorporated largely of what was only pagan, thus bringing the two factions together under the specious name, The Christian Church. The doctrine of future life, in these changes, lost nearly all resemblance to its original self. The soul was left immortal, and, if at death it had been sound in the prescribed faith of the Church, was admitted into a Paradise of unending happiness; but if not thus sound, was at the world's general judgment day hurled into an abyss of fire, of varied and unending torments. And although this doctrine was specially emphasized, if not introduced, from considerations of the good of mankind, in rendering the Church more efficient in its saving work, under its most strenuous and terrible advocacy and its enforcement by spiritual anathemas and inquisitorial tortures, the Christian world sank down to its lowest ebb of degradation. The decline was not wholly owing to this error concerning future life, though it visibly became the chief means of that most inhuman terrorism under which, personal worth becoming generally powerless, the popular mind and heart shrank away.

Those centuries of so-called Christian rule, during which the world was shrouded in a night equally dark as that of any pagan age in the historic period of Europe or Asia, must not be confounded with the Christianity of the New Testament. A failure to make this discrimination is to be untrue to science and unjust to the most beneficent cause instituted for mankind. Protestantism directed its reform chiefly at Romish usurpations, interfering little with doctrinal principles. While it did not correct the Romish error concerning future life, it yet made the correction possible by laying liberally the foundation for the freedom of inquiry. And out of that achieved liberty of the investigation of the original authorities, souls for whom it was natural soon came to believe more in harmony with the manifest belief of the Apostolic Church.

The doctrine of future life, as developed by Christ and his apostles, was that the personal self continued beyond death. Rather, it taught that death was only the dissolution of the physical body—the physical organism comprising the senses which identified the proper self with this rudimental existence. Its dissolution was therefore of trifling importance as compared with the ordinary conception of death. And beyond the incurrence of a measure of suffering likely to attend upon it, and perhaps the regret at going out from the visible presence of things and persons dearly loved in this state, there was nothing unloved or unwelcomed in the great but natural change. Death was scarcely unlike when, among friends and tender dependent ones, one is on the eve of embarking on a final voyage to a chosen home among loved ones far away. He has no doubt about the successful arrival abroad; and there is anticipated nothing unpleasant in the passage itself—perhaps a much-needed rest—but his heart aches with yearning for the ones to be left. He foresees their mourning for him, and their sighing for the aids he could render them. Besides the strong inducements of this character to tarry, there was with this people generally a fevered anxiety to depart and live farther from sin and in a more congenial world, and to meet with the many loved ones watching and waiting their arrival on the immortal land. St. Paul but speaks for the whole Apostolic Church when he says: "I am in a strait betwixt two, having a desire to depart, and to be with Christ, which is far better: Nevertheless to abide in the flesh is more needful for you" (Phil. i: 23, 24).

The Apostolic Christian was not disposed to selfishly withdraw from the world that needed him, though staying were manifold suffering. But all things being duly ready for the departure, and realizing that "all whom he stayed for were taken forever," he would accept his release with gratitude—with the gladness which the homesick child experiences when receiving the parental message to "pack up at once and come."

Hardly a clue is given of what may have been their conception relative to the location and mode of existence in the immortal state. Judgment of it is formed rather by the occurrences which the apostles put on record than by the oral teachings which they left us. The Savior's references to the character of the future life are few, but wonderfully comprehensive and clear. His reply to the argument of the Sadducees, referring to the woman who successively had the seven brothers in marriage, must be taken as his conception of that state, as to its general character. It would appear therefrom that the condition of life in that world would no longer require betrothals after the custom prescribed by Moses, of which was this unjust law requiring the brother to marry the widow of a deceased brother, possibly against the choice of both. However, it is not a necessary inference of the passage that the conjugal tie, which refers to a mental and moral as well as a physical distinction of the race, shall not continue in the immortal existence. The reply is, however, an affirmation of the soul's immortality. "Neither can they die any more" (Luke, xx: 27, 28). And as to the rank of life, he declares them equal unto the angels and descendants from God, being children of the resurrection. Being worthy of endless life after the death of the body, was proof that they were of divine substance, which children of the Deity alone possessed.

Their equality with the angels was inferable from the appearance of angels being so much in the likeness of men as to be commonly mistaken for them. The mortal origin of the angels may well be concluded from this same comprehensive reply. The angels and the souls of men are equals, in the sense that all human beings are equals. The souls of men being immortals—worthy of being raised—are God's children, as the angels among all Jews were believed to be, and hence, being essentially the same, a sameness of previous state is not only possible but probable.

Another instance of the Master's allusions to this subject is in his reference to his Father's house of many mansions (John, xiv: 2, 3). By this he argues the grouping of society by special friendships, not unlike in this life where the social spirit centers in races, nations, neighborhoods and families. And does this mean all? Does it mean races, nations, and families only? Does it not mean regions, perhaps worlds, in some way consistent with the elements constituting a spiritual universe? Does it not mean, though somewhat remotely, scenery of forms and movements, animate and inanimate, lights, shadows and colors, the eternal counterpart of the mind, and from which alone the immortal senses must feed the mind? To reason these out of existence would be to reason sanity and entity out of the soul itself.

The Great Teacher truly has left us only few words, but many gracious and most satisfying thoughts, in respect to the future life. How much the immediate disciples received of the import of these brief words we know not; but they saw enough to create a strong preference for "the world to come," and to induce them to live in accordance with the highest morality, to practice charity toward even their enemies, and to make the salvation of their fellow beings their central purpose of life.

And it here only remains to be said, that though too soon after the Master's departure this good element of faith was overpowered by the darkness of the times and the light of the world went under eclipse, during its prevalence there was attained by its believers the highest life known to mankind. And always where the Bible became accessible to the people, the highest order of society prevailed.

How much of its good influence has been due to its superior doctrine of future life may be approximately estimated by the common stress placed by believers on the hope of the "home in heaven," attainable by practicing the faith and the love of Jesus. But much of the true Christian life went out when its doctrine of immortality suffered its pagan mutilations, excluding after death a large part of the race from attaining reformation and fellowship with the higher life; thus cutting off their own hope and the hope of their friends in them. For the event of such a separation and loss, it was necessary to somewhat harden the heart against the unregenerate class, and against great fondness for any, even for children, as upon the contingency of their final failure to gain heaven, a great love for them might be a great and permanent pain.

Mainly to this sad innovation of the New Testament doctrine of future life must be attributed the outrages on mankind instigated by the Church, as aggressions and usurpations are not known to have found favor with the adherents to the simple teaching of Christ on the subject, in any age.

It will be recognized that that doctrine of future life in which man views, with the most perfect realization, his conscious self-hood beyond death in a world as real as the one he now lives in, ever attended by his fellow beings whose well-being is his own interest, is the best suited to the progress of the race, and is fairly to be regarded as indispensable. And so, to the evidence of science, history adds its confirmations of the world's great need of a more substantial hope of future life embodying the conditions referred to.

CHAPTER III.

An Important Need of the Church is the Ability to Place More Emphasis on the Future Life.

It is, by many devout people, believed that the church is not making the progress in arresting evil that it should, considering its social and civil advantages.

And allowing on account of impatient temperaments, a fair deduction from this claim, and rejoicing too, that there is in the world a power doing as much for the welfare of mankind as the church with all its defects is plainly doing, the question yet recurs: Is that great and invaluable body actually at its best, with the advantage of position that it holds?

Admitting that in the development of man's moral nature the process is necessarily slow, that there is so large a' part of the great body of the race so largely animal as that but slight impressions can be made by the best of appliances, and remembering how soon the powerful light of the personal Master was swallowed up by the same great darkness, still the lack of success is not wholly explained. It does not explain why so large an intelligence, extending throughout the enlightened world, continues to have so little effect upon the selfish motives; that so many evils which are fully seen in their enormity are still finding tolerance by so many even of church relations.

Really, one cannot help feeling that there is something of great importance being overlooked. There is too wide a difference between man's knowledge of the moral law and his fulfillment of its requirements, arguing that a much wanted motive of some kind is absent. There is needed the force of principle or conception of truth, relating to the interest of life, to bring man's moral and spiritual nature up nearer abreast with his knowledge of right. It is probable that we have in the New Testament the whole system of moral uprightness necessary to man's happiness, taught and simplified down to the easy comprehension of any ordinary mind; and yet all the appeals to the most fearful torments after death by one class, and the most powerful inducements of heaven by another class, of believers, together with the ever impressive picture of the loving, self-denying Jesus held steadily forth by all classes of Christians, have not succeeded in holding the church fellowship, in any branch of it—conservative or liberal—up to the standard of rectitude and happiness assigned to it in primitive times by even its enemies! Besides, the primitive church, as a class, exhibited a willingness, nay a happiness, in incurring bodily and social discomfiture, even to severe suffering, for the sake of the welfare of Christianity, known to extremely few believers of to-day. They were at the same time as attentive to temporal duty, practicing the usual arts and trades of life, when permitted to do so, as Christians at the present time. They were "diligent in business, fervent in spirit, serving the Lord." They had no less love for this temporal world, only they loved the world to come much more; and first of all sought to shape their lives in harmony with the requirements of that world. By this understanding, the world to come, as compared with this world, was the proper state and home for the soul. This present was every way temporary, and subordinate to the future. It could then with little sacrifice be given up. They had a satisfactory knowledge of the Master and the dear departed in that other world, and knew him to be requiring of themselves as he did when on earth. His promise they believed—that he would be with them always, even to the end of the world. He was as ever their loving Master—their Great High Priest. He was the ordained of God, and enthroned in life above them—the all-sufficient friend and Savior of themselves and theirs.

As may be easily seen, to have a thorough realization of these things, rendered their self-denial as to things in this life very natural and easy. To dispense with that which was in the way of the better—the more desirable—though it might cost suffering, was a work of cheerfulness. In this philosophical view of the matter, it is plainly possible to bring about all the great changes seen in the average people of the apostolic church, by establishing the same realization of a future life, connected with the consideration of the same great requirements of that state.

To the church more than to any other institution,

mankind are looking for moral and spiritual direction. What is there admitted is commonly considered admissible. And what it sees fit to condemn, the popular sense is likely to pronounce against. Its responsibility is therefore immense. Hence, it should be solicitous for every means that will enable it to rightly utilize this public confidence.

By the same co-ordination of accredited facts it has been conceded to be the chief repository of the intelligence concerning another world. Its precepts, its claims, have come from another world. It claims to exist by appointment from the world of spirits, where the Divine Presence is more apparent, and where, too, the decisions of the Divine Will are more perfectly realized and obeyed. If, then, the people believe too little, and incorrectly, in a future life, it is largely because the church has been unable or unwilling to intelligently teach concerning it. The failure is probably due to both these causes. In an age of science people will in some measure require scientific proof. This is forthcoming at the expense of patient investigation in that direction, and in a clearness, also, sufficient to excite belief in the future life on the part of most people who are not organically indisposed to a faith of the kind.

Apparently this investigation has not been made on account of an anticipation that in its conclusions certain dogmas, which were deemed essential, might necessarily have to be largely modified or wholly abandoned. And, as a shift, it was urged that revelation alone was sufficient; and the fact that the general instinct of mankind anticipated a future life, was esteemed all the corroboration from science that was necessary.

And, moreover, the plea supplementing this, by the rank and file of preachers and teachers, was that immortality was an inscrutable subject, and, further than a matter of dogma, was unessential to gospel work among mankind. From this has arisen a skepticism of a most dangerous magnitude in the very body of the church. From want of scientific confirmation of the traditional faith in the Bible account of future life, consistency with the prevailing habit of thought, that anything to be intelligently received must be reducible to science, rendered it necessary to discontinue this powerful element of apostolic success.

Thus is the church bereft of one of its chief powers over the souls of men, and become, to a large extent, a mere matter of social policy, and liable to stray to any point where the popular voice may be clamoring for a good time. And so this great elevating power is come to be more trailing after than leading in the affairs of mankind.

Of the extension of life to beyond the grave there is no very strong certainty, with many of even the ruling number of its membership. And the practice of the higher principles of Jesus, on account of the apparent shortness of life in this world, considering, too, the greatness of the undertaking, is usually thought as rather too much for mortals to succeed in. So, then, to live on about as nearly right as is customary in church relations, is the extent of Christian fidelity sought after or stipulated. And it may well be asked, how long can this state of things endure—at this dead level—with the church degenerating into a mere social society, ready to accept any moral state that the social taste may incline to?

JESUS AND IMMORTALITY.

Jesus recognized the importance of grounding his disciples firmly in the faith of immortality. In this simple fact he was not unlike the founders of the other great religions of the world. With the evident purpose of impressing upon them the re-assuring fact of the continuance of life in its essential wholeness and self-hood beyond the death of the body, even while yet personally with them, he took the chief ones of his disciples with him into the mountain, and in transfiguration before them, talked face to face with Moses and Elias; thus to their open vision—to their senses,—verifying the immortality of man.

To them there was but one means of verification beyond their intuition and the reliance they could place on the testimony of others. This was the witness of the senses. Science had not accumulated its present immense store of facts and principles bearing on the subject. To be the companion of Jesus was to be the witness of the "supernatural"—prophecy, spiritual power over physical substances, and angel visitations— all of which could not fail to contribute much to cause the realization of the personal continuance in the spiritual state, which so strongly characterized them while in his presence and during all the subsequent time they lived. Only for a few days following his arrest and execution was there any abatement in the zeal of their discipleship. Seeing him in the power of his enemies and dying at their hands, led them for the moment to despair and lapse into their former belief.

They even then shared the common hope of some sort of rising of the dead, held by the average Jew, which was little, if any, inferior to that of most Christian people of to-day.

But this ordinary hope was every way insufficient to support them as his chosen vessels to carry his truth before the world. And the tendency already, on the morning of the third day, was toward abandonment of the work. Their obstinate unbelief of the women, and of the men going to Emmaus, who testified to having seen him, and that he was "risen indeed," was such as to merit his sharp rebuke.

But the crisis was forever passed, when they looked upon him who had been dead, and were challenged to handle him: "Behold my hands and my feet, that it is I, MYSELF" (Luke xxiv: 39). To their minds the unnatural, spiritual ghost was now at once and forever banished from the immortal land, and the personal self of man, with all his essential appointments, took its place. When they thought the presence to be his spirit, they were in terror, but when they saw it to be himself, they were reunited with him in their old familiar love. The spirit world again became the real world, with all the great attractions of life being from that higher and greatly superior state.

They were seen to be lacking the great incentive to steadfast perseverance, while in possession of but the ordinary belief of mankind in respect to life in the future. With all which the ordinary faith could do for them, as a motive, aided by the knowledge of the value of the truths committed to their charge, and by the powerful love of Christ yet fresh in its influence on their hearts, they were powerless to face the world and to brook the required self-denials for the sake of their Master's kingdom, till the full character and certainty of that world was added.

But mark the difference from the hour of his visitation to them from the dead—his personal return from beyond physical death. The former sense of death existed no more. Death might be accompanied with fearful pain inflicted by the ingenious torture of enemies, and dreaded on that account, but as to itself, properly, it had lost its sting, and the grave its victory. From that hour they were practically occupants of a new existence, as truly so as though they had stepped out of their flesh. That they thought no longer the thoughts on the greater subjects of life the rest of the world indulged in, is sufficiently evident in what they said and how they deported themselves. Neither were they irregular in their ideas, nor fanatical in their deportment, but were the most sane of all people.

If it be said that this great change was owing to the miracle of the Holy Ghost at the Day of Pentecost, bringing about an extraordinary transformation, which is not to be under-estimated, it is not to be overlooked that prior to that remarkable visitation, they were lifted entirely above their previous level—that they were brought together in that assembly by a lofty consideration which the facts of the few weeks previous had evoked. Peter, previously slender in courage, was no longer a coward in the face of death, nor reticent before the world; being now conscious that his flesh was all of which his enemies could deprive him, which, save a short period of suffering, would affect him no more than the rending of his mantle would do. The world's wisdom respecting life and its needs was wonderfully changed from the view which was taken from his standpoint of a present endless life. The superior life universally accorded to the apostles, in the enlightened world, was but such as might be expected to follow from the view of the future life they possessed. Remembering that with them it was not faith, not doctrine written in a book and signed, not sentiment, but REALIZATION, unencumbered by doubt!

While the Master truly said, "Blessed are they who have not seen and yet have believed," the real occasion of his visit to them at the time of the announcement of this great truth, was to demonstrate the life beyond the tomb by personally returning from that state in a naturalness quite indistinguishable from his former self. That there was at this time something superior to ordinary nature about him, is to be judged from the alarm they felt at his presence, which, however, was soon dispelled by his kindly words and challenge to examine his person and be satisfied of his identity.

The power of believing beyond the evidence of the senses, he taught them to consider a greater qualification than that of working miracles; nevertheless, of the ocular demonstration of future life there was a necessity to *them, as they were,* and in view of the hardships they were to encounter in the work of his ministry. While the abstract power of believing was important, there was a need of supporting that belief by external evidence. Intuition and faith must lead the way in discoveries, but if discoveries do not follow after to confirm, the belief becomes a superstition, and a hindrance to progress.

THE APOSTOLIC AND MODERN CHRISTIAN COMPARED.

As compared with the Apostolic Christian, the average Christian of to-day is less reliant in a hope beyond the grave, in about the same measure in which he practices less self-denial for the cause of the Master. There is among believers much said in respect to death and futurity, but chiefly with reference to a necessity of a religious preparation for the final contingencies involved in them. And judging altogether from the much that is thus said on the subject, in public and private, the conclusion is justifiable that what is said is often very feebly believed by the parties themselves urging it. It is doubtful whether the Christian of to-day believes much more strongly and rationally in immortality than did the Jew in the time of our Lord, and whether he is not quite as deficient in those higher requirements of the *Christian* law, with its multiform aggressive duties, as was the Jew then deficient in the weightier matters of Moses' law, judgment and mercy. With his restricted ideas of human existence, as to duration, the Jew was too selfish, and too limited in equity and in compassion, to bear with his neighbor. Will the Christian, with similarly contracted ideas of the duration of the essential man, probably work out more successfully the great principles of his Master in sacrificing for the elevation of his neighbor and his *enemy?* is the question to be solved by the special claimants of Jesus, as well as by the Christian public generally.

Is not the steady but very slow improvement of the masses in Christian countries, more owing to the passive granting of liberties and institutions of learning, secular and sacred, by the public, together with a pulpit of more or less efficiency in shaping popular sentiment, than to a Christlike going forth to the spiritually needy, with personal sympathy and encouragement to a better life,—teaching the unconcerned and the vicious that his life is intended for higher uses than to operate on the grade on which he is now living? It is beyond dispute that this work of soul-culture, as a prime object of life, is dependent on a principle which is able to command great self-denial; which would, it seems, be largely the result of properly believing the primitive Christian doctrine of immortality,—as much so to the church of the present as it was to that of the olden time.

It is necessary that the church accept with extreme care any innovations upon its customary belief. Rashness here might be a disaster to mankind, of no small magnitude. But it should be also careful, in looking after its means to success, to know with certainty that it is in possession of every principle that can militate for human good; and should adopt without hesitation the precedents of faith and practice established by the Master himself and by his immediate discipleship, none of which is more prominent than the appeal to an immortality of a higher and more perfect life—a life of tangible realities, of the eternal companionship of man, and infallible responsibility to God—in the world beyond death.

CHAPTER IV.

Importance of Realizing Powers, Especially in Apprehending the Evidences of Science in Relation to the Doctrine of Immortality.

REALIZATION is chiefly on the plane of the external senses. The external world is to us the great reality, because we see it, feel it, and otherwise observe of it by our senses. To this we are so accustomed as to render it, in some instances, quite difficult to get life properly impressed by the facts that lie beyond the sphere of the senses. And for this reason the realities which lie interior of visible nature are little available to the understanding of a large part of mankind.

It is only by special intellectual discipline of quite high order, that one may attain the ability to recognize not only the underlying forces of external nature, but also those external phenomena which, from their vastness, may not be brought within the scope of the senses. There is a sort of mental clairvoyance by which truly scientific minds are able to realize worlds which such as rely only on the very limited use their senses can render them, hardly know of. It is not difficult to see the mind, by this means, entering world after world, as its intellectual vision enlarges to take in system after system of forces and laws that belong to special planes or strata of being, or as it is newly made acquainted with combinations of elements and forces in our own common world.

It is not to be overlooked that the enlargement of mental capacity and the advancement in knowledge are mainly from the ability to realize what is only *mentally* seen, whether introduced by the senses or caught up from intellectual reflection. No mental operation is satisfactory—becomes assimilated with the mind—till all the essential parts and their proper conclusions are realized distinctly. They must be seen by the intellectual vision in all their parts, as really as the external eye beholds an external object. A fact, in pure mathematics, requires to be realized, and to stand out before the intellect to mental view, with its elements properly gathered and joined as an objective structure, before it is satisfactory and become a matter of knowledge. Mind is creative and, in some part of it, originative. In mechanism the object may externally exist in draft or model, but before the hands go into operation, it is erected in thought and become a mental creation. Or the imaginative mind, following out certain rhythmic impulses, reaches into the unknown and originates the object and produces it to the mental senses—a real thing. Mentally holding in hand known elements of fact, the mind feels its way into the unknown, still further to obtain needed facts or principles, as the builder of wood or stone does for his structure, till a sense of completeness satisfies it, and the parts are put together, and it is a complete mental device, to be looked upon, left standing and returned to, as if it were a statue or a house.

Thus is the power of realization of essential importance in the abstract domain; but we shall find the need of it more apparent when we come to the consideration of the palpable substances of nature, where entities lie concealed from the senses; or what is practically the same, where their vastness is such that the physical senses can take no observation of their wholeness. Let us instance the planetary character of our earth. It is round—a ball of immense size. Standing upon it in the most favorable position, but little of the curvature of its surface is discernible by the unaided eye. It appears a level, extending indefinitely into the horizon in every direction, giving the false realization that the earth is of a flat surface. Even he, to whom its roundness is by the intellect unquestionably apparent, may be strongly affected by this false realization; and instead of enjoying the proper realization, of an existence elevated on the outer surface of a ball, his prevailing realization may be that he is but on a level plain or depressed below. Or to extend the principle to another phase of our terrestrial state, the realization is that the sun and other heavenly bodies move about the earth—rising from beneath in the east and going down beneath in the west, the earth not only being the center of, but itself mainly, the universe. This is the impression derived through our external senses, unaided by any intellectual device, and shows how imperfect and limited is their service in defining truth to us. The true realization, and which is a mental conception only, is that the vast earth is a satellite, rotating about the sun, which is of such transcendent vastness as, by comparison, to reduce the earth to insignificance. Or, properly, leaving the earth in all its true immensity, and thus allowing the comparison, the realization of the sun's vastness would be a globular mass whose outer limits would lie beyond where probably ordinary conception has placed infinity.

And taking yet another instance connected with our planetary state. The false realization is that our abode is stationary and the celestial scenery thus moves about us. The true realization is of the earth being one in the great panorama of worlds, moving in silent velocity through space at a rate of over sixty thousand miles in an hour. Of such a rate of traveling, and of such an extensive track, it is not to be expected that ordinary mortals can at their best have proper appreciation or distinct realization. But the approximate realization of these vastnesses is yet a necessity to the astronomer in obtaining a ready command of his most magnificent science.

By these illustrations it is seen that life is mentally transferable into states indefinitely beyond the scope of physical perception, where the deeper and more fundamental facts of nature, as well as the more inspiring, become unquestionable realities—sceneries capable of exciting in it aspirations after still higher and more gratifying attainments. Every system of principles in nature is a thing of beauty, and to realize these occult works, is to be impressed by the beautiful, and to be elevated.

But this pertains to physical principles no more than to moral and spiritual, all of which are discernible as realities analogous to substances. We see an expression of a certain nature in man adapting him to goodness. And, in the conception of its principles, it becomes an intellectual reality—a structure that we name the moral principle—recognized by the intellectual and moral senses. Internal, mental pictures exert an influence upon life hardly less potent than do the representations or the realities of external nature, if developed to a clearness attainable under a high state of excitement. One greatly important work in the moral reform of an individual is to remove from the imagination pictures of immorality, and to supply their places with those of virtue. The libertine in solitude recalls the scenes of revelry,—the fevered imagination paints new ones, and, in gazing upon them, resistance becomes overpowered, and he is the victim to a calling which his better nature despises. A change of scenery is necessary. The moral nature must gain strength by the contemplation of scenes of an opposite character, constantly presented to the mind, suggested by personal illustrations or devised and drawn from contemplation.

One is capable, then, by certain forms of mental discipline, to attain the ability to abstract himself from the power of the external senses, and to cause the hidden properties and forces of nature, reached only by the intellect, to take definite form before him, on which he may rely with all the assurance that the external senses can warrant. The success of the mental effort largely depends on this ability. Unless one can thus shape any well proved principle or fact in nature and give it substantial *form* before his mind's eye, he will be able to make but little advancement in the higher elements of knowledge in any department. The doors to the substantial realities in nature to which his outer senses are not adapted, and which comprise the major part of existence proper, are practically closed to him. And his life must remain imprisoned in about the same narrow limits of sensuous observation that circumscribe the lower animals, and beyond which, the aspirations of thought he might have could hardly rise.

The mind can grow only as intuitions lead the way, and as it places reliance on intellectual perceptions. It must attain to the power of intellectual clairvoyance. The culture of that gift must not be neglected by him who would be the subject of those happifying impressions which the Creator has placed for his inheritance. He who would acquaint himself with the inner glories of nature, and know about the primary realities— the invisible substances and powers on which visible, external nature depends for every property it possesses— must learn to behold by the light of the intellect.

He, more especially, who would do justice to inquiry after the truth of immortality, must bring this accomplishment with him to his work; otherwise, he must expect but little satisfaction from his toil. Spiritual things, it was said, are spiritually discerned. And so, too, of the principles in nature that evidence a future life; they necessarily are more refined and therefore more subtile in their character, and require not only the use of good judgment but strong realizing sense, to properly apply them. It is also necessary to remember that a strong mineralistic bias is given to science by a large part of its cultivators; and to correct this, so that science shall have its full import on a subject of this character, will require that special effort be made at realization. The spiritual side of nature has been little thought upon, or been shunned, from fear of ridicule or of being judged, by the masters, heretical in science.

Customary observation of claims to such an existence we may, then, justly suspect of being unduly mineralistic; so much so as to mislead even the most judicious of scientists. While they have rightly claimed that the student has no choice in the matter of belief, but must abide by evident truth, the external senses have been the basis of realization over the indisputable proofs of inductive reasoning. To avoid believing strongly in what has the scientific probabilities somewhat against it is natural to a conscientious scholar, but to pass lightly upon what, if true in science, would achieve a universal blessing, and that out of fear of ill favor from others, is certainly as unbecoming as anything could well be to a patron or cultivator of knowledge among mankind. While he has no choice in believing, he should be expected in his researches to have reference to discoveries that would be of the larger benefit to the race.

The disposition of science to conserve the interest of

mankind by directing investigation chiefly toward mechanical arts, is a prominent reason why the realization has been so exclusively mineralistic. By discoveries of this kind the comforts and conveniences of life have been much enlarged, and thereby discoverers have become celebrated, though too rarely requited in temporal returns. Also false teachings in religion must come in for a share of this responsibility. It has been commonly given out from a religious standpoint, that the spiritual state is in no sense material, and that necessarily nature could not be supposed to have indications of such an existence.

DEVELOPMENT OF REALIZING POWERS.

Customary thought will to some extent induce realization. Even known fiction becomes a reality, and from it persons, locations and events will have place in the reader's memory, as lasting as those of actual existence; and thus may be highly serviceable, as well as at times detrimental, to life. Hence to increase this power with respect to a desired object, it is necessary to habitually indulge the consideration of its reality. If objection be taken to this, that it may lead to the establishment of errors by allowing what is not true to be confirmed as fact, it may be answered, that scientific culture among the people is quite a failure from lack of this qualification. People are too little accustomed to enter into a realization of demonstrated truth.

DELUSION OF THE SENSES.

Besides, as seen, the senses themselves are often deceived, rendering appearances that are not founded in fact. The dictates of reason are to be ever regarded as the most reliable of evidence. Reference has already been made to instances in relation to the rotundity of the earth, its motions and state among the heavenly bodies, where the delusion of the senses is known and yet persisted in, in defiance of knowledge. The reliability of the external senses is unfavorably affected in at least two ways: in the derangement of the organs themselves and in the disordered condition of the faculties in sympathy with them. To the insane mind the aberrations are often so complete as to produce imaginary objects not having the least foundation in fact, being only the external reflections of the chimeras created by the disordered fancy within. And yet of such strength may a false realization of this kind become, as to render its victim an object of great danger. Indispensable as those senses are, their services must be received with care, as by reason of liabilities of this character they are not always able to report nature correctly. The true observation, by whatever instrumentalities, is always being made by the sane mind within. Taking for example the eye, it can only observe according to the capacity and state of the intelligence which is back of it, and beholding through it. The eye of the brute, though more perfect in mechanism than that of man, yet sees less of material nature because of a less sentient mind behind it. A very poor eye in the head of a large, bright intellect sees immensely, while an eagle eye before a deficient mind sees little more than the objects of personal wants.

It is by the ability to place reliance on existences intellectually seen—and in many cases discernible by that means only—that the greater and more inspiring truths become accessible to man. Here is the threshold leading to the grandeurs above, waiting the ability to advance and take possession. One's destiny is at the dark base of the sublime ascent, unless he succeed to this requisite means of following nature through its orderly but somewhat intricate routes from its beginnings to its summits in infinity. In ascending a mountain, it is often the case that clouds impinge upon its rugged sides, and we have nothing but the tortuous and dimly defined path on which to rely for direction. Faithful climbing upon this path results in a position above the bewildering clouds—a position from which may be clearly seen what previously baffled the understanding. So, faithfully relying on well proven principles of nature, hidden from the senses though they may be, will in due time lead to the observation of other principles, and thus onward, till by mental clairvoyance our opaque world will have become a great transparency, displaying in combination, substances and states of such beauty and order and purity—so many substantial, bright worlds lying within the same space, so many grand universes—as that there shall attach no more mystery to either spirit or spirit world.

CHAPTER V.

TENDENCY OF SCIENCE TO CONFIRM THE THEORY OF A STATE OF IMMORTALITY.

THE prevailing consideration has been that for instruction in spiritual things one must go to revelation alone. Science could testify to nothing of that character. And we find very much of that thought still, even among well-informed people. Probably from the fact that revelation itself implies a spiritual existence, and affirms the future life in such plain, comprehensive language, speaking of it with the assurance that one speaks of the objects of external nature, people have come to regard it as the source of what knowledge is to be had of the existence beyond death. And truly, revelation has not only led the way in the understanding of this great truth, but it has been to the greater and more intelligent part of the race, the only reliance in respect to intelligence of that world. And that revelation has been of immense importance in this respect, as well as in respect to the moral needs of the race, can scarcely be disputed in the light of the facts of ordinary history. The simple could understand enough of it to have a wholesome and comforting trust in a life beyond the tomb; while those of higher intelligence saw in it at least a corroboration of their intuitive belief of that state, and nothing to materially conflict with the deductions of science in respect to it; and, because of it, belief in the hereafter has been much stronger.

But there has been, nevertheless, with the scientifically inclined believers in revelation, very commonly, a feeling of disappointment that natural principles did not afford stronger proof of future life. Also those inclined to array themselves as mineralists against it, from choice of opposition or from real unbelief, felt very content to consider that nature's verdict was at least neutral on the question, and that the belief might be safely classified as a superstition to which, mainly, people of weak minds might be expected to yield credence. It has, therefore, not been easy with ordinary mankind, to cherish a full realization of a future state, or to place very strong reliance on the claims of it. A cause is not clearly established while the evidence of an important witness is not yet given. Nature, while ever unwilling to *deny* the immortality, till recently, could, by hardly any of her oracles, fully affirm. Besides, from the self-imposed, excessive mineralistic habits of reasoning referred to, scientists were disposed to pass unthinkingly over the facts therein in which the solid proofs are found.

BIGOTRY NOT LIMITED TO A CLASS.

Bigotry is by no means confined to religionists. Nor is fanaticism exclusively the product of religiously heated brains. Few great minds can, with their prancing energies, be sufficiently passive to be unbiased observers of nature. They are to be expected to come from their schools, to a large extent shaped by their schooling, with their faculties of thought directed mainly by pre-conceptions, and with their learning consisting, in a large measure, in but the transfer of the ideas of their teachers. It is incidental to the law of education, and, while it may be deplored, may seldom be overcome. Indeed, who shall rightly understand himself in respect to this, since it is not a matter of conscience or personal honesty, but of involuntary conception? The mental eye is living, sentient, and cannot help seeing the object to which it is directed. And it could not be expected to not recognize what is seen. And the hard training tends to all the more tightly adjust it to its view. So what is out of that line of vision will have little chance of recognition by the eye which, by education, is best qualified to judge of it. The ignorant one is unfitted for the work of discovery. If he were to drift about upon the domain of nature more impartially than the one of culture, and come in contact with a valuable principle, the unsentient mind would not recognize it. So here we are placed.

To change over to new views, or to introduce a new element of philosophy, is commonly the work of an eccentric, who, by certain efficient qualities of mind, well cultivated, finding the clue of some new departure, readily takes it up, and pursues it far enough to make the discovery of important new principles, which, after a time of usually hard struggle, are admitted to favor with the schools, and thus become the sentiment of the people. But eccentrics are not commonly safe people. Where they are once serviceable, ten times they may be hindrances to progress, and destructive to needful and costly institutions.

Evidently, to be at its best, and in the fulfillment of its mission, science needs the ability to vary from its customary points of view, to take into consideration other phases and sides of nature, than those commonly recognized. Too commonly investigation is pushed along only seeking the establishment of previously determined ends. And no minutiæ bearing upon this could well escape detection, while basic, large and quite conspicuous principles, unaccustomed to thought, might pass unnoticed. All great discoveries have been stumbled over and trampled upon by previous cultivators of science, because they were not suspected.

Happily among the developments of thought in scientific circles of the present time, there is a marked tendency toward the spiritual side of nature. Perhaps not from design, but more from the direction inquiries in certain branches of physical philosophy have taken during the last few years. Causes of physical phenomena have been inquired after by more persistent and penetrative search. The "affections" of matter have been considered more attentively and seen to be expressions of systems of nature farther internal than the plane on which physical philosophy has usually been regarded. Properties and forces in nature are seen to disappear from view beyond the senses and the means of physical analysis, transferring their causes as well as effects to regions unknown, and to connect with entities there no less real and substantial than are those they are identified with on the visible plane. This is not without a meaning which is strongly attracting attention.

That there is a *something* in that region, may not be doubted by him who is familiar with these facts, and is fairly disposed to credit what he sees. And that *something* cannot be less substantial—less consistent, in its own nature and state, than is the world which we realize about us. And the conclusion is scarcely avoidable that our existence, as to realization, is but with *one* of the several states of nature—the crude, physical,—with a higher related therewith, to be made in turn our abode on becoming released by the sundering of the ties that now hold us to this. That all scientists join in this conclusion, would be quite too much to affirm. Yet that such is the attainment in science, as to the existence of these occult forces, traceable from visible to invisible nature, there would hardly be found a dissenting voice among recognized scholars.

But a few references will aid in confirming this conclusion: Prof. E. L. Youmans, of our country, in the introduction to a work on the correlation and conservation of force, in which he has collected papers from a goodly number of the standard writers of the old world, in matters of science, makes these decisive statements: "There are many who deplore what they regard as the materializing tendencies of modern science. They maintain that this profound and increasing engrossment of

the mind with material objects, is fatal to all refining and spiritualizing influence. The correctness of this conclusion is open to serious question; indeed the history of scientific thought not only fails to justify it, but proves the reverse to be true. It shows that the tendency of this kind of inquiry is ever from the material *toward* the abstract, the ideal, the spiritual.   *   *
The course of astronomic science has thus been on a vast scale to withdraw attention from the material and sensible, and to fix it upon the invisible and super-sensuous. It has shown that a pure principle forms the immaterial foundation of the universe. From the baldest materiality we rise at last to a truth of the spirit world, of so exalted an order that it has been said 'to connect the mind of man with the spirit of God.'   *   *
Scientific inquiries are becoming less and less questions of matter, and more and more questions of force; material ideas are giving place to dynamical ideas. While the great agencies of change with which it is the business of science to deal—heat, light, electricity, magnetism, and affinity, have been formerly regarded as kinds of matter, 'imponderable elements,' in distinction from other material elements, these notions must now be regarded as outgrown and abandoned, and in their place we have an order of purely immaterial forces.   *   *
Star and nerve-tissue are parts of the same system—stellar and nervous forces are correlated. Nay, more: sensation awakens thought, and kindles emotion, so that this wondrous dynamic chain binds into living unity the realms of matter and mind through measure-

less amplitudes of space and time" (Correlation and Conservation of Forces, pp. 11, 12, 41).

Mr. Youmans here speaks for modern science, as advocated by many of its reliable patrons, cultivators and masters; though it may not be representing the conclusions of all the leading naturalists. He has stepped aside, for the moment, from the discussion of science itself to make this incidental statement of his conclusion, while not all others, so far as I know, have done so. That they might make similar statements, when off duty, would be true of some, and has been, and probably would be, of the large majority of them. Nothing they have said, so far as I can recall, with perhaps a very few exceptions, would be construed into dissent.

Prof. Tyndall, without question well at the head of physical philosophy both as a theorist and a demonstrator, having furnished to the world more thorough proof of the conservation and correlation doctrine than any other, speaking of the transmission of light by means of the luminiferous ether, from the glowing platinum wire across the space to the eye, and thence through the humors of that organ, impinging upon the nervous coating of the optic nerve to produce the phenomenon of sight, says: "Up to this point, we deal with pure mechanics; but the subsequent translation of the shock of the ethereal waves into consciousness, eludes the analysis of science. * * * The motion thus imparted is transmitted with measurable, and not very great, velocity to the brain, where, by a process which science does not even tend to unravel, the tremor of the nervous matter is converted into the conscious impression of light" (On Radiation, pp. 19, 11).

Mr. Tyndall's statement of the case is good and fair, characteristic of the conscientious scholar. He is brought, by scientific research, face to face with a substance which is wholly beyond the domain of the physical, so far as regards physical appliances of discovery. And yet there is no fact in nature more apparent than that of this entity into which the objective realities have by the beam of light been thus conveyed. This consciousness, so seizing and utilizing the picturing impressions of light is, finally, the very self of being.

The substance that knows is itself the thing to which he has traced the phenomenon of light, and at the domain of which he was obliged to drop the clue. But this is not all there is to this fact. This super-sensuous entity thus beyond the reach of sensuous tests, is a force resident in certain forms of physical force which it directs and impels as in the case of bodily movements. It likewise points to substances embodying those forces, though they are not sufficiently near, as to state, to be brought under any sensuous test—substances of adequate refinement for the immediate residence of the mental principle of consciousness,—"spiritual," Mr. Youmans might denominate it. But a substance is not without properties characterizing it. And properties determine laws, all of which determine a world and a universe, analagous to the one of our present surrounding.

However little direct reference may be found made to

it, the fact that the scientific thought of the day is drifting toward the recognition of a spiritual universe and the continuance of the human self into it at the demise of this existence, is very clear. While, too, by the clearness of the accepted facts of the science of to-day on which these conclusions are based, there is hardly a conceivable chance that the tendency will ever decline, but will rather all the while increase. The extreme views of evolution, that life is but a state of mineral attainment, and that to its accidental shiftings all its diversities and families are due, also are received with more caution, and on more reflection are being more commonly qualified by their patrons. Hence, not only may we look presently to see men most eminent in science openly favoring, as a matter of science, a future life for man, but favoring, also, special designs by an Omnipotent Mind, in the origin of organisms.

Dr. W. B. Carpenter, in a note appended to a recent paper on " Charles Darwin: His Life and Work," in the " Modern Review " of July, 1882, expresses his dissent from this school of evolutionists as follows: " It is, I think, greatly to be regretted that some of the more ardent advocates of the evolution doctrine are continually (by neglect of this important distinction), leading their disciples to look at 'natural selection' as the cause of particular adaptations of structure to function; whereas it simply expresses the *fact* that the creatures in whom these adaptations *had come to exist*, would be the fittest to survive, and would be likely to transmit them hereditarily. How they came to exist, natural selection tends not in the least to explain " (p. 516).

THE TENDENCY OF SCIENCE. 91

I close this chapter by an appropriate quotation from Prof. Winchell, a wide and favorably known writer on natural sciences: "The unseen world is destined to become like a newly discovered continent. We shall visit it; we shall hold communication with it; we shall wonder how so many thousands of years could have passed without our being introduced to it" (Sketches of Creation, p. 371).

CHAPTER VI.

LOCATION OF THE SPIRITUAL STATE.—INSENSIBLE WORLDS THAT WE KNOW OF.—A UNIVERSAL MINERAL ETHER.

AMONG the questions concerning a future life, the following are of frequent occurrence: Where is that world located? Is it of a palpable nature? What does it resemble? What are human appearances, habits and occupations? The answers to some of these may be given with much confidence, based on the most obvious reasons; others must be left to inferences from obscure data, of little more than conjecture. To the consideration of the first of these the present chapter is devoted; the others will be reserved for their appropriate place farther along in the book.

In respect to location, we may first point out the possibilities, and then what are the necessities, of such a state as that to which the intellect, the senses and the passions are suited. The latter must also be reserved for the proper place farther along. In order to ascertain what states may possibly exist to serve for the abode of the spirit, we must see what surrounding nature consists of, —how far it extends and what its laws and principles provide for; for however remote from this body of physical existence the qualities of that other existence may place it, the two states are connected and reciprocate in the one common system of cause and effect. Hence the spiritual is to be traced from the physical by the employment of the ordinary intellect of man directed toward the spiritual. And reflecting upon the surprising disclosures nature is all the time rendering to persistent genius, one becomes readily prepared to see that in variety of states nature is exhaustless. Worlds may exist within worlds, and, without impinging, occupy the same space. And thus planes of existence in universal extent, as to realization separate, but in space identical, may be multiplied to infinity.

That the same cup might at the same moment of time be many times filled by as many substances of unlike properties, or unlike phases of the same properties, is by no means difficult to understand, when we see that of substances so nearly alike as water, salt, sugar, and alcohol, the volume of water is not augmented by adding thereto a considerable quantity of the other elements in the order of the fineness of their ultimate particles. Glass is less porous than wood, yet will transmit visible light, which wood will not. Wood, however, will transmit electricity which glass will not. Both will transmit terrestrial magnetism which iron will not; while with more or less freedom either will transmit heat. This unlikeness of effects is owing to a corresponding unlikeness of properties in these substances.

SUBSTANCES OF UNLIKE PROPERTIES.

Wherein the properties are not common or are essentially unlike, the one substance is a nonentity to the other. Glass, so far as it is transparent, is to the luminiferous ether *nihil*. It is not resisted, not impressed by it, hence to it is vacuous. Between the magnetic poles the diamond is practically a non-existence. As to the substance that plies between the points of the needles, the interlying adamant offers no resistance, occupies no space and excludes nothing. Between the substance which draws the needle to the earth's pole and that of the cohesive attraction in the diamond itself, which grasps the ultimate particles of an impalpable gas and binds them into a mass of unrivaled hardness, there is an analogy and a distant relation, but they are so wanting in common properties as to be essentially vacuous to each other.

Substances, therefore, may occupy the same space simultaneously, in proportion as they are wanting in common properties or the same properties are affected by essentially unlike qualities. The variety of substances wanting in common properties, it is seen may be without limit; but the principle of their interlying one another, without impinging, is definitely known by the few illustrations cited. Within the same infinite space there may be universe within universe infinite in number, each complete and substantial within itself—the extreme ones having little in common, and connecting mainly through those filling the immense disparity between.

The use of the common terms "high" and "low," "far" and "near," is in reference to extension in space upward, downward or lateral; but there are extensions that do not involve external or visible space, which likewise may be infinite. The common grades in the order of nature indicate this. A few yards of coarse yarn may fill the spool it would require hundreds of yards of thread to fill, and that would perhaps contain as many miles of the fibre of silk. Of two skulls equally spacious, one may contain a thousand-fold more extent of nerve fibre than the other. And without enlarging the cranium the same brain may be immensely extended by years of healthful mental and moral culture. From its extreme ignorance to its extreme enlightenment the mind may have, in that same skull, traveled many great distances and looked upon many grades of attainment. And though there may be conveniences to facilitate the advancement of the mind from one state of intelligence to another or one state of refinement to another, without much personal effort, as railways and steamships facilitate travel from one place to another to the utmost point of the earth, distance is overcome in the one case as truly as in the other. However in the one case it is done by change of location, in the other, by change of states within the same cranial limits.

Distance in our visible state is denoted by measurement of space, because of the mutual impenetrability of substances having common properties. Such substances must lie outside of each other, and thus impress the mind of distance as the interval of space interlying localities. And so common has been this apprehension, and so natural is it to the dwellers on this or any other plane of homogeneous existence, to which resident senses must always be adapted, that it is extremely difficult to obtain an impression of distance, as applied to a diversity of states or planes of unlike substances, irrespective of visible space. And for a time, plain, legitimate proof will, of necessity, be dimly apparent and of little force upon the realizing senses. And until the evidence has been often repeated, and re-enforced by many experiences, so as to give re-assurance to the mental senses, the veils before the invisible world will lift slowly.

LITERAL DISTANCE TRAVERSED BY MIND.

Time, space and substance are fundamental realities, and are apprehended by any appreciable measure of intelligence, though never wholly comprehended. Time is the measure of duration as applied to substance at rest or in motion. Joined with substance in motion it is one of the measures of distance. The remotenesses of states of substance pertaining to thought or to sense, are approximately to be judged by the time consumed in the passage from one to the other. From the absence of any mathematical instruments applicable to such states, their measurement must lack the accuracy of the surveyor or the astronomer. But the engineer who knows the fleetness of his engine, has some idea of his whereabouts by consulting his chronometer. Even yet there are people who judge of distance only by the time consumed in traveling. So, in the progress from one state of mentality, morality, or spirituality, to another;

knowing something of the forces employed, the interlying distance may be judged of by the time required in the transit. Indefinite as the measure may be, the disparity of the states of being in their extremes is not only known, but known to be great, involving years, and, when considered by races, centuries of advancement. But, also, the attainment of each higher state of thought and feeling involves the attainment of corresponding higher planes of substance.

As the necessity of time in traveling from one locality to another, is proof of interlying distance, so, in mental and spiritual progress, its necessity is equally evidence of the most indubitable character, that mind, with its attendant life, overcomes literal distance, and advances through interlying forces that resist its movement from first to last. Vacuous space would dispense with time. The luminiferous ether having so few properties in common with ordinary matter, that matter being so nearly vacuous to it, there is but a trace of time apparent in the transmission of light—about one second only in one hundred and ninety-two thousand miles. But the traverse of the mind in the attainment of knowledge is visibly slow; and so with moral and spiritual refinement. The elements that impinge on those living substances and resist them in their progress, are, therefore, very real and palpable to *them*, however unperceived from the sensuous state.

There are, therefore, two ways in which distance is to be estimated in nature,—as on the same plane and as between planes or states; that which results from substances having essentially the same properties and may not occupy the same space—must lie outside of each other, and that which results from a want of essentially the same properties or their being affected by the same qualities, in which case substances, without impinging, might lie within each other and practically occupy the same space,—the distance being expressed by the measure of their unsameness. With the first—objects lying outside and apart from each other—the physical eye renders the mind familiar. The mass of human minds realize no other. The second is apprehensible by the mental senses alone; being effective beyond where the physical cease to avail. And to render it familiar or accessible to the understanding, this mode of perception calls for culture; as the eye, the ear, the touch and the taste are brought to any requisite acuteness and strength by training. On these the inductive nature must depend in bringing to consciousness those inner realms of elements lying away from external view, and finally those also which constitute the spiritual abode of man.

In respect to the necessity of developing the realizing powers—the quality or efficiency of mind to cause abstract principles to definitely stand forth to view, and to satisfactorily see the facts and substance of inner nature, to which I have referred in a previous chapter, the eminent scientist, Mr. Tyndall, bears important testimony, which I take pleasure in placing before the reader in this place. Mr. Tyndall says, "The life of the experimental philosopher is twofold. He lives in his vocation a life of the senses, using his hands, eyes and ears in his experiments, but such a question as that now before us (light) carries him beyond the margin of the senses. He cannot consider, much less answer, the question, 'What is light?' without transporting himself to a world which underlies the sensible one, and out of which, in accordance with rigid law, all optical phenomena spring. To realize this sub-sensible world, if I may so use the term, the mind must possess a certain pictorial power, thus to visualize the invisible. It must be able to form definite images of the things which that sub-sensible world contains, and to say that if such and such a state of things exists in that world, then the phenomena which appear in ours must, of necessity, grow out of this state of things " (Lectures in America, p. 34). Hence, not alone to those who would follow mental and spiritual forces into the unseen regions is this reliance on mental vision and power of mental construction a necessity; the student of physics needs it also in a measure, if not in as much efficiency.

The great discoveries of the world were all delayed till the arrival of this attainment to the mind of man in sufficient force. Apples had been seen falling for more than five thousand years before the inductive mind of Newton grasped the phenomenon and from it proceeded to develop the foundation principles of the stellar universe, reducing astronomy to a science as palpable as that of architecture. The force that moves toward the sun, and that which moves from it, by which the parent orb adjusts every planet, and determines its fleetness on its orbit, are no less real substances than are the iron beams of the great crane which carries so easily about it its tons of metal or rock, dependent at arm's length. In one case the forces are not indicated to the physical eye; the physical eye directed toward them rests on vacuity. In the other case force is indicated by the iron mask in which it is embodied. In both, and in all cases, it is visible to the mental eye alone. And while with the great telescope the astronomer may fill his soul with the grandeur of the great material worlds that before him swim in the great spaces, there is, in the same locality traversed by the telescope, the universe of substance embodying the forces on which these masses of matter in this wonderful exhibition rest, to which the telescope and the microscope are totally blind.

The most abundant of the elemental substances surrounding the existence of man, is oxygen, constituting one-half of the ponderable part of the globe, eight-ninths of the water by weight, and a fifth part of the air we breathe. It is universally present with man: an indispensable ingredient in all the food he eats, the water he drinks and the air he breathes. And yet its existence had not entered into human knowledge till Dr. Priestly's discovery of it so recently as 1774. Tasteless, colorless, odorless, and impalpable, it was constantly released in chemical processes, undetected by the senses to which those properties are necessary for recognition. This brings us to see how small are the limits to which our senses would restrict us, and how soon, going in whatever direction we choose in science, we must rely wholly on the mental vision—*the inductive eye.*

LOCATION OF SPIRITUAL STATE. 101

Chemistry, the basic physical science, illustrates in every process that the physical world is not only a composite unit of many elements, but that underlying these are endless systems of forces, the evidences of worlds of elements lying beyond the sensuous state. In a work of this kind, extended reference to this science is not essential. To the ordinary understanding the important truth may be fully set forth by a few illustrations, without going far into details. I take a piece of ice; it is mineral as truly as stone or metal and is capable of a large measure of resistance. I apply a low degree of heat to it; it is changed to the form of water. I increase the heat, and it is palpable vapor. I apply more heat, and it is wholly invisible. It is the same substance, however; and, but for the relaxing influence of heat on the centripetal force of its ultimate atoms, it would have continued its solidity. It is the same compound gas,—condensed in the first case and rarified in the second; capable of strong resistance in the first state, in the second it is impalpable; at one time it is visible, and invisible at the other. And so the piled-up mountains of ice at the poles may be regarded as immense volumes of gas bound down and solidified by frost; while, under a few degrees less of frost, another volume of the same gas, in the state of water,—somewhat between the solid and volitant states—is rolling about in the external cavities of the earth, as oceans, seas, lakes, and rivers. With a few degrees of yet less frost, another volume of the same is seen drifting in the sky overhead, in the form of clouds; and with a yet less measure of cold, a fourth state of this gas may be detected as invisibly suspended in the transparent atmosphere about us.

But there is no substance that may not in like manner be resolved into invisibility. We watch the process of a bar of steel, as palpable an object as could be referred to, under the influence of heat. At first it becomes red, then white, then finally it disappears in flame and is lost to view. The human body itself, fluids, flesh and bones, is likewise common material, and constitutes no exception to the rule of common resolvability. It is held in the visible state and made thus serviceable to its wonderful inhabitant, by simply that one great condensing agent, inter-atomical centripetal force. Let that be relaxed by the touch of the proper countervailing force, and the frail house of the soul, too, is vanished from sight.

No part of the mineral universe is an exception, it is perfectly safe to say. The mental eye is even now looking upon all as a transparency.

LOCATION OF THE SPIRIT WORLD.

Then as to where the spirit world may be located in space, it may be said that no substance essentially unlike it in properties or their qualities, will interfere with its existence anywhere. Our world and that, or a world of that state, may occupy the same space. That in space the spiritual universe is identical with the physical, is unavoidable. The question can only be, Do the worlds, of whatever character, of the spiritual universe, correspond in location with those of the physical? Are its inhabited centers identical in space with those that sustain the residents of flesh? Admitting the possibility that the spirit worlds are located in the spaces interlying the mineral worlds, there are special reasons for answering in the affirmative. While the outlying spaces are entirely occupied by substances cognate with those of the visible state, giving passage to light and the attractive forces that incessantly move between worlds and on which the immense stellar structure rests, the spiritual, which is like continuous, must be there as well. But in the places where are gathered and organized into shapely, lovely worlds, out of their nascent state, the elements from vast surrounding areas—where life, spirit and mind are revealed in connection with mineral forms, as seen in this world, and which seem improbable save in such aggregations,—there, too, would the finger of expectancy point as the location of the corresponding spirit world—the immediate abode of the soul that has passed beyond the flesh. The *immediate* abode; not that anything appears that would suggest a final retention to one locality—that an endless life endlessly requiring scenic inspirations should be withheld from going abroad through the splendors of a universe of that character.

But, however intimately the states may combine in location, and inseparable as the two great departments of being may finally be as universal substances, a particular physical world would hardly be a necessity to a corresponding spiritual world, any more than that a spiritual body is permanently dependent on that which is earthly. Rather as the physical body dies and goes into re-distribution with the elements whence it originated, so might the earth in the long ages to come, or sooner, be retaken by the ever-flowing currents passing by and through it, to be drifted asunder and into new arrangements, or be permanently sundered, particle from particle. Claims of such, however respectably maintained, are founded on nothing better than the unqualified fact of never ceasing change itself. Yet, the world was once without living forms and so, also, may pass on again into conditions fatal to their existence.

The question of immortality is not in the least affected by the shifting character of external nature—the formation or the destruction of material worlds. However the spiritual world may be characterized by shifting scenes, obedient to the laws of its own elements, the destruction of the physical world would not affect the spiritual as much as a thunderstorm on Jupiter would the atmosphere of our planet, when we come to consider the great disparity that must lie between the two orders of substances.

The old-time Christian thought associated the world of the blest with the upper atmosphere or far beyond somewhere. This idea was practicable enough till the shape and motion of the earth were ascertained. Then to the intelligent Christian what was above at the evening prayer was below at the morning; and the saints, who were at one time in the supposed direction of heaven, were, at another time, in the supposed direction of its opposite. With much propriety, however, do we in our time and ever, use the term high to denote the exalted state—the most refined ever being the superior. The scale running from the immature to the mature. As when we speak of high intelligence, high morality or high civilization, we have reference to extensive attainments in these elements of being. In using the phrase, "The High and Holy One," reference is had to the Deity, who is omnipresent as to location, and is as much below as above; but in excellence being the infinite superior, is only *above*. So likewise "the highest heaven," often referred to in religious discourse, is to be understood as the state of the highest perfections of life.

But while there is ample room for a world for the immortals leaving this world, anywhere where nature itself may be found, it is difficult to see what importance attaches to its location. In relation to universal space, no one can tell where our earth is located. Yet that fact does not in the least disturb our enjoyment of its delightful apartments, or afford cause for homesickness. It is more to our purpose to know what and how it is than where it is.

This chapter would hardly be complete without some special reference to the primary state of the substance we call mineral. By common consent the ultimate analysis of matter is a present and, seemingly, a final impossibility. Back of the impalpable state is the irresolvable aggregate of substances, permanently inaccessible to all physical means of apprehension. And yet while the analysis of science is at this point unable to proceed, the mind, by means of its inductive powers, may extend the search far toward what may be settled as its primal form; thus attaining conclusions by a process hardly less reliable than that of sensuous demonstration itself. The known forms of substances, as rocks and metals, are plainly the result of adequate causes, to be seen in the properties of their essences which bring them into crystallization, under favorable surroundings. These several essences point back to an ulterior oneness, by the oneness of sympathy, however remote, that connects them all,—and also in the fact of their many common properties and strong resemblances.

And, incidentally, from this it seems necessary also, in order to account for the origin of these forms, to resort to the theory of an adequate mind presiding over this oneness, and by special, designing volitions impinging upon it the special modes of force required for these forms,—ordaining thus the constitution, laws, and features of nature, as they appear to us.

These states are not alone inaccessible to the faculties of sense, but to the mental eye only their *necessity* is visible. As infinity is known and talked about as familiarly as a household object, and yet its necessity is the nearest approach the finite mind can make toward its reality.

However their origin, the mineral universe is an aggregation of special mineral ethers as numerous as the several kinds of substance that appear in nature. And of these, again, many ethers may be necessary in combination to render them recognizable objects. To each, also, there is a place in the order of nature that no other supplies. Each is a link in the chain of mineral being that may nowhere be wholly absent. A mineral universe is but an all-pervading mineral ether, generalizing all the special forms, which, under favorable circumstances, would pass into crystallization and become tangible, and enter into the composition of worlds, but otherwise would remain in their imponderable states. Then, though there might be no rocks, iron, silver or gold on another planet, their ethers, more or less plentiful, would be there; while our own earth must contain many elements no chemist yet has found, and which may abound in tangible forms on other spheres.

This, then, is the external surrounding of man in his present state of living, of which he is embodied, of which his bodily senses are organized, to the perception of which they are adapted, and where the mind performs its first evolutions. From it, then, let us proceed to other states of being and their ethers farther inward.

CHAPTER VII.

INSENSIBLE WORLDS THAT WE KNOW OF, CONTINUED.—THE VEGETABLE REALM.—A VEGETABLE ETHER UNIVERSAL.

THE last chapter calls attention to the worlds of substances lying beyond the reach of the external senses, but more especially those of the mineral kingdom, and with reference to ultimately defining the location of the spiritual state and abode of man. Before proceeding to the next topic, the definition of the word "mineral" should be given. By doing so, it will be seen quite inclusive of all sensuous substances. Prof. Dana observes under the head, *What is a mineral?* "It has been observed that Mineralogy, the third branch of Natural History, embraces everything in nature that has not life. Is, then, every different thing not resulting from life, a mineral? Are earth, clay, and all stones, minerals? Is water mineral? All the materials here alluded to properly belong to the mineral series. * * * *
Water has no qualities which should separate it from the mineral kingdom. All bodies have their temperature of fusion; lead melts at 612 deg. F.; sulphur at 226 deg. F.; water at 32 deg.; mercury at—39. No difference, therefore, of this kind can limit the mineral departments. Ice is as properly a rock as limestone; and were the tempera-

ture of our globe but a little lower than it is, we would rarely see water except in solid crystal-like masses or layers. Our atmosphere, and all gases occurring in nature, belong for the same reason to the mineral kingdom. Several of the gases have been solidified, and we can not doubt that at some specific temperature each might be made solid. * * *A mineral, then, is any substance in nature not organized by vitality, and having a homogeneous structure.*

"The *first* limitation here stated—not organized by vitality—excludes all living structures, or such as have resulted from vital powers; and the *second*—a homogeneous structure—excludes all mixtures or aggregates" (Manual of Mineralogy.—pp. 14, 15).

This definition of *mineral*, in respect to a distinction as to the mineral and the vegetable and animal forms of matter, representing also, as it does, the common view of the subject, is such as to leave, after all, all visible existence of the order of mineral elements, only that in one instance it has been in the hands of the vital forces, and in the other it has not. Vegetable matter is composed of the substances of the earth and the atmosphere, and may be resolved back again into the original gases and ethers from which it was evolved by these special forces styled "vital." Before it was appropriated by the vegetable it was in its gaseous or ethereal states, and might have been reduced to, perhaps, corresponding rocks and metals.

Then, associated with these mineral substances or ethers, are to be seen, by the individual forms representing them, the *vital* elements or ethers, but higher and farther inward on the grade of being, the lower of these being the vegetable. The lovely plant, existing partly in the earth and partly in the air, and deriving subsistence from both, represents the first in the order of this indefinitely numerous series of universes interlying the mineral.

And thus it is seen that inner from and beyond our external and visible surrounding, there is a state with a substance of very unlike and superior qualities. It presents not only much greater activity, but also a species of instinct. The plants that are standing about my table as silent witnesses to my labors, as to all that I see of them, are minerals, constructed into these lovely forms by the real plants operating upon them from the vegetable state within. The structures are easily enough comprehended, but the construction—the putting together—by these adequate internal agents from within executing the work, is confessedly a superhuman difficulty. They are too orderly to occur from accident, and too much operating toward ends to be without a species of sense. The symmetry is pleasing, the coloring in richness and pattern is matchless; while the distilled odors are in the highest measure exhilarating. But all this, so far as chemistry can enlighten us, is only inert material, owing the delightful arrangements to vital organisms within inaccessible to chemistry, existing as the adequate causes. These vital individuals, as they themselves enlarge, and their individual needs increase, erect about them these material trellises, enveloping themselves with myriad prismatic splendors and loading the adjacent atmosphere with the most enchanting aromas. "I say unto you that Solomon in all his glory was not arrayed like one of these." And for the incense that filled his royal apartments, this prince was indebted to the labors of these lovely, living laboratories of nature.

THE PLANT NOT A MINERAL DEVELOPMENT.

That the plant is not due to a phase of mineral forces, or a spontaneous production from that kingdom, is made certain by several well recognized facts: The soils and atmospheres most suited to its growth are unproductive till the living germ or cell is properly inserted. Voluminous speculations concerning spontaneous generation have failed to obviate the difficulty which this single fact interposes. Though it is extremely difficult, if not finally impossible, to determine when soil, water or atmosphere may not contain some form of living germ which extreme heat or chemical erosion may not have destroyed, the facts that in the most favorable conditions, vegetable life does not issue from the soil without having been deposited there, and that from it it is in no form seen originating, are strong evidence against spontaneous generation. Also, the nature of vegetable life, —descending through all time by families and types, is in conflict with the theory of its production from the mineral state. The properties of the mineral kingdom are such as to render it of almost interminable variety; and the vegetable, to be the product of the mineral, or even to be primarily dependent on it, should be of corresponding variety. The plowed field, instead of yielding vegetation in well marked types and families, as wheat, oats, corn, apples, grapes, etc., should issue heterogeneous mixtures of these, somewhat in correspondence with the soils producing them. If the typal characteristics of these families should be continuous, maintaining their typal identities, as the several ingredient minerals persistently retain their elemental identities, then as minerals in the soils are aggregated in very unlike mixtures, so the vegetable forms resulting from them, should be found in corresponding confusion,—various typal characteristics jumbled into the same individual product. In the language of chemistry, the plant might, accidentally, in one example, be pure wheat, in another, the oatate of wheat or the bicornate of wheat, according to the combination of the evolving minerals present. Unless there be attributed to the mineral, *per se*, the voluntary power to suppress its own properties in accordance with the requirements of this family or typal persistence in plants, the last probability of their being forms of the mineral state, disappears.

It could be of no avail to say that vegetable life, with its forms once attained—evolved as we see it—is now advanced to the superior position where, by an inherent conservative law of selective subsistence, and by reproduction from seed or other form of cell, it maintains its types, and is quite independent of any *originating* qualities of the mineral compounds from which it is subsisted. This were only shifting the difficulty to a more pleasing distance, without, in any measure, getting rid of it! Let it be admitted that, at the point where our agriculture takes vegetable life, it is too far developed to be any longer susceptible of the soil's originating qualities; then we need only to go back to the alleged beginning—to protoplasm, the conversion of mineral into organic forms; and here the same difficulty presents itself. Again, it requires to be explained why, from the indiscriminate aggregates, should ascend such orderly conservative types? And, suppose it be said that the ethers, in requisite densities, properly formed the simple slime of protoplasm; does this explain why, in this proper assembling of elements, parts of the general mass are retained and other parts are rejected, in such precisely suitable measures as to establish even the mere typal structures or embodiments, saying nothing of their tendency to persistence, and why this assembling *itself takes place?*

But the same protoplasmic process is present in all vital forms, in the highest as truly as in the lowest. The mineral aliment for the germ, incased about it in the seed, becomes available by the action of the adjacent elements rendering it pulpy and viscid, and thus, suitable to be wrought into cell-structure, to which purpose it becomes, in part, appropriated by the liberated life of the incipient plant. Then, the same state of mineral substance relied on for spontaneous generation being present in all orders of vegetable production, spontaneity, if true at all, should be true and visible everywhere: —as well in our cultivated fields as on sea bottoms! The aliments of the same seeds, instead of being restricted to the production of but the one type, should produce in variety, as the constituents of the aliment could hardly in any two cases be wholly the same or of the same proportions, and the excitants are never exactly the same.

With a nearly total want of resemblance between the vital and mineral forces, an apology were due to the reader for occupying the space with arguments for their separate substances and planes of being, but for claims of the doctrine of spontaneous generation that have been extensively and ingeniously urged upon the attention of the popular mind. From what is obvious of the two kingdoms, their relationship is scarcely more than that of the builder and his material.

As has been said, the facts in the orderly construction of the human habitation, in which the builder reaches forth and intelligently selects the material suited to his purpose, correspond well with the facts in relation to the production of the plant. From the surrounding material in earth, water and air, this instinctive individual of internal vegetable life, extending its invisible hands, selects and appropriates the elements needed in constructing its requisite body; proceeding in this way until the internal—the plant itself—has attained the full development of its individual nature.

By this it is not only seen that the vegetable subjects the mineral, but that it is all the time *preceding* its mineralization,—that it is a substance affected with typal instincts and forces, and is as truly, though not as completely, independent of the elements which it selects as is the mason of the stones which he builds about himself into a wall.

It undergoes *modification* in great variety, from the mineral state. When growing in localities differing in soils and temperatures, it varies correspondingly in structure and habit. But that these conditions have not influenced the typal form itself, is manifest in the fact that it is not any more available for hybridizing with other plants than before. It has not left its orbit and come nearer to others. Its relation with other plant lives is left wholly unchanged. All that is apparent in these modifications is to be explained by reference to the fact that its development is amid surroundings which impinge upon it favorably or unfavorably according to the indications of the special modes of growth that are seen. The food supplied from soil and atmosphere has been more favorable to one part of the organism and less to another, according to how the modification has tended.

By the same principle, the application of intelligent cultivation enables the plant to display qualities and forms quite unknown in the original representatives of its family. Like man, the unaided plant is never at its best.

But, however such changes may be effected in it by the mineral state, each family must be regarded as a separate form of its general life, with a fixed and distinct order of qualities, which, by a system of germination, is conveyed along from generation to generation, the tendency always being to enlarge the number of its representatives.

IT IS UNIVERSALLY PRESENT.

Its universal presence is assured by what assures a universal mineral presence: namely, *its forces!* These are possible only with a universal wholeness of the substances embodying them! "Nature abhors a vacuum" in one order of substance no more than in that of another. It so abhors because of its universal tendency to equilibrium. The vegetable element, with its typal lines, in the process of developing its forms or in latency waiting, in rareness or profusion, is to be considered as extending universally—co-extending with the mineral and spiritual universes.

Hence, on every mineral world, swimming in the serum of infinite space, of requisite mineral representation, and of proper density and temperature, vegetation may safely be supposed to be decking the surface of nature as on our own. Every such terrestrial floor throughout his many mansioned house, the Great Father has overspread with this living beauty.

VEGETABLE IN THE SPIRITUAL STATE POSSIBLE.

But there is yet another view to be sought of this vegetable universe; not for anything that it might contribute to the theory of it as a separate entity, but with a purpose to approximate an understanding as to how it may be related with the spiritual side of being. For concluding that, as shown, it is not identical with the mineral, through which it manifests its existence, the question to one who is in love with this form of nature, may readily occur, May not this vegetable soul reveal itself on the spiritual side as well, and perhaps in still more lovely ways and forms? Part of what may constitute all the answer that may be safely given to this, is deferred till farther along.

Knowing why or from what this element makes its appearance in the present visible state, and knowing also what must be the qualities of substance in the spiritual realm, one might legitimately judge of the probability of the vegetable manifesting itself there as well. The most probable way of accounting for its presence *here* is to consider that its requirements bring it,—that finding in these material elements a required subsistence and means of development, it appropriates them to its use. Should then the substances of the spirit state correspondingly afford supplies to the nature of any of its forms, it would follow that they, in such modes of life as would harmonize with the peculiarities of that state, would be represented there. In modes of being, human life conforms to the peculiarities of the present state, and will, it may be assumed, have no trouble in appearing even more perfectly in the next, however unlike this it may be. So, likewise, might the vital forces of the vegetable exhibit extreme variations in their modes of manifestation in the same two states in which man is represented; and without the loss or change of identity. That it operates on this mineral side for the sake of subsisting and maturing itself, may be true to a limited extent. That is, subsistence and maturity result to it by the food it derives from the material world. But when we consider that bodily food does not assimilate with life at all—even the life which it sustains—but only acts as an excitant to life by transferring certain forces to it which are wholly immaterial, we no longer see the strict necessity of mineral food to even the support of life, *per se*, unless we show that from no other source than the mineral that excitant may proceed. Appetite does not call for additions of elements with a view to placing them into life. It is more like the mason calling for brick to lay them into the surrounding wall, when he is only seeking the impressions of comfort the house supplies. Or, what may more clearly illustrate, the electrician who needs more electric force does not call for more electricity, but orders up repairs and more cups to his battery. The battery is but the bridge over the interlacing atoms of which that certain force issues to impress itself upon the adjacent medium, there to be transformed into special modes of force as the new recipient may direct.

This is precisely the office of the material body. The ultimate fibers of food taken into the system in response to appetite, go only into the formation of minute cells—cups of batteries—for delivering force upon life itself, or upon some interlying semi-vital ether which conducts it thither, by the impulse of which is produced the satisfying sensation of vital activity. Not a single mineral fiber or atom goes beyond the cups, some of which are barely, though distinctly, visible by the most powerful microscopic aid.

That these visible cells are of the innermost line, immediately against which the life functions are arranged, it is at present neither possible nor important to say. It is, however, entirely safe to say that while their variety is necessarily great, answering to the great variety of functional wants, beyond where the utmost microscopic power is effectual, there may be many classes of cells much more diminutive, which, by their special natures, are delivering special impulses and awakening the required special activities.

Every atom, of whatever substance, stops in or within the walls of a cell. Thence, after being "broken down" by the traversing force, it returns to the earth as it was, to be followed by the new atom taking its place, in turn to be also broken down to retake its place among the elements of its kind.

That I may not seem to the casual reader, who may not have followed closely the researches of science on this point, to be advancing peculiar views, I will here insert a brief quotation from Dr. Wm. B. Carpenter, the eminent English physiologist, who is so favorably known throughout the educated world, especially in that branch of science. The quotation is from a chapter specially devoted to this subject, and given to the world in a compilation of scientific papers edited by Prof. E. L. Youmans, already referred to:

"Thus, during the whole life of the animal, the organism is restoring to the world around both the *mate-*

rials and the *forces* which it draws from it; and, after its death, this restoration is completed, as in plants, by the final decomposition of its substance" (Correlation and Conservation of Force, p. 443).

At first reading this language might appear to affirm quite too much for the purpose for which I have here introduced it. But the reader will observe, that the professor affirms of the *organism* exactly what I have affirmed. At its death both the materials and the forces which the organism *drew from* the world are returned to it. None will have disappeared into and become a part of the entity which evoked and wove them into form. And of course when released they return to the state whence they were taken; as the materials of the ordinary battery, having been "broken down" by the passage of force, are, together with their own inhering force, returned to the world from whence they were taken. The life entity itself, however, the agent in the construction of the plant form, not having been of this world, could not return to it, but must, at this death, return back on its own side of nature, a continuous plant, or to be redistributed with the ether of its own elements, possibly to reappear in new individuals of its order.

If, then, we were to propose to answer the question suggested by this train of thought, May this vegetable ether develop any of its types on the spiritual side of nature, to contribute a floral beauty to the attractiveness of that state? we would need only to consider whether that state is characterized with substances analogous to the mineral; that is, of an inert, passive quality, which might afford it this requisite nourishment—the passage of the stimulant impulses that it would require to have impinge upon itself in order to excite its life to growth.

The slight traces of semi-rational instinct that appear, are to be referred to the general law of appetite (not all of which, however, refers to material food) and to some extent indicate that the vegetable has means of gratification and growth which do not necessarily involve the use of the substances of the mineral state. However, these traces are too obscure for data on which to rest any decisive observations. Though the disposition often seen in the plant to seek light, warmth and water, is to be classed with the general promptings of its nature to go after bodily subsistence, whether that be mineral or of some other order of passive existence. But, at least, the propagative disposition, in which is something of the nature of the selection of kind, is not to be classed with appetites of this character. It is, however, the evidence of a want, the supply of which is on the side of its own domain, and which is a principal motive in the development of the individual life. Also, the vegetable being graded between the mineral and animal states, where the semblance of the mineral substance is found in association with the animal, rational or irrational, the presence of the vegetable kingdom might well be expected.

It might, also, be well here to refer briefly to the modes of vegetable life as bearing on this question.

The ordinary plant subsists by being inserted partly in the earth and partly in the air,—very few being more in the earth. But while this is true of the largest number, it represents only a portion of the kingdom, and is not at all universal. And of these, the weight of their forms impressing their bases in the earth, may be assigned among the causes of their taking this position, which, being habitual, has resulted in a class of mouths that are suited to obtaining nourishment under the surface of the ground. For, granting that their organization unfits them for any other mode, there is meaning in the fact that the rootlets are most abundant near the surface, where the soil is more rare, and the atmosphere circulates with greater freedom. Other plants, however, are of aquatic nature, and live chiefly or entirely in the water, drifting from place to place. Others live entirely from the atmosphere, even in the arid atmosphere of tropical deserts. The *Epidendrum* will for years live and bloom, suspended from a ceiling in mid air, and nourished from the atmosphere alone.

But it is apparent, that while any state, to be characterized with order, figure and fixity, must be characterized by forces corresponding with those of the external world—cohesion, gravitation, etc.—they might not be in the same proportion to each other, from which the mode of being might not be the same. Besides, what is *greatly* important, with the higher orders of existence, new forces, more intimately related with *volition*, are found supervening the mineral; as in the case of the will dissolving and resolving the magnetic energies of the living body, at discretion. And though the law of gravitation is, in the mineral state, without a known solvent that may neutralize or mitigate its hold, or reverse its tendency, is such a power not to be anticipated in the living ethers with their special and superior forces? In animal economy mineral forces become reversible or subservient to those of volition. The demonstration of this fact, by even so small a circumstance as the movement of living muscles in obedience to the impulses of the mind, is some assurance of the prevalence of that principle of force sufficiently great to produce, in a state so superior as that which must be accorded to the spiritual, possibly great changes in the modes of being. This might be true alike of its passive substances and of the inhabiting life, vegetable and animal; while the character of the modification would be favorable to their existence rather than otherwise.

It is hardly possible to conceive of a state having individual existences, as the world of spirits must be allowed to have, without having palpable scenery, responding to their needs; but, with the active presence of some, and possibly of many, forces little known or wholly unknown to us, no settled conclusion as to its *details* can be indulged. This encouraging fact, however, remains; the state is not *inferior* but *superior* to our present. Hence its greater gratifications to our superior nature would seem a necessity. The prevailing evidences also are in favor of a correspondence in the essential features of that world with the one we live in. The evidences that apply to its existence, determine its being of a cosmical character, and as being remotely allied with this visible existence. But astonishing little would be the alteration required in the forces of this existence to render many of its details very unlike what they now are, to which vegetable and animal life would need to conform. But as the type of the vegetable is not determined by mineral conditions, to appear in any existence at all, would be to appear in its own nature and form to the extent that surroundings would admit. And so with the animal. So, then, of that land that lies far inward of this, spread out into a radiant universe, the substance may hold in modification, but may not change the type of any life which may extend there from any other world.

Moreover, the vegetable extending inward to the realm of the spiritual would, necessarily, be of the highest types contained in that ether. The history of vegetable life on the planet has been extensive enough to substantiate this claim. In the gross, unsettled state of the mineral world, vegetable life has been correspondingly gross. The vegetable growth, during the ages when the elements contained immense quantities of carbon, was dense and vast as at no other time; growing and perishing in rapid succession, and thus carrying the carbon with it down into the earth in reservation for the future comfort of man. The varieties seem not to have been numerous, but of the crudest types, developed in the grossest fiber and forms; in the main, leathery, spongy, unseemly, flowerless, colorless, vapid and vile. The finer elements, which emit the agreeable odors accompanying the bloom of fruitage, had not yet been reached by nature's laboratory; nor was the material yet in hand whereof to overspread the petals with radiant *spiculæ*. The rainbow had not yet been set in the heavens, nor on the plant. And the types then prevalent have either wholly disappeared, or shrunken from giant trees to the trivial diminutiveness of a few inches.

The history of the vegetable kingdom is thus described by a distinguished writer: "We see only detached bits of that green web which has covered our earth ever since the dry land first appeared; but the web itself seems to have been continuous throughout all time; though ever as breadth after breadth issued from the creative loom, the pattern has altered, and the sculpturesque and graceful forms that illustrated its first beginnings and its middle spaces have yielded to flowers of richer color and blow, and fruits of fairer shade and outline; and for gigantic club mosses, stretching forth their hirsute arms, goodly trees of the Lord have expanded their great boughs; and for the barren fern and the calamite, clustering in thickets beside the waters, or spreading on flowerless hill slopes, luxuriant orchards have yielded their ruddy flush, and rich harvests their golden gleam" (Testimony of the Rocks.—Hugh Miller, p. 502).

The vegetable has thus far well proven its ability to keep pace with the progress of the mineral world in promptly issuing higher and more lovely forms as the mineral substance became refined. Hence the probability is that though the specimens may be stationary, or floating in the diviner atmosphere; and though they might germinate after the earthly manner, and so likewise fade and die; or, by insensible gradations, might rise into and recede from view; or, like the banyan tree, beset their appointed bounds by ever renewed growth, it is not in the nature of things that the loveliest plants of earth should equal those inspiring the senses of the immortals in the gardens celestial.

CHAPTER VIII.

Insensible Worlds that We Know of, Continued.—The Animal Element in Nature.—Its Position Interior of the Vegetable.—Its Special Superior Forces and Prerogatives.—The Animal Ether, Etc.

SOME strong resemblances may be seen between the vegetable and animal kingdoms. In certain forms they appear to be of the same order of existence. Each is divided into families and types, and these again into varieties, maintaining, for the most part, strict genealogies and descending in races. Sex lines and the propagation of their species are characteristic of both. The propagation by conjunction of the sexes is about as common in one kingdom as in the other. Their nutritive apparatuses are also in strong resemblance to each other. However, they are unlike as to the selection of the elements of subsistence. The vegetable takes its food from inorganic, while the animal depends on organic fiber.

Both are of nutritive instincts, conserving their general plans of organism, which results in that systematic adjustment of the materials in the arrangements of their bodily forms. Both the animal and the plant in all their states and forms are living beings, inhering in vital ethers of the properties and qualities indicated by their individual representatives, and attain to maturity by the common principle of the development of their internal, constitutional forces. These are progressively evoked or liberated from their latency by the augment of external forces, which, through the instrumentality of their surrounding material cell systems, they induce upon themselves. The bodily organisms in both kingdoms, as to extent and manner of organization, may be regarded as only the requisite material embodiment of the forces essential to their relation with external nature. And when the constitutional functions, with their corresponding organs, are all fully outlined, the body will have attained its full size and shape.

To this there is a seeming exception in that the vegetable appears, in some of its types, limited in size only by the producing powers of the elements; and, by continually issuing new branches, is all the while undergoing changes as to individual appearance. The resemblance to its type is, however, not lost thereby. The oak at a century and at a dozen centuries is the same as to its characteristics; and, bating the mutilations from disease and external causes, maintains the pattern of the oak. The same is to be observed of the polyp in the lower forms of the animal kingdom. But these are not, properly, exceptions to the law of bodily production referred to.

Up to this point the vegetable and animal are strongly analogous. But beyond this, it is seen that the two natures are widely different. The vegetable in its highest forms, exhibits no traces of the distinguishing features and forces now appearing in the animal. Here is a system of nerves, interlying the organism, on which are plying forces not met with in the kingdoms below.

Plants are to some extent affected by an apparent sensitiveness, as already referred to. Some being of so refined an order as to be impressible, favorably or unfavorably, by the atmosphere of human life. It is a common trouble of florists, that with some people, and with the most appropriate treatment, some plants will wane and die; while with others, by the best care, they remain sickly and dwarfed. Also, contrariwise, the plant is at times seen to do specially well with the care of certain ones; all owing to the impressibility of human temperamental peculiarities. The same, to be sure, would be true of association with other forms of life. In some plants (*genus Mimosa*) this trait is so prominent as to suggest the name of "Sensitive-plant."

But this impressibility seems not owing to any functional arrangement in the plant, there being no corresponding organization. Hence, it is rather a chemical than a vital phenomenon; rather the nice general cell arrangement by the refined plant within, yielding so readily to the neighboring emanation, than that it is owing to sensation properly. All that is apparent in the most perfect plant, in its most satisfied condition, conveys no reason why it should be experiencing happiness. And, when drooping from exhaustion or shriveling by heat, nothing is seen to justify the consideration of pain. The shriveling contortions are from the inflating gases and dissolving fiber, and are in like manner seen in the decomposition of lifeless structure. Its beauty in health and its convulsions in the process of fire might suggest sensations of happiness and of pain, but the anatomist would find no occasion to suspect their existence.

But, regarding the plant as a thing of *life*, without taking into account the fact of vegetable and animal life being different entities with different properties and different organisms, it might be no small difficulty to overcome the impression that the sense of pleasure in some way belongs to it; that though no organism indicates it, it may by some secret way yet exist, to be some day uncovered by a better science; and that thus the thing of life, of beauty, and of sweetness, is also a thing of happiness; or, alas! of pain at times. But, while the conjecture might be entertaining, that the floral universe is an infinite throbbing happiness, the proposition at best could never be more than a sentimental conjecture.

The plant is as old as the animal, but no trace of an organism for the embodiment of sensation has yet been evolved in it. Besides, without it, its mission and plan of being are complete. And though the vegetable is a living entity, and greatly superior to the mineral, the presence of sensation is as probable in the one as in the other. The hair of the human body is also a thing of life, of animal fiber, and is dependent on animal forces; has a selective function, or mouth, at its root; no stomach, no heart, no nerve, no sensation; but is complete, and all it should be, and all it was designed to be, without these.

But the differences between the two kingdoms are more apparent when we come to consider their higher forms. Saying nothing of man, one will readily note many particulars in which the sagacious horse is entirely unlike the great tree that overshadows him. The tree is a truly wonderful object to contemplate, but the horse is immeasurably more so. Though characterized with life and working out a design half intelligently, the tree remains stationary, rooted fast in the soil, and is dependent for life on such materials as are within reach of its bodily appointments; while the horse has the power of locomotion, and conveys himself after the objects of his gratification, when necessary to obtain them. At this high grade of the two kingdoms the difference is prominent and the classification easy. But in the simpler forms, the naturalist has been made to doubt whether he should classify his subject with the animal or vegetable. Being but little advanced in the scale of living nature, and with characteristics imperfectly developed, it has been difficult to agree that the sponge is or is not an animal, or the polyp is or is not a plant. The natures of the two kingdoms often, in those lower forms, seem so much confounded in the same individual.

Then in contrasting the two kingdoms, it is necessary that we take them at the points where the highest forms obtain—where these departments of nature are most fully characterized—that no constituent element will be overlooked for want of proper development. And, doing so, we see that above the highest attributes of the vegetable realm, the animal brings to our consideration a series of functions that evidence the existence of an essence much its superior as well as much farther inward in nature. Here are sight, hearing, touch, taste and smell, employed in the uses of this existence, subserved by organisms correspondingly wonderful in their mechanism.

The device of senses were absurd but for the consideration that they are fitted to an entity whose nature requires means of this kind to facilitate its development and the accomplishment of its mission. Some of these are serviceable in the selection of the ordinary bodily supplies without contact therewith, by conveying their several kinds of apprehension of outward nature to the inward principle of voluntary thought, as by sight or by sound. And but for that thinking principle within to seize and reflect upon the impressions thus derived from nature, and relegating the intelligence they awaken to the powers of volition, out of which the rational action comes, which chooses this and refuses that out of the aggregate presented for bodily food, these faculties would be as useless to animal economy as the microscope to the stone; and for the same reason were as unmeaning in the unthinking vegetable as in the mineral. No correspondence or analogy is to be noted between the simple instinct which builds the fiber in the vegetable or the animal tissue, after an immutable pattern in nature, and the designing power that is apparent in the uses of these senses.

And by no possibility can these senses be considered as belonging to an entity to which they are alike useless and meaningless. Their existence is no more a certainty than is also that of the sentient substance which alone they so perfectly conserve, and for which alone is the purpose of their existence. The design of their existence may not be apprehended without at the same time apprehending the intelligent entity for which they are designed. These senses also refer to a nourishment demanded by this higher essence, which is not required by the kingdom below, and on which it is dependent for the development of its attributes. This development is not, strictly speaking, by the use of assimilating forces, as in vital recuperation, but, purely, by apprehension, which it is the special office of the senses to perform, and which, when it has been attained, is by a *mental* selectiveness relegated to knowledge, and in this form is satisfying to the yearnings of the thinking principle in the animal economy.

Apprehension itself is by impression, plainly enough, and thus far the process of nourishing the mind is analogous to that of nourishing the ordinary vitality of vegetable or animal tissue. Through its vibratory properties, nature makes its impressions indifferently upon its surroundings, to be utilized by any receiving entity to the extent and in the manner that its own properties call for. In the lower, or vegetative, processes, there is need manifested for rudimental cell force—the structural force—obtainable by immediate atomic contact of homogeneous substances. The force craved and acquired on this plane and in this manner, supplies this simple purpose and manifestly no other. It indicates the presence of a capacity to receive and respond only to so much of nature's various operations. All the other of nature's pulsations are without a recognizing echo in the entity of that simple form of being. The mind is the only entity seizing upon and utilizing the aspects of nature—the mere spectacular forces.

THE PROCESS OF KNOWLEDGE.

To answer the demand of the thinking principle, in respect to external nature, mediate elements are necessarily employed; the mental entity being so much higher in the order of being, and hence, too, so much farther removed inward, its commerce with the external phase of existence is possible only by proxy.

The thinking entity, as a substance, is a matter of force, and so are the interlying entities between it and outward nature over which the apprehending powers of the mind proceed and the impressions are returned; but the apparition apprehended, *per se*, is not characterized by any of the attributes of substantial force, as that supreme agency in nature is manifested to our understanding. The pictured substance may be styled a condition of force, and so, too, the vehicle of light by which the resemblance is transferred; and impingement on consciousness is by a mode of force: but the picture, the resemblance, the variegated abstract fact, imprinted, and now contemplated, is without the recognized attributes of substance, outside of which substantial force may not be found.

From these immaterial realities—these pictures and the work of harmonizing them—the mind satisfies and extends itself. They respond to its hunger. They are its food from the external source. Their presence, by a sort of catalysis, confers a yearned-for release of the expansive properties of the thinking entity. Hence these gratifying sceneries or apparitions of nature, thronging upon the hungry senses, whether of sight, sound, touch, taste or smell, are to be regarded as the outlets rather than the inlets of mental force.

Strictly considered, therefore, the development of mind, the highest merely animal attribute, is from its own side of nature—the mental ether—partaking of neither the mineral nor the vegetable domain, save of their intelligible aspects as portrayed upon it by the action of the senses. These apparitions pass over the vital fiber which acts as the mere vehicle of the picturing powers. The forces that rebuild or replace that vital fiber itself are entirely unrelated with the picturing forces,—as the microscope itself, is not supposed to be conscious of the apparitions it supplies to the sense of sight.

ANOTHER IMPORTANT DISTINCTION.

But in yet another essential particular is the animal distinguishable from and superior to the vegetable.

Without exceeding it in bulk we find the animal far exceeding the vegetable in the activity and variety of its forces. The animal entity, revealing itself by an organization of voluntary functions and also by the attribute of mentality, as above referred to, is at the same time characterized by a voraciousness, so to speak, for force impingements, such as is nowhere found in the vegetable. This evidences an internal subtlety of being far exceeding that of the lower kingdom; while at the same time it proves plainly that the animal represents a state of life correspondingly more intense, active and powerful. It is greatly important to see not alone that the appointments of the animal nature are more varied, and of an order apparently wholly separate from and above the vegetable, but that these functions have far more capacity for the employment of force than is seen in the vegetable; which fact is a clear confirmation of the claim that the animal state is farther inward and nearer the great heart of universal power.

In what may be termed the vegetative department of animal economy, the nutritive formulæ in all the modes and places of fibrous construction in the body, the analogy between the two kingdoms, as before seen, is very strong; but the requirements in respect to this process, by these entities of nature, are very unlike. While the slow, leisurely currents of unaided capillary action are quite sufficient to supply the vegetable with the materials it requires for repairs and growth, the animal, in its true representative types, to meet its demands, has need of the most thoroughly efficient system of transfer imaginable—beyond the best engineering skill yet developed by the human mind. Here is placed a harmonious network of arteries and veins, suited and extended directly or indirectly to every part of the body, however minute and concealed. And these are made not only strong, but active. They are supplied by a well-knitted, elastic, muscular integument, not only to hold securely, but to assist in propelling the freighted fluid along on its rounds of delivering the needed fiber and fuel, and carrying away the debris and cinder.

But these alone are not sufficient. A throbbing engine, with powerful muscular walls, is placed at the head of these works; while wires of nerve fiber are distributed to all the contractor muscles upon these living freight lines, by simultaneous impulses to augment the flight of the transporting fluids. And to further increase the efficiency of this system, thorough provision is made to apply to this machinery the great motor of heat, in various suitable measures. A special and very intricate device—a pair of lungs—for transferring oxygen from the atmospheric air to the blood, in exchange for the extinguishing carbonic acid, is placed in the most protected cavity of the body, and is incessantly operated, pouring a constant blast of this fiery agent into the organism, for the use of the economy. While, at the same time, there is carbonaceous fuel, mainly of fat, distributed to the numerous magazines or receptacle cells that impinge upon this living network, from which to supply the waning fires.

Besides, that there may be as little waste of force as

possible, and that the small bodily limits may not be occupied by foreign substances, the admission of aliment is presided over by a selective taste, by which nearly all that is not serviceable as food is excluded. Moreover, the admission of the food is first into a most complete laboratory of muscular grinding and chemical erosion; dissolving, combining, eliminating, and thus putting it into the most complete readiness to finally pass on to the myriad cell mouths, who, from the urgency of the demands which this inward living energy begets, are gasping for it.

In contemplating this wonderful device of the animal organism—this inimitable machinery—it is to be remembered that the erection and using thereof are wholly from an invisible world, the existence of which may hardly be doubted by the observer whose gift of reason is adequate to the understanding of the physical or apparent part itself of this phenomenon. Neither will it be easy for the same measure of mind to fail to locate that invisible world, which contains this greater and more subtle motor of animal life, farther inward and nearer the perfect than that of the vegetable entity.

Another very important distinction is to be seen separating the animal from the vegetable. It is in respect to the element of affection or the love of individuals for individuals of their kind. Whether any such attribute as affection, properly so called, characterizes the vegetable kingdom, has, so far, not been fully demonstrable. But enough is known to say confidently, that what might be found, could differ but little from mere chemical affinity.

The only trait of the plant in respect to affection for a member of its kind, and in which it resembles the animal, is that of sexual adaptation.

This, to some extent, is in the likeness of the sexual relation in animal economy. But it is passive and seemingly passionless. And, in many instances, this sexual want of the plant is all supplied in the same individual, by self fructification. In other examples the pollen reaches its destination by drifting in the air or being conveyed by insects or by some other accidental means. But in all cases, so far as may be judged, there is a complete absence of any recognition or desire of conjugality or even companionship. It is but analogous to what may be seen in the selectiveness of chemical affinity. Iron atoms combine more readily with those of iron than with those of any other substance. So the vegetable entity will be found to be bonded in a sympathy or unity with its kind. And as iron atoms are massed by the property of polarity, by their opposite poles seeking each other in affinity, so the vegetable masses or multiplies its individuals by the law of mutual attraction of opposites—opposite halves of the same orders, if we may use the illustration.

Higher than this, the attribute of affection is not traceable in the plant life. At its best it is but an unconscious and feeble instinct, exerting little visible influence upon the organism.

Herein, therefore, is another instance of the superiority of the animal over the vegetable, little less marked than is that of intelligence itself. The element of affection in the animal is of such subtlety and power, and of such intensity, as to often overcome the powers of volition themselves, though aided by the strong reinforcements of reason, and to completely change the sentiments and current of the whole life.

Besides, while in the vegetable at best but one form of affection is indicated, namely, that which pertains to sex, in the animal—in the human or rational department—we may enumerate the conjugal, the fraternal, the filial, and the reverential in at least two varieties—for parents and for Deity. And these affections all refer to corresponding basic entities or substances of which they are the reciprocative and unifying bond. Affection, the same as all modes of common attraction, implies a commonness of essence in the objects drawn and united. These objects so drawn, being individualized states of that substance, are in sympathy as a brother with a brother; or as individuals of its opposite phases love—as one sex loves the other; or as child and parent love each other; or as the Deity may be said to love the humanity, and the spiritually enlightened human being loves the Deity. These phases are also endowed with corresponding peculiarities. Fraternal and parental loves are chiefly denoted by an expressive tenderness and social fondness, to which the conjugal adds an endearing sweetness, all expressed in yearnings analogous to those of appetite; while, also, the reverential, to that of social fondness, adds submissive confidence, etc. Then, the variety enlarges to view as it is seen that each circumstance draws its special form of sympathy;

as pain excites that which expresses itself in sorrow and tears, and happiness that which manifests itself in smiles and rejoicings.

And now it is to be uniformly remembered that these all are forces embodied in their respective substances, congenital with the soul in which they inhere, and lying wholly within the animal realm; part of them appearing in the irrational, and all in the rational orders of animal being, in some measure of development; that these forces, recognized and denominated affections or loves, are not denoted by any form of organization in the lower kingdoms, and are wholly without representation or even imitation in those more external states.

A word of explanation in reply to the hypothesis submitted by some, that the animal and vegetable entities are identical, from their frequent close resemblances in the lower forms, may properly here be added. Reference to these resemblances has already been made, but for another purpose. Then, if these entities are intrinsically so different, and are ranged in states so unequal, relative to the central, innermost and governing perfections of being, why do these mimicries and resemblances in their structure and habit, exist? And why may we not say that they are fundamentally the same life, extending thus widely, from the lowest vegetable to the highest animal characteristics? We may answer, that allowing the existence of an interlying medium, impressible from both states, analogous to what we have in the catalysis of chemistry, where by the mere presence of an element essentially foreign, elements derive important modifying influences from each other, all is explained: The relation being one of impingement rather than of affection. And the fact that, beyond what may in this simple way be wholly explained, resemblances do not continue, but in the higher and stronger orders of both, are lost, is proof of the most conclusive character, that the essences are not the same, and that the phenomena occur according to this explanation. The lower animal types, which are the least perfect, and therefore the weakest of the animal ethers, would of course suffer more readily restraints and modifications from the lower kingdom, and be more readily suborned into its resemblance, in form and habit. For example, in the coral, which is a community of homogeneous animal lives, the community or the plant-like structure, often extends itself upon the form or typal design of the vegetable. Feeble animal souls, as they are, they are readily trellised upon the vegetable patterns. It is the mutual impingement and transfer of force of the two elements, resulting in the adoption of common forms, rather than two branches of the same element joined below in a "loop."

The principle is seen to operate in other forms of the lower grades—worms, beetles, moths and butterflies, who do not only mimic vegetable life, but also animals of the lower forms. Interesting examples of these are to be seen referred to by Prof. Mivart (Lessons from Nature, etc., pp. 244—247), and by Wallace (Natural Selection, Chap. 3), where, in color and form, insects are so disguised by resemblance to their surrounding vegetable nature as to readily deceive the beholder into believing one to be a leaf or twig of the kind where it is found, and where it habitually lives; and whereof, also, it most probably derives its temporary modifications, but with which its diverse and superior attributes can in no sense combine or unify. The animal is of and for its own superior domain, and not to be confounded with that below.

Prof. Gray, the veteran botanist of Harvard, in his recent lectures to the theological class of Yale, intimates that the vegetable and animal kingdoms unify below; from the fact "that there are multitudinous forms which are not sufficiently differentiated to be distinctly either plant or animal;" and also because "in respect to ordinary plants and animals, the difficulty of laying down a definition has become far greater than before." From these facts he feels justified in expressing himself in the rather precipitant conclusion: "In short, the animal and vegetable lines, diverging widely above, join below in a loop" (Natural Science and Religion, p. 11).

But the professor would hardly concede that mineral elements chemically combined, and in that condition yielding their true characters for one greatly unlike either, must, because of this, be but the same element there joining in a loop.

CHAPTER IX.

Insensible Substances, Continued.—Intellect Further Considered.

IT will be observed that I use the terms "substance" and "matter" in somewhat separate meanings, in which essence is always substance, but not always matter—after the old time way of employing them. Of course no very fixed line of distinction can be drawn; but by this view matter would be that form of substance which is allied to the sensuous state, the substance of sensuous nature. In this sense mind, soul, and spirit, being embodiments of force, are substances, while they are not to be classed with material substance, or, strictly, with the mineral domain.

In thus conforming to this old time conventional use of these words, it is not to be understood that in matters of law, where the same conditions are involved, they are subject to different systems. The principles of force and of cause and effect, can only be considered as of one and the same universal government, extending over, and affecting alike, in like conditions, all forms of substance, whether of supreme mentality or of inert mineral. To be sure, the same conditions throughout are not to be expected in wholly unlike phases of substance. Hence the mental and the moral forces we would not look to find operating a piece of granite; nor would it be certain that we would find in the mental state what would fully correspond to the specific gravity of the stone, though the same principles of cause and effect are necessarily operating in both of these substances which in all other respects are without any relation soever which is defined to the human understanding.

In the previous chapter, which has been mainly devoted to the state and general attributes of animal life, in contrast with the vegetable, reference has been made to the element of mind; but necessarily in brief and quite general terms, and without the close discrimination that should characterize a presentation of the subject of mind in a fullness adequate to the present purpose, in which it is designed to exhibit its types, with respect to the superior and interior, on the general scale.

Even to the ordinary observer the kingdom of animal life is seen to be of great variety in form and grade. But as the simplest part of it is vested with a seemingly impenetrable mystery, the different phases of its phenomena are not commonly classified and grouped as the more palpable facts of lower nature are seen to be. Hence, too, fundamental causes for the differences of mental action have not been commonly suspected and looked for; and so this crowning manifestation in animated nature was, by a sort of common, hopeless consent, regarded as derived from a single entity, with all these differences as but from so many of its own intrinsic properties, or versatilities of the same properties.

But the mental universe, whose phases are denoted by the various animal types, spreads out into broad extremes, presenting differences as abrupt and wide as those noted between itself and the kingdom below.

Mentality in its lower forms, where the capacity is barely sufficient to apprehend and impress upon consciousness the most external features of nature, and possibly also the registered experiences of the organism, is indeed a wonderful phenomenon, denoting an immeasurable exaltation of being. But when we observe the majesty of that special form of mind whose office is to apprehend abstract principles—principles lying wholly away from and independent of sensuous substances—we strike out again into a new universe, the innermost order of existence; where are associated, co-operatively, in an inseparable oneness, all the supreme elements of being; which, in their limited but endlessly unfolding and ever advancing individual forms, constitute the finite or human phase; while in the infinite and unattainable heights and absolute perfections thereof, is the undivided sphere of Deity,—the state of the Supreme Jehovah!

DIVIDING LINE BETWEEN INSTINCT AND REASON.

Setting aside, for the present, a full discussion of the question that in connection with this subject so commonly arises, as to where—between what merely two classes of animals, that is, between man and what animal that is next to man—the line of distinction between irrational and rational mind is to be drawn, let but a brief passing note be made of the mental habits of some of the vertebrates, as they represent the highest order of the animal kingdom. And further, let them be of the mammalia; that our selection may be from the highest in that order. And here we see a very visible difference in the mental habits of the horse, the ox, the dog, and that most sagacious of lower animals, according to some naturalists,—the elephant, and those of man. This difference is more apparent as we remove each to his own sphere and away from the influences of the other; removing the brute, for a few generations, from the influence of domestication under man, away by himself; and man away from the wilderness and preponderant brute associations.

By near proximity, the brute, under the guiding hand of man, might, in time, become influenced by his mental habits, and thus, by the imitative quality of his mind, temporarily assume his traits—rational traits—that do not belong to him. Science would allow even more than this. The brute, by his necessary close, servile attention to man, might receive temporary mental impingements from the human source; where the higher element of mind might, unconsciously, diffuse itself upon the lower substance, and execute its special office through a lower organism, while in no way identical with the resident mind of the brute itself, as will be seen illustrated in a future chapter. The element in common, on which the action would be predicated, would be animal sensibility, lying within the lower nature of man and the brute alike, and available to either mental state, so far as the physical mechanism would be adequate to the execution of the requisite movements. Such transfer, through a rare temperamental condition on the part of the brute, might occur according to well known biological law, analogous to chemical law, referred to in the previous chapter in connection with "mimicries" in nature. Further along it will be seen also that it is not an unusual occurrence for a function of mind to employ a part of the nervous organism below that of its own immediate seat; as, for example, the wounding of a limb by a great mental force precipitated on it, but more especially in cases of rational acts being performed during periods of somnolency.

But the alleged phenomena of brute rationality would generally, if not always, find a ready and natural explanation in the brute's instinctive recurrence to the modes of its experience, incurred in its management while under training. Hence such deportment might be only of self-repetition, and not of original device.

To the beholder, who has not gone back and observed the long, careful training, and the minute adapting of beast to master by voice and gesture, the deportment of the animal on exhibition will be strong proof of its endowment with human reason. But recurring to the painstaking training, and mechanizing of the animal into essentially fixed modes of operating, of which the exhibition is but the last example—the last evolution of practice, he sees no need of recourse to rational mind for all that the facts reveal.

The extent to which this training may influence lower animals, may not be apprehended by even the skillful artists themselves, who, on their own part, do not have the same need of utilizing every experience and co-ordination of circumstances, by which to be directed in supplying the foods and conveniences of life, as the lower animals have to do, but who from their different mentality, can, to some extent, forget experiences, and draw on inductive intellect for the devising of current necessities. It is materially otherwise with the brute, who for want of the devising powers of reason must, unconsciously, substitute the remembrance of co-ordinated experiences, and essentially repeat himself—each time adding another evolution to his training. As the blind man, who has not the benefit of sight, must make more extensive use of his other senses, the irrational animal, from want of reason, attains the ends it needs on its simple plane, by a more diligent recurrence to the register of its experience. And, considering its limited mental range, the brute, as also many others of the lower forms of life, has ever been remarkable for its exact memory.

As an illustration of rare development of mind in the lower forms, facts connected with the death of an elephant, with some of the details, were related to me, in which it was evident that the animal was a good representative of his sagacious race. Prostrated upon his huge side and suffering intensely, his eyes followed his keeper, who, besides other modes of relief, was applying the soothing cold water; and when at any time it was discontinued, the sufferer would gently seize the hand of the keeper and convey it from the water to the wounded limbs; also in the same manner calling his attention to other seats of pain.

Here then, was, apparently, a phenomenon of the human mind. It was doing about as sensibly as a human being would do. And without the use of language, it was quite the same method by which a human being would, under the circumstances, undertake to relieve himself. And the question is, how is it to be accounted for without according to the elephant the reasoning attribute of the human mind? But what are the facts in this mental phenomenon? And what are its conditions? Do these necessarily involve the element of reason? Will not the theory of recurrence to co-ordinated experiences registered in the mind of the animal, and, indeed, assimilated with his bodily functions, readily account for all that so strongly indicates reason in these sentient deportments? In the first place, the animal was affected by pain from which it sought relief by its accustomed modes, so far as they were applicable to the case. In the second place, its movements with reference to the desired result, were the effect of certain modes of mental force—the highest and most efficient of its mental endowments would be called into service by the deadly pain. His movement was toward a compound object of relief,—the water and the hand, and from thence to the wounded part.

INTELLECT FURTHER CONSIDERED.   151

These facts, proceeding from a reasoning intelligence, would be explained, substantially, after this formula: the causative power of the hand must be directed to communicate with the water and effect its deliverance to the suffering part, implying also, a knowledge or a belief of the existence of the requisite ability, and also of the agreeable result following. And all this to be perceived independently of experience or example, other than the ideal act rationally constructed from principles found in combination with outside circumstances. For, though having experienced the treatment and the consequent relief, and perceiving the probability of its being followed by the same agreeable result, the man, without necessarily noting or remembering these facts, would proceed from their known principles to originate the application, as the keeper himself had done.

After this manner, substantially, would the rational mind have proceeded to produce the actions referred to in the case of the disabled elephant. The same acts assigned to the irrational mind, would, however, be explained by reference to a quite different mental process, involving a much less capacity. Though the distressing heat might have suggested a bath to the elephant, no signals indicated the *bringing* of the water, nor its application, prior to experiencing the act from the keeper, although a large body of it was near at hand, and his organization would have permitted their use. Recourse to experience of correlated circumstance, is the short and sufficient means of explaining the methods of the irrational mind in procuring the somewhat singular deportment of this animal.

But the animal had, for years, and probably during the whole of his long life, been the constant companion and servant of a keeper, from whom he received every privilege he enjoyed and every supply he needed—had often experienced severe punishment and kind restoration from the same hand; and from the same source had received constant training. His instinct, therefore, could not be otherwise than largely modified into human habits, as his experiences were almost wholly from the traits and treatments of his keeper. Besides, his main experiences, as to his own acts and deportments, were of close observation of the keeper's movements, with a constant retention of their effects upon himself.

Then that he should have recurred to his keeper's hand, with a view to mimic the mode of relief that he just experienced, was but in accordance with his organic nature and his lifelong training.

That the motion should be so human like—so like one using his arm in handling an object—is from the peculiar proxy arrangement of his organization, and is not essentially unlike extending his trunk to his food and conveying it to his mouth, or the bird seizing the twig and adjusting it to its nest—a mode of motion that it never learned nor otherwise acquired, but was part of it at its birth—a wonderful piece of mentality, yet wholly below reason.

People are often led to misjudge that because such phenomena are in strong resemblance to acts of reason, they are necessarily attributable to reason alone; not having fully considered the domain of instinct and the variety of purposes to which it may be extended by training, and what results may, and often do, thus follow from the many correlated chains of experiences at the disposal of an acute mind which is yet wholly on the plane of instinct.

Then, again, it is often the case that the *absence* of the power of analogy—one of the cardinal elements of reason in its lower forms—leads, substantially, to the same results that follow from the use of this great attribute of mind.

The indistinguishable grouping, simultaneously or in succession, of similar facts upon the mental apprehension, having a resemblance so strong as to cast, essentially, the same impression and awaken the same states of consciousness, would also call forth the same deportment, the one fact or experience as the other, and would from the sense of *oneness*, without analogy, apply to the same uses; which would very readily occur on a low plane of mind. But the more sentient mind, knowing them as *separate* and, by the power of analogy, judging them to be suitably *alike*, would be disposed to also apply them each to the same use, the same as in the previous case. In the one case, because they are *indistinguishable*, the one object or experience, may, by instinct, be mistakenly taken for the other; in the other, from a consciousness of their *distinction* joined with the fact of their resemblance, reason might decide that they may represent or substitute each other. In the former case, the substitution would be from a mistaken identity; in the latter, a device emanating from the mind.

Where the resemblance disappears in an absolute oneness, analogy or reason is impossible; but where there is a difference—a separation—a space—as between independent units, analogy erects her ideal mathematical lines, and mentally conveys them over the interlying differences, and by them measures and computes the resemblances, forming thus a judgment as to the extent and manner that one may take the place of the other and yield the same results.

A main distinction, then, between mind on the level of instinct, and that on the level of reason, is, that in the former it is actuated from without, by the impingement of current experiences correlating with those that are registered in the memory, and thus exciting the volition whereof the mind proceeds, in its accustomed modes, to influence the organism to select results in harmony with the major stress of appetite, passion or any form of yearning; while in the latter it is self-actuating and originative—devising within itself and issuing from itself, new modes and reforms of modes. The former being but adapted to *echo* devices of thought, the latter to create them. On the lower level, ideas reflect, on the higher, they originate.

But, as both of these forms of mind are resident in man, who, under Deity, is probably the only example of the attribute of reason, and as they combine in nearly every form of his thought and conduct, it requires very careful and penetrative analysis to avoid confounding the one with the other, while, when rightly separated, their unlikeness is readily apparent. And it is from the fact of the uniformly unlike and unequal mind of the brute, as compared with that of man, that the suggestion first proceeded that a radical distinction existed in mind, separating it into the irrational and rational forms.

But how different from imitation or repetition of experience, is the phenomenon of originating the treatment—the part acted by the keeper of this elephant. While it is not the best illustration of the attribute of reason that is to be given, the part performed by the man is yet essentially unlike that performed by the beast. It is supposable that he was then for the first time in the presence of these facts in exactly this combination. It was, on the whole, an entirely new impression. And, as a combination, it could not connect with any of his experiences. There was no continuity of this composite fact to unify it with one of previous experience or observation, by which the remedial act in respect to it could be prompted, as there was in the case of the elephant. But the keeper, it is to be supposed, had seen cases in which facts similar to these were present. However, they were combined with others not similar; so that, as aggregates, they were dissimilar and unsuggestive of the mode of procedure, till sentient and creative reason could administer upon them, separating the similar from the dissimilar, and from an estimate of how far the modes of relief in the former might supply the same good in the present case.

Possessing the power to perceive abstract principles and their properties, from which to select and construct the ideal fact of relief, after which the literal fact should be formed, the unarranged factors of relief, lying strewn through nature, were at his command, to the extent to which this divine attribute of induction was attained in him. With this pre-eminence of mind—appointed for unlimited voyaging in a limitless sea of principles, concrete and abstract, this assuaging device, seemingly so impossible to the brute, was so simple and easy to the man.

REASON IN LOWER ANIMALS NOT POSITIVELY DISCLAIMED.

For the purpose of exemplifying the realm of instinct, the animal kingdom under man has here been held to view, as being without the element of reason. That is, however, not finally insisted upon, as already intimated. That is to say, that a latent germ of the reasoning mind may be imbedded in the lower organisms, which by some future possibility may grow into recognition, it would be unsafe to positively deny. Only, in the support of that hypothesis, it were necessary to explain why, when surrounded by the same nature that man is, and preceding him in the world, the highest brute has not produced what is necessarily an act of reason? Also, why their mental state as families, remains absolutely fixed—neither gaining nor losing? All modifications are well shown to be temporary only—disappearing with the removal of the special causes to which they are due; thus rising, or settling back again, to the typal character to which they belong, when released from temporary constraint.

Evidently for want of rational capacity, rational experiences by which they are in rare instances influenced, are immediately lost when the rational agent disappears. Thus far it is evident that the reasoning element may impinge its facts in every conceivable way on the mind of the beast, and leave with it no reasoning trait. On the contrary, we observe that in man, abstract principles, apprehended by one mind, are, even without sensuous illustration, readily impressed upon its kindred minds, where the same elucidation may continue on indefinitely unfolding new combinations of principles, from which human life shapes itself into ever varying habits.

From what has been said of instinct, it is apparently a form of mind that is resident upon the senses only, and is limited to the apprehension of sensuous phenomena; only apprehending the properties of external nature. It may take observation of colors, as identified with visible objects, but not apart from them. It may distinguish yellow and blue, seen by the physical eye, as characterizing some forms of nature, but could not possibly translate them from their respective substances into the ideal realm, and there combine them into green. It, too, may take observation of the association of properties, as color and shape, with some form of taste, and anticipate the latter by the accustomed combination of the former, as is to some extent illustrated in the selection of food. But it cannot perceive the ideal act of placing upon an object the designating property of color or shape.

Then, when we come to give our attention to that form of mind whose office it is to apprehend principles out beyond the sensuous state and abstract from material nature, there to see those principles not only, but also their properties and relationships, and be able to arrange and combine their units into immutable chains of logic; and in this manner proceed to construct reliable ideal systems which may be, and often are clothed with material forms, as seen in every new device that falls from the hand of man, we are in a realm of mind which is essentially and immeasurably different from that, the movements of which are limited to the sensuous state. Such capacity, it is to be remembered, perceives the immaterial,—properties that are not and never can be associated with matter,—as the perception of thought itself, for example! Here we deal with another class of attributes, which imply the existence, also, of a corresponding class of functions and substances and a more inward and more controlling realm.

CHAPTER X.

The Moral Element and State.

AMONG the features that adorn the higher state of life, the moral is especially conspicuous. Like intelligence or like reason in intelligence, it is of a domain of its own. And while it is difficult to separately identify it—intimately joined with life as it is, and being itself a living entity,—yet its place and state are approximately definable by its visible effects on the volitions of the human mind.

As to its relation with mind, by its own conditions as a sense allied to the perception of abstract properties—the qualities of sense and of thought—it can appear in connection with *reason* alone. It is in accord with affection and very prominently reveals itself in that way, yet is in no respect identical therewith, but at once separates itself therefrom when by the light of reason it discovers in affection conditions of unfitness with its nature's requirements. That it is a sense in itself, as we see sight or taste to be, and not to be confounded with a mode of mental perception, is apparent in the fact that it is primarily a matter of taste, and reveals itself essentially alike in all human life. Man might see, with absolute clearness, the conditions of right and wrong, and, beyond personal convenience, choose the right no sooner than the wrong, but for the taste we here call the moral sense,—sometimes, in one phase of it, conscience.

Being a sense within itself, its own peculiar nature is not describable by reference to another, further than in the matter of mode. So far as may be judged, it derives its satisfactions by its special capacity for apprehending those forms or adaptations of life that we designate by the term moral. We could not describe the sense of sight by reference to the recognized quality of another sense, and therefore could not possibly convey an idea thereof to one who is mentally void of it; but we could indicate some of its uses by reference to the sense of touch, which joins with sight in the observation of figure and extension. So, also, while the moral taste could not be described to one who is inherently void of it, however intelligent and cultured otherwise he might be, yet some of its uses and importance are to be seen by reference to the social convenience and refinement that result from it. For the immoral man may still be a lover of the beautiful and of his kindred life. And thus some of the *effects* of morality might be apparent and interesting to him, as shape and dimensions are to the blind; but if given to right doing, it would be for the effect's sake and not for right's own sake; as the invalid might eat food for strength's sake, and not for the sake of pleasure which a perverted or absent taste could not afford. But as animal economy would be very insufficiently supplied with food without a taste for it, so would society be speedily deprived of its essential virtues, when no longer induced thereto by the cravings of its moral sense.

One will readily recall the fact that that simple element of morality called honesty, is mainly advocated from the consideration that it is a matter of commercial necessity,—that without integrity business would be impracticable. Hence, "honesty is the best policy." But this is desiring the result, merely, and not the thing itself. The moral principle is not, in this way, recognized at all,—only its effects. And that men do honestly is not always evidence that they are honest—that it is from the sense of honesty seeking gratification; of which the many depleted individual and community estates can testify. And until this sense is sufficiently enlarged to make its demands for gratification the controlling influence among the tastes of life, eradicating the false sentiments of exclusive selfishness, and founding honesty on a less precarious principle than mere policy, these inflictions must be expected to continue to distress the business world.

But that the love of honesty itself is recognized as a fact, and is also appreciated, is manifested in the fact that certain ones of whom it is believed to be strongly characteristic, are universally at a premium in business circles.

While at this stage of human development, this form of the moral sense—as indeed all moral sense—is not commonly well developed, yet scarcely a civilized community is to be found where there are not examples of it sufficiently strong to indicate its special character,—where public confidence, in respect to its possessors, would not rest secured in the presence of a very large measure of temptation. And the saying that "every man has his price," is a cruel injustice to many on this better grade of human life, with whom neither money nor position is availing to divert from the course of pure equity.

Then related in this same moral sense with honesty, but more comprehensive in application, and not so particularly commercial in import, is the sentiment referred to in the word DUTY. It implies obligation or binding by the appearance of fitness in life, in all its modes—in the personal, social, commercial and esthetical. And while it includes the principles of justice and honesty in all their applications, it does not recognize them by their commercial values, but by their abstract merits of satisfying the taste of equity. To illustrate: One may be so situated as to be interested in the musical taste of the community, and be desirous of musical attainment in society; but his interest extends only to its commercial value—the profits of its *trade*. This value may cause him to be a very enthusiastic advocate and patron of music culture. But, plainly, it is not for music's own sake. It is not responding to the passion of music,—only to the passion of money. It does not suggest to us the principle that is apparent in the one who pays his money for the privilege of enjoying the music. The former is yielding to the taste of commercial value, the latter to the taste of musical value.

Then the one fact of music readily employs these two very unlike sentiments of life. In like manner may the facts of justice and honesty be appreciated and demanded from the same unlike considerations,—the one for their own sake, the *other for their effects' sake.*

So while DUTY makes requisition for all beneficial conventionalisms of society, it does so from the *sense* and not the *convenience* of equity.

Another peculiarity of this form of the moral sense consists in the fact that its motive, or objective claim, is to convey a good or gain from self to another, rather than the reverse, and often expresses itself in acts of self-sacrifice. And where self becomes the subject of its desires, it is by the way of that lofty sentiment that counts on self only as a necessary factor of the whole, and subservient to the general good, and whose impartial participation in the good to be bestowed individual-wise, becomes a common necessity. It actuates life unselfishly by finding its own objective good in yielding good to life beyond the limits of self. It is the source of that feeling of obligation to the disinterested good of fellow beings that is so adorning to the habits of human society, and is referred to in the words of the Divine Teacher: "Therefore, all things whatsoever ye would that men should do to you, do you even so to them."

That, however, is not necessarily unselfish, nor what is meant by the term *duty*, which prompts the bestowment of good on an object of special personal interest, as upon a friend controlling one's affections and thereby his volitions. When done by the universal law of equity, it is in *accord* with the sentiment of duty; but even then it is due to another,—a more common and inferior, though very precious, principle of life—selfish friendship, or self interest in another,—a principle that is expressed in the provisions that most animals make for their offspring; and which the rational and more diffusive mind of man extends to kindred and other affinities in life. But *duty* refers to pure equity, without regard to sympathy of any form. It is deferring to the good of another in pursuance to the cravings of equity in the presence of manifest worthiness, and not with a purpose to obtain gratification to selfish sympathies, however rightful and holy in their place such may be.

Justice (another name for equity) is often symbolized by the blind eyes, the even balances and drawn sword; denoting that the feeling of self interest affected by love or by fear or by commercial advantage, is not observed in determining its awards; and that justice is not a mere expediency determined upon by man while legislating for the advantage of aggregated humanity, but is part of an original sense for taking cognizance of the moral qualities of life, indicated by cravings of this special character.

MORALITY DEFINED.

Taste of fitness as to parts and modes of rational life, designates the function of morality. The fitness might exist and be distinctly apparent to the intellect, without affording us a morality, were the taste therefor wanting. Fitness or harmony of sounds might exist, and a knowledge of them attained by ingenious students of acoustics, but were there not taste whereby melody were appreciable, we would have no music nor be aware of its existence, and its most sublime executions would be liable to excite disgust. The same observations, substantially, would be seen to apply to all our pleasing arts, in which such great accomplishments are attained, and of which we have such immeasurable good.

It is to be still further observed that by way of these several tastes of life, by which the arts are appreciated, these lovely harmonies, so characterizing nature, serve immeasurably to awaken life and to extend its powers. So also the pure moral sense perceiving the charms of a life of true morality, is the source of a constant and surpassing joy not alone, but of the enlargement of life. Hence, too, the noted fact that morality is life-giving and immorality is devitalizing to the mind. While, therefore, the moral sense suffices to promote the indispensable principle of equity, the high order of happiness it confers by bringing into consciousness the beauty of fitness in social and divine relations of life, is a surpassing blessing to the race, by stimulating life to all proper attainments.

THE MORAL SENSE AND THE BRUTE.

As the element of reason has been claimed in small measures, or in incipiency, for the lower forms of animals, so also has it been claimed that the moral sense, or the beginning of it, is a factor in the brute economy. But as we have seen an absence of that superior mentality in all forms of life below the human—no phenomena occurring there that are necessarily acts of reason—so, likewise, do we find upon a most thorough and careful examination of the facts adduced in evidence of this claim, that they lack the conditions of life that render the presence of the moral sense a necessity. Admitting without questioning as to possible extravagances in the reported examples referred to (for most of them are taken on trust), they are yet inadequate to satisfy the requirements of a final test for that divine sense. All the notable feats referred to are easily traceable to selfish instinct in harmony with personal ends in these animals—the good falling *within* the limits of self interest and not *beyond*. They are but instances of sensing a good wherein self is, directly or indirectly, the sole end, and not where the abstract principle of right—sensing the equity itself in the mutual modes of life, already set forth—is the motive.

As the late Mr. Darwin's views on natural history are authority with what may be called the Darwinian school of naturalist, outside of which we find but few scientists of note claiming the moral sense for the brute, it will not be necessary to introduce examples other than the most important of those he has seen fit to give. This would be especially proper from the fact that he seems strongly inclined to correct what he regards as an error, that which would limit the moral sense to the realm of man, and may be expected to support his cause by selecting the most convincing examples; and also because his range of observation in the field of natural history has been quite as extensive as that of any one of this greatest age; and still further because his work consists more in tabulating statistics than evolving theories of this great science, and that he is, on the whole, as unbiased and fair in his conclusions as any one we could name. It is important also in accepting statements in evidence, that they come to us from competent witnesses—that no essential fact has been overlooked. Hence it requires one who knows what facts are needed and to be looked for, and who has no undue prominence of faculty for drawing facts from the imagination or confounding a fact of one class with that of another. And so while thousands of good people and good judges in their specialties, might be anxious to submit their observations on this subject, being confident that in a favorite dog, horse, cow, cat or bird they had witnessed as distinct a morality as that in man, we could take no risk on their judgment, till there was proof of their qualification to apply the proper tests.

The pure scientist in our specialty, who, besides his love of truth, has his reputation as a scientist at stake under a thousand closely dissecting eyes, who is never satisfied with superficial appearances, who moves toward conclusions slowly and allows no secret possibility to escape him, is the proper one from whom to have the facts we wish to apply to our inquiry. It is, however, true, that an expert may draw from a witness in respect to a case more than the witness himself knows.

The instances adduced by Mr. Darwin (Descent of Man, vol. 1, pp. 71—75) in support of the theory in question, are few indeed, and, with perhaps two exceptions, are of very commonplace character. His method is by exhibiting deportments supposed to be parallel with the moral sense in man; namely, of mutual aid. But mutual aid may be prompted by a variety of animal motives without any necessary reference to the moral element. The idea of the mutual in life plainly partakes of the selfish character, and of a personal good. Also, mutual aid may occur where even the idea of it does not occur—by incidental arrangement. Thus when the timid, nervous rabbit, sheep or chamois, whose safety lies in the power of its legs, unconsciously, in readiness to spring, stamps the ready foot on the ground, the act would at once startle its equally suspecting companions. The leader, too, of a troop of monkeys, whose place is necessarily in the line of march and ranged in the eyes of the whole company, may unconsciously display a warning to his companions, from the fact that danger would be first apparent to his advanced position. He may well "act as a sentinel" and be unconscious of acting for any one but himself. So of the bird that is perched aloft. To it not only is danger more apparent, but its more lonely position renders it more cautious; and while its first discovering and first moving in flight, alarming its companions, would suggest the idea of "sentinel" to a rational being, all could as well take place from this accidental arrangement. And does not the baboon attract more attention in an effort to overturn a stone of unusual size? And may not the rush of companions to his assistance be from the prospect of more abundant insects, rather than from consideration of friendly aid? The better proof of friendly aid would be that these baboons, after having overturned the stone, would leave their companion in the undivided possession of the uncovered morsels which were his by right of discovery!

One may imagine, who does not know, how distressing is the presence of parasites, and that the relief from them would be greatly desired; and when done by a rational being would be accorded to the motive of benevolence. And from these appearances our distinguished naturalist is considering the act of monkeys searching each other's persons for these troublesome concomitants, as evidence of moral principle, or at least, social aid; and it might be difficult to account for the seeming generosity on other grounds, if these parasites were not relished by them as food! The tormented one becomes quiescent under the sense of relief, while the motives of the relief are the little relishes on the neighboring skin. And by these facts, we may easily explain the not very wonderful fact cited by him (p. 72) from Mr. Brehm, who states, with much confidence, that after a troop of monkeys "has rushed through a thorny brake, each monkey stretches itself on a branch, and another monkey sitting by, 'conscientiously' examines its fur and extracts every thorn or burr." Essentially the same irritation of the skin as produced by parasites, would at once also suggest the same mode of relief, and its invitation by the recumbent position; while the search for the usual objects would result in the removal, incidentally or by way of testing their fitness for food, the foreign substances that might be lodged there, without necessarily involving the least measure of sympathy.

Still another class of facts he represents by statements, first, from Captain Stansbury, who "found, on a salt lake in Utah, an old and completely blind pelican, which was very fat, and must have been long and well fed by his companions;" and, secondly, a corresponding one from Mr. Bly, who saw blind crows fed by their companions. But one will readily recall the quarreling carnivals of these birds, especially the latter class, abstracting food from each other's mouths by the very opposite from friendly sentiments. Then it is also to be remembered with what special care blind animals adhere to their companions, and to what remarkable extent they make their other senses supply to them the use of sight; and by these the solution of what there is in these examples, if not easy, is yet very possible, by the possibility of pursuit and robbery yet remaining with these afflicted ones. And if then there is no miscalculation in respect to these last instances, just reviewed, all instances of mutual aid thus far adduced by Mr. Darwin as evidence of moral sense in the lower animals; are fairly and easily explained by the theory of mere selfish instinct operating under casual allotment, and without reference of any sort to the welfare of companions.

That moral intelligence would dictate arrangements for mutual aid, and, to some extent, in form like the foregoing, were most natural indeed. But that they may occur from the most dissimilar causes is equally plain. And the question as to which of the known causes shall be assigned in a given case, is always to be answered by reference to the grade of life to which the animal concerned, belongs.

But the facts adduced which are entitled to the most consideration, are those in which there is so evidently the feeling of behalf or sympathy, and which is seemingly quite another sentiment from that of mere desire of companionship. The latter, though often partaking of sympathy, may exist without it, and is sometimes equivalent to mere affinity with surroundings,—which surrounding may be of animate or inanimate nature,— as one feels pleasure in the presence of flowers or in mountain or water scenery or works of art, and may be so strongly attached to these as to leave kindred associates for their companionship. The fact is probably due to pleasure derived from certain expressions of form or movement on the part of these objects, which harmonize with a corresponding consciousness or taste in the attracted life. To be sure, companionship of this kind is usually of much less power than that of animate life, which may also be from the fact of its representing less of the conditions that are required in response to the great and intricate variety of animal sentiments. But the love of companionship is no certain proof of an interlying sympathy; while, on the other hand, the most tender sympathy may be without a corresponding measure of desire to associate,—indeed may exist with no desire of companionship by the mutually affected parties. In fact, finding the two sentiments happily going together, as in the case of love and sympathy, is no evidence that they are related or spring from the same cause.

SYMPATHY DEFINED.

Sympathy, the chief basis of friendship in society, is one of the many forms of that oneness of life denoted by the general term affection — self represented in another by a living, reciprocating bond that interlies and pervades all of life that ebbs and flows on the same level. This bond may be illustrated by reference to ordinary magnetism—material affection, which, though it is manifested only in its individualized or polarized forms, is nevertheless the same active substance at all the points of the seeming vacuums between, and is that by which the self of one individual substance is identified with all others on the same plane.

Hence sympathy is realized in the home heart when want is agitating another.

But the sympathizing bond cannot extend beyond its own element, nor can it be realized at all, speaking of it in the customary way, save in the negative or wanting state of another. From this fact we have the adult's tenderness toward the young offspring; and in it, too, considering the intimate nearness of the child in the order of nature, and hence the correspondingly increased power of the bond, we see the cause of that wonderful self-denial of the mother in behalf of the infant nestling in her provident arms.

From this principle also the child may feel sympathy for the parent or the weaker for the stronger, when the latter is regarded by the former as affected by some form of yearning or pain.

And need we to look farther than this for all that is essential to account entirely for those sympathizing deportments of the lap-dog and the monkey cited by Mr. Darwin? In the first of these examples he related an instance of a somewhat common occurrence, "a person pretending to beat a lady who had a very timid little dog on her lap. * * The little creature instantly jumped away, but, after the pretended beating was over, it was really pathetic to see how perseveringly he tried to lick his mistress' face and comfort her" (ibid, p. 74). How readily to a moral being, accustomed to the use of the moral sense, this demeanor would suggest a moral faculty in the dog; while in fact it is but an instance of sympathy matured into a prominence sufficient to actuate the ordinary instinct of the animal; though much weaker than that with which the parent dog caresses her young progeny when seeking to restore them when abused, or to supply food to their hungry mouths, when their clamor indicates their want of it, for which acts of routine life, no one has claimed a moral quality.

It is all within the provisions of self-interest. The example of the monkey is as follows:

"Several years ago a keeper at the Zoological Gordens showed me some deep and scarcely healed wounds on the nape of his neck, inflicted on him while kneeling on the floor by a fierce baboon. The little American monkey, who was a strong friend of this keeper, lived in the same large compartment, and was dreadfully afraid of the great baboon. Nevertheless, as soon as he saw the keeper in peril, he rushed to the rescue, and by screams and bites so distracted the baboon that the man was able to escape," (ibid, p. 75).

In this case of the *abused* as well as *petted* monkey, it is rather difficult to decide whether its conduct was prompted more from sympathy with the keeper than from consideration of revenge on the baboon, of which the conflict afforded an opportunity. But let us suppose that it was the former, and we shall have but another of the numerous illustrations following this law of oneness or sympathy pervading the same level of animated being; in the nature of which there is always at least enough of self and self-consideration, so that the acts arising therefrom may be regarded as prompted by self-interest. No sentiment higher than this is required to explain this not at all remarkable transaction.

Another instance from our author in this same connection, and again cited from Brehm, is that, "When the baboons in Abyssinia plunder a garden, they silently follow their leader; and if an imprudent young animal makes a noise he receives a slap from the others to teach him silence and obedience; but as soon as they are sure that there is no danger, all show their joy by much clamor." Now his statement as to these procedures is easily accepted. But not quite so with his inferences. Thieves of any order of animals operate as much as possible in silence and under cover; and noises likely to betray them are no doubt aggravating and suggestive of the customary means of resentment, which with lower animals commonly fall upon the weaker ones. And that the slaps referred to are for discipline, whatever they may incidentally result in, is far less probable than that they are for the more ordinary purpose of easing a passion! But why did our observing naturalist not state the fact that these baboons usually leave their quite young ones behind when engaged in these depredations, and infer that they do so from a desire to not have them fall under the influence of stealing! With respect to dogs possessing " something very much like a conscience," it were not wonderful that under domestication, and their special intimacy with mankind in that state, for many hundreds of generations, the many observations of the traits of man, as to carefulness and trusting, should often produce temporary modifications of their character into resemblances of these. But as in respect to apparent reason in lower animals, so of these modifications,—they are not reported of the dog away from the influence of man—his favorite companion.

The error from which the supposition arises that morality is resident (incipiently) in the brute, consists in assuming that, as seen in man, it is a consummation or superior form of a lower and more simple element, probably the social instinct. Mr. Darwin says: "The following proposition seems to me in a high degree probable—namely, that any animal whatever, endowed with well marked social instincts, would inevitably acquire a moral sense or a conscience, as soon as its intellectual powers had become as well developed as in man" (Descent, vol. 1, p. 68). But this statement, so fairly presenting the theory under review, fails not to bring to notice the objections in which it is involved. It assumes this possibility not for all social instincts. Only those within a certain undefined limit—those of "well marked social instincts"—are capable of attaining a moral sense. But where does this limit lie? And what does it consist in? Is that which is not so "well marked," lacking the basic principle of the moral sense? are questions whose answers are of essential importance in the analysis of this problem. By this it is apparent that the mere unqualified social instinct is without the properties requisite for the moral sense, and that only that social instinct is sufficiently marked which is supplemented by the requisite property or element; which would most naturally be the superior or moral sense itself. Then, still further, the acquisition is made contingent on intellectual powers "as well developed, or nearly as well developed, as in man;" assuming, substantially, that those favored animals must wait for their moral sense till they become human! Well, that will do!

But this conclusion is justified by his own statements further on: "There can be no doubt that the difference between the mind of the lowest man and that of the highest animal is immense. An anthropomorphous ape, if he could take a dispassionate view of his own case, would admit that though he could form artful plans to plunder a garden—though he could use stones for fighting and for breaking open nuts, yet that the thought of fashioning a stone into a tool was quite beyond his scope. Still less, as he would admit, could he follow out a train of metaphysical reasoning, or solve a mathematical problem, or reflect on God, or admire a grand natural scene" (p. 100). With these admissions, in the face of his proposition just reviewed, conceding the "immense" difference that he here finds lying between the mental and moral states occupied by the lowest man and the highest animal, it signifies little that he adds that the difference "is certainly one of degree and not of kind." And this is especially true, as some ever present deficiency, which none of his school have hinted at explaining, has thus far prevented the latter from overcoming that difference; while having the same world, and the same chance as that of man, and an earlier start in which to accomplish it.

However, let the social instinct be understood to consist of all that this school of thinkers claim for it—let it be regarded as being from the bond of sympathy, from the sense of mutual aid, or commercial obligation, yet it is not the moral sense nor the element from which the moral sense is derived. Its essential requirements are not supplied by any of these conditions; while, nevertheless, it is the chief motive and authority for their wise use; for to the Taste of Fitness, as to the parts and modes of rational life—the equity between its members and the esthetical in its manners—we must ever look for the persistence of the spirit of rectitude and of virtue among mankind. And of this taste or sense, after all, perhaps no one would expect to find even so much as a trace, in all the living domain below man.

Man is of the very latest arrivals on the planet. The lower orders were in the exclusive possession of this same world for untold ages before his arrival, and since his arrival, all its advantages and all its good influences have been as free and liberal to the brute as to him. And now that with all these the brute has yet no taste for the moral qualities in life, can only be understood by the theory that that element is without representation on so low a plane, but is of a state of life which is superior and farther inward.

And now, too, the pleasing fact is before us—one which tends to move the profoundest sense of gratitude —that with the superior state of being, wherein are all the superior forces, there also resides the moral sense— the taste for the moral qualities of life; and that on beyond the finite—in the realm of the Supreme—in the soul of the Deity—its absolute perfections mingle with the volitions from which the finite universe derives its laws and limitations. And, in the same view, an equal cause for thankfulness is in the fact that where this moral sense does not extend, there also are the smaller measures of power to secure ends of injustice; it being always the weaker and less capable side of nature, and that the enactments of which are at most temporary— in time yielding to that spirit of supreme goodness whose beneficence extends finally to all forms of feeling life.

CHAPTER XI.

The Religious Element and State.

IN human economy the several manifestations of affection are not attributable to the modified uses of the one general function, influenced to operate in these several ways by a conscious obligation to the several related conditions of life. This were the more convenient way of judging of the matter; but, however evidently appropriate were bonds to strengthen these human relationships, the fact of appropriateness, clearly seen and appreciated, were wholly inadequate to account for the several forms of fondness expressed in them. The many instances of lost affection, of either of the forms, where the appropriateness for its continuance remained fully apparent to all concerned, are sufficient evidence that they do not arise from the sense of their necessity, fitness, or desirableness.

Besides, by a more thorough examination, instead of merely *one* general function so widely versatile, we find a *group* with their special attributes adapting life to the several forms of its relationship and impassioning it accordingly. Neither is it in all cases very difficult to separate the parts into their distinct natures, to be thus seen to be original factors of the indissoluble self of man, and of the most essential and beneficent arrangements of human economy.

Without the requisite form of affection, one might know another as a *convenience* but not as a friend. Friendship would suggest a convenience readily enough at all times. But not so, reversely. The friend is associated with the highest uses in life; but these uses, apart from this requisite form of affinity, would not induce the consciousness of friendship. Without still another, one might know his properly wedded companion as a *friend*, but not as a conjugal mate. Without the filial form, one might recognize another as his special benefactor, even as his progenitor, but yet not as a parent—an object of filial gratification. With it, there is realized a sense of deference for life in the parental state generally—prominently when it is ranking in seniority, and ardently for the immediate progenitors of self. In the final and the highest use, it excites sentiments of adoration for the Deity—the Supreme Progenitor—in him to find, with no lessening of its force in respect to human parentage, its final gratification. Still another illustration: One might be providently disposed toward a child; not alone from the consideration of its dependent condition and possibly an interest in it as the beginning of the unfolding of the rare qualities of a human life, but from the more forcible consideration of its owing its origin in the world to him, and yet, without the requisite form of affection, fail to be moved toward it by the greatest—the all-over-shadowing motive of parental love.

Now it is to be conceded that some of these forms are not readily so separated as to be separately viewed. However, the difficulty is easily enough explained. It is, in part, from the presence of the customary disposition to view all phenomena of this character as emanating from one and the same principle of life. Besides, occasions which evoke these several forms of affection are transient or intermittent, giving the appearance of an oscillating action of the mind, moving responsively to the various occasions eliciting it, rendering the impression that it is but the one principle of mind in all cases. But in these disappearances instead of anything like an arbitrary discontinuance of the special form in a given case, it should be understood as having simply dropped into latency, from the presence of conditions unfavorable to its manifestation; the same as life is known to do under exposure to devitalizing influences; ready, however, to reappear with the recurrence of the required conditions.

Then, again, some of the forms are feebly developed, even on the human plane. Some are occasionally, and others probably altogether, absent from the lower kingdom. There the conjugal rarely appears and, for many reasons, the filial does not exist; while of friendship properly, the probability is that what is taken for it, in the lower animals, is nothing higher than merely love of companionship. The fact then that they are weak and not fully demonstrative, would, of course, render the work of distinguishing them more difficult. And hence no difficulties of this character can properly constitute objections to the claim respecting affection, as above set forth.

Then, likewise, a special psychical sense for apprehending the Deity is made necessary by the uniform presence of a persistent tendency in human life to acts that have solitary reference to such an existence. The filial sense will not account for this. One may know another as a parent and not as a deity. Or he might know an object as a deity and not as a parent. From the parental nature being found in a deity, it does not follow that the deific is found in a parent. Neither is the sentiment, subjectively, a product of the mental state. The human mind, with more or less clearness, is universally apprehensive of a sublime living existence which nothing in the limits of the finite domain fully comports with. It is possessed of a certain sense, in varying prominence, that in no nation, cultured or uncultured, the highest mere human ideal will satisfy to adequate fullness.

Mind would be able to locate a cause back of phenomena; and so, also, prior to all finite phenomena, whatever they might be, a *first cause;* but it could not apprehend, in respect to the attributes and character thereof, any thing not functionally represented in itself. It could not recognize in it the moral quality, unless in itself resided a function of the moral nature to render it morally sentient. So, then, while the unaided sense of philosophy would readily *confirm* a suggestion of the Deity, it could not *suggest* Him. It also entirely confirms music; but, in the unmusical mind, it could not suggest *music!*

Besides, a purely mental or psychical sense is without external organization, as mental sight, for example; and is denoted only by its special form of force persistently developing its characteristics to view in life. And the presence of the characteristics is, unavoidably, proof of the force and of the substance or essence from whence they emanate; as truly so as a sentient mode of life denotes the sense of sight. Correlatively, also, the existence of the sense is proof of its objective's reality.

But an argument for the existence of the special sense through which the supreme is impressed upon finite consciousness, were well-nigh as superfluous to one who has considered its prevalence, as were one made for the existence of the special sense of sight. And it may in this connection only be said that this variously employed sense, joined with the sense of fitness in the modes and relations of life, constitutes that super-ethical sentiment known by the venerated name of Religion. And it is from this sense of fitness being joined to that of the recognition of the Deity in his supreme worthiness that the human mind so commonly recognizes in religion its supreme obligations. Also, in accordance with this fact, this same high deference to religion, when correctly formulated in the mind, is indispensable to a well-balanced and properly sentient life.

This function of consciousness of the existence of the Supreme Being is induced to activity by the powerful taste of fitness in life joined with it; while, by a similar relation, it derives from the faculty of reason sentient confirmation and also the power of discerning suitable modes of its gratification. And in combination with these chief senses, it constitutes religion not only a controlling, but, in the same measure, a refining and an accomplishing power in life.

In all examples of religion this taste of fitness has appeared as its main impulse; but when not associated with a lucid reason to apprehend proper principles for its observance, the impulse, thus deprived of its mental eyes, has often staggered through blindness to the perpetration of gross improprieties and dreadful crimes, of which history has been a ready and commonly a very willing witness.

As a matter of course, in the less sentient minds, the conception of worthiness in the Deity is mainly limited to his more obvious attribute of supreme power, in its external manifestation; while, to the more sentient, the qualities of his *life*—the tastes and the forms of affection in the deific Being—are measurably apparent. Hence on this grade the divine worthiness is estimated by the standard of a totally different and greatly superior order of values, awakening also a correspondingly higher and stronger sense of obligation.

From this greater eminence of life, less value, comparatively, is seen in the mightiness and the intelligence of the Deity to do as he pleases, than in his endearing attributes which respond to the sentiments of affection and the taste of fitness,—even though in his supreme power and wisdom he is seen maintaining the constitution of nature by a system of absolutely perfect and unchangeable laws, as we so plainly see him to be doing. And it is on this plane of life—where these realizations in respect to the Deity are duly strong in human consciousness—that religion becomes a supreme adoration. On this plane, too, by the nature of these facts, man becomes unalterably inclined to attain the accomplishments of his mental and moral nature in more and more of the perfection in which they appear in the Divine Personality.

And, now, along with the superior qualities of life, seen to be belonging to the inner and superior state —with reason and the moral sense—we add, in conclusion, the sense of consciousness of the Supreme Being; it being the essential factor of the religious element in man. This sense is, less than reason or morality, claimed to be represented in the brute plane of animal economy. We might turn to a few alleged examples of gratitude occurring in the brute, and referred to as evidence of the religious principle. But gratitude—a sentiment of obligation that characterizes the higher practices of religion as well as also the more enlightened forms of social life—*is* religion in no sense. Besides these examples are so improbable as to evidently afford little assurance of their soundness to those submitting them.

However, in the lowest human society there is a worship, and in the darkest human mind a glimmer of the deific, traced by the rude symbols of ideal divinities.

Yet in the highest and most favored brute there is a characteristic absence of all these. And religious modes of life being in man universally present and in the brute universally absent, can only signify that he is the representative of a domain of life lying far inward from the brute, and unto which the element of the mere brute never attains. And though man's entire nature is not now, and for good reasons, may never be wholly inside of this boundary, those elements of his being which properly designate him as man—his reasoning mind and his moral and religious senses with all their attendant wide range of sentiments,—with all their present wonderful achievements, and with all their possibilities in an unlimited future in pursuit of the ever-increasing attractions leading the way toward the deific perfections above,—*these*, towering above and obscuring every other part of his nature, are wholly of the innermost state of life,—the inexpressibly glorious domain of man, THE ONLY REALIZING COMPANION OF HIS CREATOR!

CHAPTER XII.

MAN IN HIS ESSENTIAL SELF CONTINUES BEYOND THE LIMITS OF PHYSICAL EXISTENCE.—THE OBJECTIONS REVIEWED.

"To be or not to be; that is the question" which underlies all others in contemplating the future. All speculations and beliefs in respect to what is to be in the state of life beyond the grave are at last contingent upon the fact itself that there is such an existence.

The evidence—the universal anticipation of it—on which the human family have so commonly rested their faith in the continuance of life after death, is to be regarded with great respect, and as by no means without foundation. Aside from the testimony from competent fellow beings in respect to the dead seen in life again, and the fact that the religion having the approval of the highest order of mankind, originated amid circumstances of this character, and within the historic period —aside from these, the fact of such a belief being common to mankind, regardless of state or education, and hence being *organic* rather than of an accretive character, stands as proof thereof from nature itself.

This, until recent years, has been regarded as the only scientific aspect of the question. All nature otherwise being looked upon as at best a sealed book in respect to the subject. Theologians of the best culture, with few exceptions, were content to say to the non-theological minds, "We agree with you that a future life is not determinable from a stand-point of science. We rest our faith therein on the authority of Revelation alone,—claiming, however, at the same time that from nature there is no voice against it."

The mind, by its indulgence in so strong a faith in the future life, and withal one so hopeful as that represented by much of Christendom, has in many ways been largely benefited. But there have all along been many good minds, though less credulous, who have not been able to so largely take advantage of a faith mainly resting on the representations of history, however credible as such; who sought confirmation by evidence from the field of obvious nature.

This evidence has, over many difficulties, been slowly advancing to view; but not from the source toward which expectation has been mainly directed. The facts first available are not from the domain of nature surrounding man, but from that higher which his own personal existence embodies.

It has in previous chapters been seen that by tracing the elements of life in the several kingdoms,—in that of man, in that of the animal below him, and in the vegetable yet lower and more simple, that there are universes of substances lying inward of this—the one with which our present senses connect us—worlds inward of this material world of our present state. And this is surely the most natural, if indeed not the only practical route by which we could proceed, hoping to discover internal universes—by closely observing the individual phenomena of plants and animals that bear traces of those states.

As to the existence of those states, doubt is not so extensive on the part of the learned as casual observation of their works treating on other subjects than that of other universes, would lead one to believe. Few treatises from men of science are found having special reference to the subject. And treating of physical sciences, they very properly use terms in their physical sense, and may mislead theological minds into the belief of their exclusive mineralism. Hence, not infrequently, they arise and explain. Also, very evidently, many being so much preoccupied with their specialties, have little room or liberty for the work of tracing out new paths of science. Be this all as it may, the concessions to the claims of a spiritual state coming from this source, are sufficient in numbers and character to largely commit the science of the age to its support. In the words of Prof. Youmans, already cited, "The tendency of this kind of inquiry" (modern science) "is ever *from* the material, *toward* the abstract, the ideal, the spiritual." * * "From the baldest materiality we rise at last to a truth of the spirit world, of so high an order that it has been said 'to connect the mind of man with the Spirit of God.'" This would legitimately follow from the habit of philosophy being to deal more with the forces than with the materials of nature—their correlations and conversions, through the unending variations of mode, from ordinary mechanics up to the volitions of mind.

But whether such a state is for the occupancy of beings separated from this—beings originated in that state or entered there from this or some other subordinate state, is evidently less clear to them. And we find them, when they come to devote themselves specially to the question of the soul's future personal existence, hoping and believing from the old forms of evidence—historical revelation and common intuition—rather than from settled principles of science.

Prof. Huxley's reply to Mr. Frederic Harrison's rather singular position in respect to the question of a future life (A Modern Symposium, — p. 82.— Rose-Belford Pub. Co., Toronto,) probably represents the thoughts of the majority of the distinguished writers of science in the present day:

"I understand and I respect the meaning of the word 'soul,' as used by Pagan and Christian philosophers for that which they believe to be the imperishable seat of human personality, bearing throughout eternity its burden of woe, or its capacity for adoration and love. * * And if I am not satisfied with the evidence that is offered me that such a soul and such a future life exists, I am content to take what is to be had and to make the best of the brief span of existence that is within my reach, without reviling those whose faith is more robust and whose hopes are richer and fuller."

The sympathy with, and evident tendency toward a

belief in a future life, which the distinguished biologist has here committed himself to, is seemingly by way of assent to it as a current religious sentiment. And he is so disposed from a common spontaneous impulse to believe, rather than from anything which his exacting habits of thought would justify as evidence.

But with greater assurance does Prof. Wm. B. Carpenter, the most widely accredited authority in physiology living, notwithstanding the frequent references to him as a skeptic, close his great work—" Principles of Human Physiology "—with these profoundly believing words: "But the Death of the Body is but the commencement of a new Life of the Soul; in which (as the religious physiologist delights to believe) all that is pure and noble in man's nature will be refined, elevated, and progressively advanced toward perfection; whilst all that is carnal, selfish, and degrading, will be eliminated by the purifying processes to which each individual must be subjected, before Sin can be entirely ' swallowed up of Victory ' " (American Edition of 1862—p. 870). Although often drawn out on physical and physiological topics connected with the recent developments of science, in which his language, used comprehensively, but with *special* purpose only to physical science, may seem to antagonize the sentiment of this quotation, he has not, so far as I know, given expression to views that are *necessarily* opposed to it. But he has rather said a good deal to corroborate it—enough to assure us that though these words are not words of argument deduced from the established principles of his favorite science, they are surely as liberally suggested from that source as from the more commonly accepted evidences of revelation and intuition.

At the present, scientific research has not fairly reached the ground where the question of man's survival of physical dissolution comes unavoidedly into view. And only here and there do we see an accredited leader snatching a special opportunity to step in advance to apply the rules of scientific evidence to the problem of such an existence. The preliminary work is not yet sufficiently advanced. The problems in respect to the more obvious forms and modes of life are not yet sufficiently well solved—are not yet so undebatably clear in all respects as to make it necessary to proceed in force to the next, the final and all-overshadowing question. But as the researches in biology come to uncover more completely the motives that are incidental to the forms of life, and the destinies that are deducible from the nature and arrangement of their functions, their orbits will be called for and must be computed, which will render the question of an after death life impossible to be avoided, leaving the mineralistic scholar, who is indisposed to such an issue being made in science, to decide whether he will part company with his prejudices or with the issues his times will inexorably bring up for solution.

RELATION OF MIND AND BODY.—CONSCIOUSNESS.

The part that physical science has to act in settling the question of a future life, is to determine the relation of mind and body; from which it is to be ascertained that the mind as well as the soul with which it is identified, is or is not, in its essential wholeness, separable therefrom. Then, when such a separation is found possible, that, at the death of the body, it is actual as well—that the essential being is continued, and that the dead are not dead—that death extends to no more than the body, and that the sorrow of this is all that the facts of death merely will justify, and, when fully seen, will call forth. To a carefully thinking being, however little he might realize thereof, this evidence of a future state would be as uncontrovertible as would be a residence in the land of spirits itself. The conditions incident to that state might still be matters of speculation and doubt, but the existence itself would be a fact—a fact in science. Though it might not then be fully and forcibly impressed on consciousness.

And now in proceeding to consider the evidences, it is manifestly proper to first review the doubts and negatives on the opposite side. For though they are not numerous nor very often repeated, they have yet at times been so forcibly stated as to have in many quite strong and clear minds well-nigh extinguished belief. Commonly the first negative met is a claim that, so far, attempts at scientific proof that individual human life may or does exist outside of a physical body, have failed, while the improbabilities have also largely increased. While this has much truth in it, it yet is far from being altogether true. Then a more common, and, perhaps, a more sober trouble is in respect to consciousness. The expression usually is, How shall we know of a matter of which we are so completely unconscious? How shall we be made sensible that life exists on the other side of a state of *unconsciousness,* and that it is not itself ended with the dissolution of the organization with which consciousness inheres or is manifested? Or how shall we have knowledge of a state of consciousness unconnected with our present mode of being to which our senses are limited? This form of doubt, out of which these questions arise, is deserving of much respect, as it may readily result from the prevalent method of dogmatizing in science, which so uniformly inclines to exclude claims to facts of a psychological character.

But what shall we say of consciousness? What is it to be conscious? It denotes but the detention of the senses, psychical or mental, in their active relation with their objective states, while ministering to the individual life from the side of nature or of being to which they are adapted. Hence it can only be maintained in respect to the state on which the senses are employed, whatever side of being that may be. Whenever, therefore, our system of senses and faculties should be embodied in an organism related with another order of existence, or objective world, and be discontinued with the one relating us with this, we should be conscious of *that* state and unconscious of *this.* By this view, this negative would lose much of its force; as evidently, a want of consciousness of another conscious state would not constitute the least measure of proof *against* its existence. And besides, it would render the mind more open to perceive what proofs of such a state might be forthcoming, which is of great importance in this investigation.

BISHOP BUTLER ASSAILED.

In his Belfast address (Advancement of Science), this form of negative is introduced by Prof. Tyndall, in a problematic manner, and by way of testing the strength of Bishop Butler's position in defense of the doctrine of future life as set forth in "The Analogy of Religion." The position is honored with liberal concessions of its strength; yet not with being absolutely invulnerable. Fatal flaws are believed to be discovered in the argument. The bishop's well-known position is that the proper self and the body bear the same relation to each other that do the mechanic and his set of tools, which he renders very firm by numerous forcible illustrations. Against this the professor brings his "disciple of Lucretius," armed with the philosophy (the atomic theory) of his distinguished master,—that the soul and body are one and the same, and live and perish as one.

The "disciple" proceeds to intimate that the bishop's statement that the removal of parts of the body, as limbs, etc., does not remove anything from the consciousness of a complete self, is without much force; and suggests the experiment be continued by removing the brain, or by temporarily paralyzing it; saying: "You begin at one end of the body, and show that its parts may be removed without prejudice to the perceiving power. What if you begin at the other end, and remove, instead of the leg, the brain? * * Or, instead of going so far as to remove the brain itself, let a certain portion of its bony covering be removed, and let a rhythmic series of pressures and relaxations of pressures be applied to the soft substance. At every pressure 'the faculties of perception and of action' vanish; at every relaxation of pressure they are restored. Where, during the intervals of pressure, is the perceiving power? I once had the discharge of a Leyden battery pass unexpectedly through me; I felt nothing, but was simply blotted out of conscious existence for a sensible interval. Where was my true self during that interval?" (p. 45).

Somewhat anticipating the reply, he continues, "You may say that I beg the question, when I assume the man to have been unconscious, that he was really conscious all the time, and has simply forgotten what had occurred to him." Truly, so might it naturally be, in harmony with the "instrument" theory, and with no offense to any sense of fitness. And certainly in these illustrations that theory has suffered no damage nor inconvenience. "Where was my true self during that interval?"—so enforced by the passage of the electric discharge from the battery. Well, so far as the theory is concerned, it is a matter of entire indifference as to where the true self was at the time. *That* only provides that the true self and the organism of nerve wires that continued the discharge through the individual body, were not one and the same thing. The self might have been separate from the prostrate instrument; insularly connected therewith; or even in a measure participant in its fate. It is not incumbent on the theory to show where or in what condition the self was during the tragical instant. When the refractory lightning leaps from the clouds on to the wires and thereby into the operator's room, it may also penetrate him; but that would not necessarily follow. Neither is it probable that his mind would be so much more active than what is common of man, that it could take note of what transpired in the interval—the flash.

Substantially the same answer will apply to the removed or disabled brain,—it is simply disabled—disqualified for use, in both cases. In the one instance, it is not only sundered, but the vital circulation on which its supply is dependent is also sundered, and it could no longer be the instrument of consciousness. In the other, essentially the same explanation will apply. The instrument is broken and unable to represent its agent, and hence consciousness has disappeared. But that it has ceased with its manifestation, requires proof of a class this school of Lucretius would be the last to admit—evidence from the state beyond the unconscious hiatus itself, testifying from knowledge that the consciousness has not survived.

Without varying the principle, or scarcely the form, our "disciple" submits a further illustration in this same connection: "A telegraph operator has his instruments, by which he converses with the world; our bodies possess a nervous system, which plays a similar part between the perceiving powers and external things. Cut the wires of the operator, break his battery, demagnetize his needle; by this means you certainly sever his connection with the world; but inasmuch as these are real instruments their destruction does not touch the man who uses them. The operator survives, *and he knows that he survives*. What is it, I would ask, in the human system that answers to this conscious survival of the operator when the battery of the brain is so disturbed as to produce insensibility, or when it is destroyed altogether?" (p. 46). In connection with the answers already returned, it need here only be replied that though the operator himself knows of his survival, the fact is not within the reach of the consciousness of the outside world till the wires and battery and delivering apparatuses are all up again. During the interval his relation with the outside world would be the same as would be that of the conscious entity in question, whose presence is rendered vacuous to external realization, by the disabled vital mechanism—a severed or paralyzed brain. And, but for the force of analogy and inductive evidence, the operator so separated from the outside world, would, also, be reasonably supposed *not to exist*. His existence it would be impossible to affirm. Operators, however, have been, under similar circumstances, known to survive; and the ready inference would be that this one, too, has not ceased to exist; though the means of sensuous knowledge have for the time disappeared. But this is all the basis for belief in the existence of the unseen and unknown one in this case, save what induction from a knowledge of the nature of the wire, the battery and the man, might certify. For the operator, his fallen means of communication is re-erected and his survival is made apparent. That consciousness that is finally deprived of the essential instrument of the brain, is not so well favored. No master workman is able, at that final time, to revive it, to re-erect the fallen fiber. And the occupant must be content with another state of being and to know of those in this world what he may have means to, without the satisfaction that a definite knowledge of himself reciprocally exists with *them*. Confirmation of their hope of his existence, is to be had mainly, if not only, by the inductive method; which, in the good fortune of our present day, is, with many, scarce less to be relied upon than would be a verdict from the fickle senses themselves.

"Another consideration " he urges in his negative, as pressing upon him " with some force." It is the well-known fact that " the brain may change from health to disease, and through such a change the most exemplary man may be converted into a debauchee or a murderer." And to illustrate, he cites the melancholy case of Lucretius himself, who was so terrified by promptings to lewdness, that, out of fear of yielding to the base impulses, he slew himself. In respect to this he asks, " How could the hand of Lucretius have been thus turned against himself, if the real Lucretius remained as before? Can the brain or can it not act in this distempered way without the intervention of the immortal reason? If it can, then it is a prime mover which requires only healthy regulation to render it reasonably self-acting, and there is no apparent need of your immortal reason at all. If it cannot, then the immortal reason, by its mischievous activity in operating upon a broken instrument, must have the credit of committing every imaginable extravagance and crime " (p. 46, 47). In this, and in what immediately follows, our " disciple" is disposed to develop the moral aspects of the case. Who is the party properly chargeable with the moral delinquencies of life, but immortal reason itself, if the brain be but an instrument in its employment? is the substance of his objection; averring in substance, that it would harmonize more with enlightened sensibilities to think of the brain as being alone concerned in the lamentable result, rather than the cherished immortal reason should be obliged to appear capable of immoral tendencies.

How far, to be sure, pure reason would be chargeable with the results of using instruments that are so much out of order as to be dangerous, would depend upon the nature of the case. There are combinations of machine and operator, where the machine may overmaster the operator and inflict great damage. In such a case the operator is not chargeable with the matter; while also it is of little consequence that we charge it upon the machine. Whether the brain is the parent or the instrument of the element of reason, can make no difference as to the necessity of its best possible condition.

But suppose the mental economy to be a congress of functions, each, in some measure, acting in its own sphere, as may readily be conceded; then suppose the operator (a single function) has his wire fall upon another's or another's upon his, in such a way as to mingle or divert the currents, and at a point beyond his means of knowledge; will his conscious reason enable him to obviate mistakes? And is he, under these circumstances, to be arraigned for misdemeanor, or evil intent?

One would think that the professor, of world-wide fame, and abundantly deserving to be classed among the very first of this age, rather misanticipates the bishop in imagining him " thoughtful after hearing this argument " of the " disciple " of the great poet philosopher. The bishop has not written in this direction without some mistakes—some important omissions; but in the main he has taken correct grounds, and built his superstructure so well as that it has stood the assaults of a century and a quarter, showing little damage, and promising to stand in the future as strongly as in the past.

But our " disciple " might have submitted, perhaps, a more difficult objection for the bishop's consideration; more difficult, because in the main it is new and involves new principles. He might have added, " But the survivor of the broken medium of communication was enabled to relate at least somewhat of the state of his consciousness during the interval of his isolation; whereas, usually, parties on regaining consciousness are unable to do so. And assuming that there is but the same seat of consciousness in the individual life on which all experiences register themselves, why, during intervals of external suspense, are there not vacuums as to conscious life, in all instances where nothing concerning the interim may be evoked from the memory?"

We shall be helped to the answer of this by noting the fact that *sometimes*, however, they *do* recall. And that what is regarded as inability, is but circumstantial inability; only depending on the arrival of the proper condition when external activities do not monopolize the apprehending powers, and when the kindred fact by its association, will awaken the memory in respect to it. We may unconsciously drift over many fine pictures, easily enough seen were the right circumstances calling attention. Our memories during consciousness are largely due to the interminable series of awakening incidents.

But to be troubled with doubt concerning a future life, arising from a disposition to discredit existence where it is not within the sphere of sensuous observation, would put one on the defensive in respect to a theory of self's continued existence in the present state of being,—that the self of yesterday evening is *yet*, and is the self of this morning,—that it could possibly have passed through the intervening unconsciousness of the night's repose.

THE MAIN NEGATIVE.

The last negative, now to be considered and already indirectly reviewed in the foregoing criticisms, and the one the most confidently advanced among unbelieving men of science, is that mind and all animate conditions result from organization, and are finally and always dependent on it; and hence, also, terminate with it. I say, "the one most confidently advanced"; for very few, so far as I am able to judge of their observations, consider the claim with entire confidence. It, also, is more problematically than assuredly stated. Prof. Tyndall, in this same Belfast address, referring to the relation of the vital organism with sensation and thought, says, "We can trace the development of a nervous system and correlate with it the parallel phenomena of sensation and thought. We see with undoubting certainty that they go hand in hand. But we try to soar in a vacuum the moment we seek to comprehend the connection between them" (Advancement of Science, p. 80). This is the difficulty commonly seen and confessed. The coincidence is striking enough to *suggest*, but not to *prove* that the mind and soul are of a physical origin alone. A vacuum, as to physical demonstration, must be soared through to attain the necessary elements of its proof. In the lower forms, the connection and co-ordination of mind and life with the organism may not be doubted; but that fact alone settles nothing more than that they are in the arrangement so well adapted as that they may act in exact accordance, or are so combined as to influence each other to action, that the state and act of one would, uniformly, correspond with the state and act of the other. But to determine the causative side—to determine with which of the related parts to locate the origin of the force impinged, recurrence must be had to other sources of knowledge. One may, standing apart from it, consider a locomotive moving, and from that point of view alone, be unable to decide whether the moving cause is located in the cylinder or in the wheel, or somewhere back of both; whether the advancing and receding of the piston revolves the wheel or the revolving wheel inserts and retracts the piston. The actions of the piston and the wheel are exactly co-ordinate.

Much like this position is that of the scientist viewing from physical science alone, the activities of human economy. Is it the mental or the psychical state delivering the actuating force on the vital organism, or is it the reverse, is the troublesome question. All that we here see is embodiment and action, and that it is, at times, rational. As to how this action transpires in ourselves, we only are conscious of having will, thought, and experience, and that in response to will, much of this action takes place. But the manner of these in us, and their source, may not be known by physical analysis alone. Also, the question as to the location of the moving cause in the locomotive would be very liable to a mistaken answer, if the engine were of invisible substance. The appearance would unavoidably deceive. Finding the wheel itself only capable of action in response to force applied to it, would measurably rectify the mistake; rendering it necessary to locate the cause outside of it, and derived through one of its points of connection—the rail below or the piston rod or walking bar. But in all these, though suitably combined, there is present no cause for such movement. And if they are rightly understood, it must be looked for elsewhere. But heat and water are necessarily in attendance upon this machine; and, in combination, are generating an adequate force. And although no engine—no point or means of communication of this power is visible, the justifiable conclusion would be that in this force, however unknown is the medium or mode of application, is the cause of the manifest movement.

Similar to these are the facts in relation to body and mind, or soul, as so far developed. The body is an organization of substances identical with the common elements of nature. It is of the earth, earthy. But it is of the most minute perfection in respect to all the details necessary to the multiform uses for self-preservation—present and future—and is qualified to serve at least many of the requirements of voluntary intellectual processes; is accordingly characterized by feeling and mind. Mind and feeling, like heat and water, are manifest to mental observation and to self-consciousness. So, too, the body. But from which of these the causative power proceeds, and what are the element and mode of connection or of communicating the power, are the matters in obscurity to all observation from purely physical data. And judgment as to from which state this motion is communicated, must depend on a knowledge of their separate properties and possibilities.

But we must here first attend to a prior consideration, before proceeding to weigh the probabilities in respect to which of the allied parts is the true agent of the living, rational phenomena of human existence. Having done so we shall resume work on this line.

MIND AND SOUL AND ORGANIZATION.

Speaking of mind and soul as results of physical organization, implies that by them is meant only modes of physical motion—that these are but physical evolutions, or physical gymnastics, rendered possible by requisite adjustment of its atoms. However, the terms mind and soul can scarcely be used without conveying the impression of their separateness in identity, and that they are substantial realities. Results of *organization* can only be considered as *mechanical* effects— movements corresponding with modes of combination; not the evolution of properties of the substances of these parts, previously concealed in latency, as in chemical unity. And here we must be on our guard yet again. The organism may be regarded as being not only an attainment of more subtile and favorable unions of atoms than occur in the ordinary mixtures and combinations elsewhere in nature, but as embodying in these living results, atoms of specially required properties, which are wanting in forms denoting the absence of the vital principle. Thus did the Greeks speak of divine atoms, love atoms, hate atoms, etc., which went into combination with the atoms of common matter, in the formation of these living organisms. But, by such considerations, separateness of mind and soul from the physical organism, was not to be regarded as impossible at all, nor improbable, where other probabilities pointed to it. This, indeed, might satisfy now, as it did then, a philosophy of biology that provided for a future life.

This, however, does not represent the mineralistic school of to-day. With them no such atoms are required in explanation of living phenomena. With them a "two-faced unity" of substance supplies all data required in explaining all that pertains to life and intellect; and seems preferable as thereby avoiding troublesome complications arising from the necessity of providing a means of *union* in the admission of distinct orders of substance. The mineralism of to-day resolves the problem of life and mind into simply one of *mechanism—spontaneous mechanism*. The concession, however, is that, of course, it is not at all easy even with *this* method. There are *vacuums* to soar in, and *"paradoxes"* to elucidate, while, at the same time, suffering the inconvenience of the ever two-fold appearance of this "double-faced unity." It is ever " mind *and* matter." The idea cannot all be contained in the word " matter." Nor is the word " mind " a whit more accommodating. Nor is it wholly the fault of our concededly poor human language. It is quite as much because two distinct states are unavoidably apparent, and that in consequence the logical mind refuses them oneness of sense and admission to be expressed by the same term, or by terms of the same meaning.

MATTER, ESSENCE OF LIFE.

In still pursuing the theories in respect to life and mentality incipiently or latently consisting of a proper union of atomic forms or properties of atomic matter, a sort of compromise position we find suggested by Prof. Tyndall, in the address already quoted from at the point where he approaches that peroration that brought to his consideration a world of unmerited abuse, from ecclesiastics and also the religious laity, in which he professed to " discern in that matter * * * the promise and potency of every form and quality of life" (p. 77). As he is here, as usual, remarkably clear, I take pleasure in representing him in his own words: " Two courses, and two only, are possible" (in accounting for the origin of life in relation to matter). " Either let us open our doors freely to the conception of creative acts, or, abandoning them, let us radically change our notions of matter. If we look at matter as pictured by Democritus, and as defined for generations in our scientific text-books, the absolute impossibility of any form of life coming out of it, would be sufficient to render any other hypothesis preferable; but the definitions of matter given in our text-books were intended to cover its purely physical and mechanical properties. And taught as we have been, to regard these definitions as complete, we naturally and rightly reject the monstrous notion that out of *such* matter any form of life could possibly arise. But are the definitions complete?

Everything depends on the answer to be given to this question. * * Is there not a temptation to close to some extent with Lucretius, when he affirms that, 'Nature is seen to do all things spontaneously of herself without the meddling of the gods?' or with Bruno, when he declares that nature is not 'that mere empty *capacity* which philosophers have pictured her to be, but the universal mother who brings forth all things as the fruit of her own womb" (pp. 76, 77). This in effect is submitting, not very confidently however, the supposition that the blankness of matter in respect to the vital principle, may be deceptive, owing to the imperfect common view; and that in a form not yet apparent to science it really is but a state of life, which state, by suitable atomic combination and environment, becomes active—enlarges itself, till it appears in the animal and finally mental forms known to us.

From this supposition, which perhaps represents the extent of his belief in respect to the primal state or essence of life, the professor does not see himself as being fairly a materialist or mineralist; as it abrogates the common mineralistic views of matter. It would indeed leave him the representative of an absolutely pure psychism. His is not matter and soul joined together; nor a two-faced unity; but soul and nothing else. And that which is necessarily spoken of as matter, by himself as well as by others, is, strictly speaking, *essence of life;* but in a state so remote from that at which it is recognized life, as that no means of measuring the disparity from one to the other are known to exist,—no parallex of sufficient extent may be found from which lines erected across the chasm would describe an angle of sufficient distinctness for measurement. Seeking to comprehend the distance of their relation, would be trying "to soar in a vacuum."

Whatever may be his belief in respect to a future life (of which I cannot confidently speak), this theory, at first view, would seem to provide a quite satisfactory explanation for the phenomenon of life; and thence possibly also would be reconcilable with a theory of a future life. However, only to the extent to which this vital form of matter may be made to conform to the view of its being a substance quite separate and independent from that of the visible organism,—erecting, inhabiting, and using the organism as a convenience or an instrument, which, without detriment to itself, it might discontinue,—would it be possible to derive from it any form of theory of future life.

The prominent objection to this speculation of the professor is that the inference on which he founds it is not justifiable. Observing that in following the order of vital evolution backward, from the highest forms down, one finally sees the vital principle disappear in a mere viscid state of matter, and that there are parallel facts in the affections of matter,—for example, the successive decrease of polar force at each subdivision of the mass, while yet some measure of it remains, however enfeebled, with the last possible or imaginable division,—he infers that a sympathy and ultimate oneness not only of these phenomena, but of their essences, may exist,—that life and physical attraction may be but widely sundered states of the same substance—"the universal Mother."

But here the necessary sequence is plainly lacking. From these facts nothing follows to fairly establish even a probability of oneness; and the inference is without a real justification. All the sameness here brought to view is in respect to quantity—the idea of more and less as applicable to each. And we might gratuitously add that, without having reference to any other order or side of nature, the individuals on the same side are mutually attracted. But the fact that phenomena are parallel, although suggestive, avails nothing as evidence that they are in any way identical or even remotely related. Besides, the simple fact of quantity does not determine the quality, state or substance—that it is black or white, substance or sentiment. We find therefore by the best presentation of the professor's ingenious speculation no valid reason for its acceptance.

THE DOUBLE-FACED UNITY.

But more common, though less plausible, is the theory of "a double-faced unity" advanced by Prof. Bain, of Scotland. By this theory, substance, in its imaginable ultimate first state, exists of two faces, sides, or aspects, the material, or bodily, and the vital, or mental. And these sides, or aspects, are analogous to what is understood by the properties of matter. And by similarly uniting they constitute this underlying first form of substance; from which all other forms and phenomena of universal being have ascended.

THE OBJECTIONS REVIEWED. 213

The difference between this and the previous theory by Mr. Tyndall, in respect to the first form of matter, at first view would appear slight, if indeed they would not seem identical with each other. Nevertheless the difference is very important. In the previous, substance, primarily, is life itself,—all visible distinctions thereof, such as the many forms of matter, being but of its phases, and due to some unexplained law. It therefore requires no "union,"—is just the thing in this respect that this of Mr. Bain in vain hopes to be—a solitary oneness, and in no sense a composite. On the contrary this of Mr. Bain is unavoidably beset with the ever embarrassing dualism in its "*unity,*" being always a *double-facedness*. Even though, as provided by the terms of the proposition, the *joined* faces constitute its *verity*, so that apart from the *unity*, substance and faces are alike without existence, the troublesome idea is not effaced. Taken in any way imaginable, while unity and plurality fail to convey the same thought, a two-faced unity will only be understood as a two-fold representation! In this case the one of the representations, or faces, of the *unity*, supplies the *material*—the mineral, purely passive quality,—while the other supplies the *immaterial*, vital and sentient.

But as to what about these states which these factors of substance severally represent, this theory is utterly silent. It seems wholly unaware that it has solved nothing till the problem of the *states* belonging to these facial representations is solved. These states could be no less facts than would be their representatives! The mineral or passive "face," or aspect, representative, would be due to anterior mineral forces with their embodying mineral substance, though not yet arrived at a state of matter; while the vital, mental, etc., representative would be equally inexorable in its logical requisition of a prior vital and mental domain of being. But this fact seems persistently overlooked by this school of writers.

There is a notable want of confidence and clearness, of conception, also, on the part of writers in defense of this theory, necessarily seen in the embarrassment of their efforts to vest its conditions in satisfactory statements. Professor Bain, Aberdeen's eminent logician and physiologist, champions this theory in his usual able style. He is concededly one of the ablest advocates the theory has been favored with up to the present time. His work entitled "Mind and Body," contains the most direct, painstaking and satisfactory effort at stating and solving its conditions, yet published. But, while invincibly adhering to his purpose, with his most careful and artful use of language upon it, he frankly concedes his inability to wholly set aside the objections referred to. The following are examples of the estimation he places on the difficulties he encounters, and of the darkness in which he is obliged to leave it after endeavoring to render his theory available. In the undertaking he submits a series of labored attempts at relieving the "undivided twin" and the "two-sided" cause in respect to the facts of mind and body from the persistent *realness* of duality in their union. This is to be so done that, in the first instance, the twin shall not after all really be a *twin*, and, in the second place, that the two-sidedness of the "cause" shall not have reference to two effecting potencies jointly contributing to the existence referred to.

This is necessary with a view to getting rid of the two-fold reality while still retaining a necessary adherence to the two-fold aspect, leaving it consistent to speak of *mind* and *body* separately without conceding that they really *are* so and represent different existences. After this troublesome undertaking, he sees proper to submit this important concession: "While admitting that there is something unique, if not remarkable, in the close incorporation of the two extreme and contrasted facts, termed Mind and Matter, we must grant that the total difference of their nature has rendered the union very puzzling to express in language. The history of the question repeatedly exemplifies this difficulty" (p. 134).

Of like character with this is the following concession: "This, then, as it appears to me, is the only real difficulty of the physical and mental relationship. There is an *alliance with matter*, with the object, or extended world, but the thing allied, *the mind proper*, has itself no extension, and cannot be joined in local union. Now we have a difficulty in providing any form of language, any familiar analogy, suited to this unique conjunction; in comparison with all ordinary unions, it is a paradox or a contradiction" (p. 136).

The trouble is that Mind and Matter are "two extreme and contrasted facts" and cannot be referred to one and the same subjective fact or state; and the admission of this is fatal to the purely mineralistic theory. To recognize the union is unavoidable,—it is a *mineral*, selected and wrought into flesh and blood, etc., made into a living phenomenon, by the presence upon it of a force of an *adequate* nature! And yet to speak of it in this way, is to speak of two forces not only but of the *substances* whose natures they represent and of which they are respectively embodied! Hence a lack of the *language* (?) that will express the desired result!—that will give us a "unity," a "union," a "conjunction," an "alliance" without the *reality* of the constituent *parts!* In the professor's last effort, in this work, to give an intelligent statement of the theory in question, after all his faithful labors have been expended upon it, he leaves it as much as ever in the dark. Although he seems to have won his own assurance in respect to it, and is willing to assume that doubting ones, who have followed him, are all safely transposed to his side. He says:

"The arguments for the two substances have, we believe, now entirely lost their validity; they are no longer compatible with ascertained science and clear thinking. The one substance, with the two sets of properties, two sides, the physical and the mental—a double-faced unity—would appear to comply with all the exigencies of the case. We are to deal with this, as in the language of the Athanasian Creed, not confounding the persons nor dividing the substance " (p. 126).

This, so far as I know, is the first service that the

creed has rendered to science! My impression also is that it was formulated quite independently of scientific considerations, and was never hoped nor expected to express anything that was possible in nature. And with this understanding of it in the present case, the professor has honored himself in selecting it as the closing tribute of labor in behalf of the "double-faced unity." I apprehend, however, that, outside of this subject, he would consider "ascertained science and clear thinking" available in more tangible terms.

As a matter of science, this theory, then, is to be objected to on the ground of the seeming irreconcilable self-contradictions in which it is involved. As touching the doctrine of future life, its conditions seem utterly incompatible with the theory of life separate from the physical body; and, aside from this, it makes the basis of positive existence itself *mineral* or at best limited by mineral conditions. Cutting off entirely all conditions upon which a future life may be projected, it bleakly points future-ward as regards life that now is, to an eternal nothingness. The soul with the body returns in common dust, to the earth from which, by undirected chance, it aggregated into being, its sundered particles to stray hopelessly apart upon the ever changing drifts of endless time.

But, disagreeable as is the impression the theory legitimately tends to make on the full and healthy mind, that is not the motive that happily sets it aside. It is rejected only because, as seen, it fails to accord with the facts with which it is related and to which itself appeals.

MINERALISTIC THEORY OF LIFE.

The last negative to the theory of a future life here to be considered, and one already referred to, is that mind, with vitality generally, is the result of organization, and, therefore, must also end with it. For, considering either of the several theories of matter just reviewed, by neither of them is matter available for actual life till it is brought into requisite form. There is no life—no living phenomenon—till organization is achieved—till in requisite proportion and requisite relations with each other the ultimate molecular atoms are brought together. This having occurred, life has occurred.

In proceeding then to consider this negative, it is important to first set before us what its advocates regard life itself to be. And for this purpose Mr. Herbert Spencer is perhaps the most available. He is more explicit than any of his contemporaries, so far as I have seen. After submitting various definitions tentatively, none of which seem to him entirely free from objection, he concludes that "the broadest and most complete definition of life will be—*The continuous adjustment of internal relations with external relations*" (Principles of Biology, vol. 1, p. 80). This definition he applies to it in " all its manifestations, inclusive of intelligence in its highest forms " (First Principles, p. 85). Also these internal relations are defined to be " definite combinations of simultaneous and successive changes " (Principles of Biology, vol. 1, p. 81). The continuous adjustment of these with "co-existences and sequences" (ibid)—that is, continuous adjustment with adjacent nature and its phenomena, constitutes Life. And this is what we are to understand Life to be from the standpoint of this philosophy.

Now, by this definition of Life, it is the result not alone of organization in individual forms—of some requisite group of forces by a corresponding group of their atoms, but it is the result of the *joining* of such with the related external forces. By this, then, Life is contingent on three several facts: the internal relations, the external relations and their continuous adjustment. And with *either* discontinued, Life is discontinued.

Of whatever nature he may consider the internal relations to be, even though they were purely psychical, the *external* are purely mineral, and the separation from them would be the ending of this mysterious molecular complexity called Life.

Life, then, "in all its manifestations, inclusive of intelligence in its highest forms," by this mineralistic school of philosophy, represented by Mr. Spencer in the preceding, is to be regarded as merely *a condition* of certain phases of the mineral element! *Self* is but that *condition*, and nothing more.

In considering the attainment of organization and the fixed variety of organization as well, from the bare mineral state, it is necessary to bridge or leap over an immense chasm. The great unlikeness of the organized and the unorganized aspects of nature, with hardly an analogy between them, would require a mode of insight that would certainly be extraordinary if not miraculous, to show that they are of the same order of existence.

As to how Mr. Spencer arrives at organization of matter—how the unorganized becomes organized, the pivotal point of the whole question, and where light were more valuable than anywhere else, and where the eye of solicitude rests and ever has rested since the issue first arose, he fails to be explicit. Referring to the interesting facts of chemical evolution, resulting in increased complexities having correspondingly increased sensitiveness, he follows the principle along upward by illustration and then by inference, from simple or binary relations, till he arrives at the delicate colloidal aggregates, where he abruptly introduces us to "organic molecules" or "organic atoms," without thinking it worth while to account for their presence.

It is true that he tells us that "organic matters are produced in the laboratory by what we may literally call *artificial* evolution" (Principles of Biology, p. 482). But by this he is to be understood as referring only to *organizable* matter and not matter formed into organism. The *artificial* evolution refers to the attainment of chemical complexities "ending in organizable protoplasm." So much he finds it possible to explain quite satisfactorily, but at the very next and *supremely essential* point—"the molding of such organic matter into the simplest types," he *conjectures*, "must have commenced with portions of protoplasm more minute, more indefinite, and more inconstant in their characters, than the lowest Rhizopods—less distinguished from a mere fragment of albumen than even the Protogenes of Professor Haeckel" (p. 481). And "to reach by this process the comparatively well-specialized forms of ordinary *Infusoria*, must * * have taken an enormous period of time" (ibid).

This is rather obscuring than defining the great transition of matter from the dead to the living state. It "must have commenced" with a substance practically indistinguishable from albumen and in inaccessible ages past, is by no means a clear statement of how a piece of mineral jelly became transmuted into life!

Also, without any further attempt at explaining how from dead mineral substance they came to be such, except to say that the process "likely * * took place at a time when the heat of the earth's surface was falling through those ranges of temperature at which the higher organic compounds are unstable" (ibid), "living particles" and "physiological units" (pp. 180, 287) are taken in hand and invested with "an innate tendency to arrange themselves into the shape of the organism to which they belong" (p. 180). That is, to follow obediently the typal design of which they are predestined parts.

And now we shall see that trouble which was insurmountable at the very first steps of this theory, thickens with its progress. While no light was at hand to show us the mode of the great transformation from the passive mineral to the subjective living state, and we were obliged to proceed *without* a solution, now even greater will be the difficulty when the theory is to be carried into organization—the accounting for the presence of those units in the peculiar arrangement seen in a living being. That this aggregation of so-called physiological units has proceeded upon method is unavoidable. And to account for the method, it must be placed in a general system of co-ordinating forces, characterized by fixed typal tendency, aggregating and distributing the " units " as they are required to complete the design; or it must be placed in the units themselves, each of which must know not only the animal, but the place in the animal to which it belongs. So that when each one has attained to its place, the animal is the result, physically and sentiently.

The theory assumes the latter. Mr. Spencer says in respect to this, " We have seen it to be necessary from various orders of facts * * * that organisms are built up of certain highly complex molecules, which we distinguish as physiological units—each kind of organism being built up of physiological units peculiar to itself. We found ourselves obliged to recognize in these physiological units powers of arranging themselves into the forms of organism to which they belong " (Principles of Biology, vol. 2, p. 8). The passage in which he refers to this is where he has made full application of this theory, and is the following: " We have therefore no alternative but to say, that the living particles composing one of these fragments, have an innate tendency to arrange themselves into the shape of the organism to which they belong. We must infer that a plant or animal of any species, is made up of special units, in all of which there dwells the intrinsic aptitude to aggregate into the form of that species: just as in the atoms of salt, there dwells the intrinsic aptitude to crystallize in that particular way. It seems difficult to conceive that this can be so, but we see that it *is so*" (Principles of Biology, pp. 180—181).

This view not only credits each of these wonderful units with an "intrinsic aptitude" to aggregate itself to its own species and its exact place in the organism, but also with the sentience of the complete being of the animal or plant to which it belongs! Otherwise, by what means would be avoided a hopeless jumble, extravagance, and indefinite multiplication of the several parts? How could the tail units determine, relatively to the other parts, where the tail is to be developed? How, when a lizard loses an arm, these caudal units do not happen to rush to the spot and build out a *tail* in the place of the new arm that appears? How could the claw and the leaf units come to discontinue their additions when the claw and the leaf have attained their standard size? And, as said, how could the tail units limit their construction to but *one* tail? And how could the eye units come to not all double up into only *one* eye, but must distribute themselves into exactly *two*, or as the species requires?

Now if there is not sentience here employed, covering the whole of the details of the organism, how shall we be assured that such a principle as sentience has *an ex-*

istence? And if this "intrinsic aptitude" covers all there is of this, where but in this intrinsic aptitude is this super-human sentience to be located?

It is of no consequence to the argument that we say it, and if these deductions of our author are *facts*, there is no objection to be raised; but while we are about it there could be no impropriety in taking a view of the picture which this theory places before us. By the immutable law of sequence, these postulates make us to see an astounding picture of the vast body of nature. We see this whole cosmical existence as being a field in which a densely crowded panorama is revolving, —not only of these far-seeing units, on the alert for formative opportunities to come into proper and appointed relations with each other, but all the myriad swarms of vegetable and animal beings, in all their complete personal appointments in a pregenital existence, are suspended therein; their distributed atoms waiting in turns at the door of generation the signal for the assembling of their "units" and the completion of the practical organism.

This may be observed to transpire somewhat after the circumstance of the pioneer going to make a home on a western prairie. He has his house built before going, but ships the parts in a promiscuous package to be properly joined on their arrival. Only, in the case of the house, the beams and braces and boards and shingles, do not come together from an intrinsic aptitude on the part of each to take its place in the arrangement, as Mr. Spencer sees his physiological units doing.

THE OBJECTIONS REVIEWED. 225

Not knowing how to account for it on other principles, the conclusion would be quite justifiable that each of these "*units*" of the house by an intrinsic aptitude took its place,—that it foresaw in detail the shape and character of the structure that it was included in; but it were more in accord with current facts to say that the aptitude and the intelligence were in an attendant artisan and not in the beams and boards themselves.

It will be observed that in endeavoring to gain a substantial footing for the origin of life, consistent with what life truly *is*, Mr. Spencer abandons, for the time, his favorite doctrine of evolution by environment, in this theory of physiological units, above set forth, by endowing them with inherent powers to *escape* environment and voluntarily build *themselves* into living organisms. And yet, in making the immense sacrifice, no relief is gained from the ever troublesome fact that to that anteceding force, necessary to their existence, which can resolve itself into nothing but a sentient volitience, no form of mineral aspect can be made to apply. And this leaves it so that even the theory of *special creation*, for which he has so little charity, may, after all, be the last resort in accounting for the existence of these units and the beings they represent!

OF THE GENESIS OF NERVES.

It is not in the province of this work to follow this mineralistic philosophy into its details very extendedly; but Mr. Spencer, in seeking to account for the origin of nerves, seeks again to get on without crediting the existence of a prior typal life principle to act upon the mineral aggregates; now again reverting back to his favorite theory of development by environment. In respect to the origin of nerves, he observes that "in all cases, motion follows the line of the greatest traction or least resistance, or the resultant of the two;" and that "motion once set up along any line becomes itself a cause of subsequent motion along that line" (Principles of Psychology, vol. 1, pp. 5—11). On this principle, protoplasmic matter in incipient organisms, having nerve filaments, becoming impacted with force from the environment, the passage of the force taking the route of the least resistance, leaves in that direction, first a general outlet or inlet for force, and lastly by long use of this kind, reduces it to a channel or thread, into which the sensitive filaments drop and constitute a nerve (p. 515).

At least two facts are hopelessly in the way of this otherwise plausible theory. In the first place, environment, without intelligent or instinctive direction, is without requisite uniformity of condition; and, in the second place, without the operation of antecedent typal forces on these colloidal or protoplasmic masses, these "lines of the least resistance" would be utterly without conformity. And, save by mere accident, the individual developments would be radically unlike; and as under this state of things *repetitions* of force passages over the same lines would rarely, if ever, occur in more than the same individual, this theory of nerve genesis becomes extremely improbable, if not altogether impossible!

While nerves may be and seemingly are formed after this general manner, this method as truly as all others, renders it necessary to include a differentiating power back of this external process to *shape and maintain* the requisite conditions. And so at this second stage of vital development, as truly as at the first, the mineralistic philosophy shows itself powerless to get on without involving the existence of a domain of vital substance, from the instinctive and sentient forces of which, operating upon the mineral domain, the whole list of vital phenomena proceed.

Now this is the *entire lore* of the mineralistic school of philosophy, claiming the mind and the vital principle generally, to be results, or rather states, of physical organization. Of all their voluminous works covering this subject, none embodies statements or arguments more strongly maintaining that claim. There is not a bottom principle that is not fully comprehended in what has been here brought forward and examined, in all the volumes, worthy of consideration, that have been contributed to the illustration and defense of this theory. And the reader must judge whether, after all, there is in them the strength—the conclusive evidence of soundness, that has many times been claimed for them, or whether they do not show evidence of hurried conclusion on the part of men who looked upon the subject as more or less hopeless of a solution in harmony with a cherished theory.

CHAPTER XIII.

Man in His Essential Self Continues Beyond the Limits of Physical Existence, Continued.—The Argument for the Affirmative.

HAVING now considered, in all their essential details and to an extent which the limits of this work will hardly justify, the doubts and negatives respecting the continuance of man's existence in a state beyond death, we turn to the argument for the affirmative. And we begin by restating the position taken at the first of the preceding chapter, that "the part that physical science has to act in settling the question of a future life, is to determine the relation of mind and body; from which it is to be ascertained that the mind as well as the soul with which it is identified, is, or is not, in its essential wholeness, separable from the body. Then when such a separation is found possible, that, at the death of the body, it is actual as well." To this last proposition a more full consideration will be given in the next chapter.

In considering our existence, we first of all contemplate our nature as a sentient self. We pass through hours of time without our clothing or our body having come into our thoughts at all. The current ap-

THE ARGUMENT FOR THE AFFIRMATIVE. 229

prehension is that our self is in some sense residing *in* or *about* the body. The body concerns us mainly in two respects: Our feeling extends into it, and our consciousness or life (external) depends on it. In minor respects, we are concerned in its parts for the *uses* they are to us, and the *aspect* of ourselves they constitute. But did our feeling extend into our clothing, our cane or crutch, our sense of *self* would be found there quite as much as it is in our skin or arm or leg.

Indeed, the material part of our existence can hardly, if at all, be brought into realization as *self*. Taking a survey of our whole anatomy, part by part, or in its effective wholeness, the sense of it as an *external object* is irresistible.

Now, this being a fact which we need to refer only to common observation and experience, we must treat it as such and give it its due weight in the discussion. It is, to be sure, not cited as *positive* proof, but as a corroborative circumstance—a cumulative proof. This manner of mental disturbance is not without adequate cause, and one that cannot be wholly attributed to education. It prevails with people of little education of any kind, and whose state of intelligence would most readily incline them to the *opposite* view and conclusion.

That, then, this disturbing cause lies in a *fact* somewhat in accord with *the impulse*, would be the legitimate inference,—that though so related with it that the forces of the two are interlacing each other, the *self*, in its effective wholeness, is in a sense separate from and not at all identical with the body. And now it is our next business to see what corroborations can be produced from the facts of human existence to confirm this common impression respecting ourself and our embodiment. And here we need not be long considering where we will begin. All sentient operations exclusively pertain to the nervous system.

In viewing the voluminous mass of brain, securely lying within the bony integument of the skull, and from it proceeding directly, or indirectly, by way of the great spinal cord, the meshes of white or of silvery gray strands, threads and fibers of microscopic fineness, one beholds all there is in the physical aspect of man that is at all concerned with any form of mind or feeling. The masses of bones, flesh and the substances incident to the flesh, that constitute the chief mass of the human body are as remote from the mind as are the hat and the coat. The feeling that is realized in connection with them is from the presence of these nerves lying through them. An insensuous connection is seen to exist between certain nerve filaments and the muscular fiber. However this is by way of the induction principle known in electricity. The nerve itself is wrapped about by an insulating integument; and in this manner of exclusion ramifies the physical tissue; and by the inductive process effects muscular activity. In respect to this Dr. Lionel S. Beale, of London, an authority on Microscopic Anatomy that will be conceded by the learned everywhere, whom Professor Bain extensively follows in his celebrated work on Mind and Body, observes:

"I have given a drawing taken from a beautiful specimen of muscular tissue, in which the ultimate ramifications of the nerve fibers are very clearly demonstrated. Many points here illustrated have long been and are still disputed by anatomists. Some think the motor nerves pass into the substance of the muscular fibers, others that they are connected with special organs imbedded in and in close contact with the muscular tissue, but at least as regards the particular muscles represented, I feel sure that the arrangement as I have given it is correct. In my specimens the fine nerve fibers traversing the muscular fibers can be seen very distinctly. The bioplasts often come very close to the muscular tissue, but they are not imbedded in it. * * Although the bioplasts of the several tissues are very near to one another, they never interfere with each other's growth, or coalesce" (Protoplasm, pp. 255, 256).

Here, not alone the nerve and muscle fibers are in their ultimate ramifications wholly separate, but their bioplasts (the pabulums of their subsistence and growth) are also peculiar and separate from each other.

This is not saying that *remotely* the very *highest* mental element may not, by way of the successively lower elements, impinge upon and control even the *mineral* forces in the states below the lowest vital state, and without reference to organization. The fact thereof, as already seen, lies at the bottom of the *origin* of organization itself. But in man's physical aspect, all sentient transactions take place by means alone of the forces that are incident to the nerve circuits.

THE MODE OF NERVOUS DEVICE.

In principle of arrangement and operation the whole system of nerves is quite like the magnetic telegraph; the nerve fibers being tractile to what is called nerve force, the same as the telegraph wire is tractile to electrical force. Batteries of cups or cells are found connected with these lines of nerves to supply the nerve force with which they are charged, after the manner that in *telegraphy* batteries are placed to the wires to supply them with the force with which electricity is resident. In confirmation of this Dr. Beale, above referred to, says:

"The nervous apparatus, through which alone the vital power of the highest bioplasm of every creature acts, consists essentially of fine fibers which form, with the mass of bioplasm, uninterrupted circuits. The fibers are continuous with the bioplasts, and grow from them. * * The smallest nerve fiber instead of resembling an ordinary telegraph wire, might rather be compared with a bundle of wires, each having its battery (mass of bioplasm in the case of the nerve) connected with it. So that even a very short piece of nerve fiber would contain numerous bioplasts, or little batteries, which continue to act, that is, give rise to nerve currents for some time (the period varying in different cases) after the nerve has been removed from the body" (Protoplasm, p. 317).

In this quotation Dr. B. is in substantial accord with the learned in this department, everywhere; and while it is seen to entirely confirm the statements just made, it also anticipates my next observation by saying that these cells "give rise to nerve currents for some time after the nerve has been removed from the body," and that "the fibers are continuous with the bioplasts and grow from them." The next fact, then, to be noted, and one that immensely concerns this subject, is that the force called nerve force, which is subservient to the higher forces of mind, feeling, etc., *is not originated in the nerve fibers* at all but is *delivered to them* out of a form of substance that is simply adjacent, and much less complex, and at most of barely any organization; while often it is simply a tractile mass with no form of organization visible.

Now that the nerve forces and the construction of the nervous fabric, as we have seen, proceed from the bioplastic cells, it is plain that by way of those cells, mainly, the unconscious and the conscious operations of the mind upon the body take place, and that the forces that so sentiently actuate the nerves and give expression to the whole organism, in whatever form it may be that they exist, hold only a certain form of *relation* therewith. If the mind were in any way identical with or dependent on the organization, we should certainly see its presence first with the *highest* forms of organization—in the nerve fabric itself—and not in the *lowest*, and least elaborate, even in that that has not yet attained to the simplest form of organization. This, it would seem, must cut off all means of *presuming* that the mind is within or in any proper sense limited to the enclosure of the nervous integuments; and would leave it only possible to consider *self* as a separate party; though an occupant of the same space described by the bodily limits.

In this connection it is still further important to be observed that seeing, as we do, that the mental element is in no fixed relation with any part of the nerve substance, but is in a state of incessant transference,—is not fixedly, but transiently actuating the parts, we find again this *self*, with respect to the body, to reside externally of it, and with no such connections with it visible, as would render its efficient individual completeness contingent on the union of the two.

DR. FERRIER'S EXPERIMENTS.

The fact is fully established that the co-ordination of muscular action results from local cerebral arrangements. The application of electrodes to different parts of the gray matter of the brain, which is the external layer, next to the membranous coverings and the skull, is followed by muscular action in different parts of the body. Quite recently, Dr. Ferrier, of England, submitted a series of most thorough experiments of this kind made on the lower animals, cats, monkeys, rabbits and dogs, finding the principle true in every instance. Dr. Ferrier, in these observations is thoroughly endorsed by both Dr. Beale and Prof. Carpenter, and the reports of his experiments they have extensively embodied in their works.

Dr. Ferrier has carried his experiments quite into detail; and of the several kinds of animals examined, has mapped the brain, showing the locations of the groups thus actually found, much after the manner of phrenologists. The following statements from his conclusions concerning his experiments will sufficiently illustrate his views:

"1. The anterior portions of the cerebral hemispheres are the chief centers of voluntary motion and the active outward manifestation of intelligence. 2. The individual convolutions are separate and distinct centers; and in certain definite groups of convolutions (to some extent indicated by the researches of Fritsch and Hitzig) and in corresponding regions of non-convoluted brains, are localized the centers for the various movements for the eyelids, the face, the mouth and tongue, the ear, the neck, hand, foot and tail. Striking differences corresponding with the habits of the animal are found to be in the differentiation of the centers. Thus the centers for the tail in dogs, the paws in cats, the lips and mouth in rabbits, are highly differentiated and pronounced" (Dr. Beale on Protoplasm, p. 323). Dr. Hughlings Jackson has made similar observations on the human system.

THE SELF AND ITS INSTRUMENT.

Now, in the lower portion of this gray-matter layer of the brain, whereon these electrodes are applied, "the number of nerve fibers, like that of the bioplasts, is altogether beyond calculation. A portion of the gray matter upon the surface of the convolutions, not larger than the head of a very small pin, will contain portions of many thousands of nerve fibers, the distal ramifications of which may be in very distant and different parts of the body." And these masses of bioplastic cells and their attendant nerve filaments, are formed into *local groups by kinds,* with reference to special destinations and offices, as is seen in these experiments. However, is it not the same mental element?—the same sentient volitional force?—indeed the very and complete *Self*, that appears as the disturbing—the actuating cause of each of these several groups from which the voluntary muscular action occurs? Is it not *Self* that appears in the voluntary movements of the foot, the eye, the hand or the tongue? Does not *Self* say, *I am doing it?* There certainly is no plainer—not a more pronounced fact of *any* kind. But it is also no less plain, that this mental element—this sentient, volitional self-force, passes, without contact with intervening ones, from one of these groups over to another. While one set of bioplasts, or more or less sets, as the case may be, which are correlated in the execution of one given purpose, are being impacted by it, it is absent from others, and, in turn, will also be absent from these. The mental element is to be seen operating these groups of bioplasts and nerves upon the same mechanical principle that the pianist operates the keys and the wires of the piano in executing a sentiment of music: Now the ravishing hands fall on *these* keys, and now, completely leaving these and passing *over* others, descend on *those*, striking only such as are grouped in the strain and which the spirit of harmony foresees and dictates to be used on the occasion.

Recognizing here that it may be judged that in this

illustration I have not covered all the ground,—that as there are, besides the fully defined intelligent movements and expressions, many that are vaguely intelligent and often barely traceable as such, after all the *inactive* groups may be retaining their appropriate parts of mind, but in a state of comparative latency; and that in some sense the mind is still identical with the brain and of it. This, perhaps, solitary objection, is readily set aside by the fact that conceding it, it were still required to admit the existence of an outside and essentially independent mentality to impinge upon and arouse the latent part in such unison with other and *not all* parts as to obviate confusion and produce intelligent results! But for the purpose of rendering an explanation for the mixed phenomena referred to, it may be said that in these separate actuations of the brain groups the *entire* self may not always be employed. The effort or intent may be feeble from indifference or hesitancy, or from being tentatively distributed to a variety of objective motives; so that the action may be aimless and irrelevant or seemingly automatic. Like as when the operator's mind is loosely floating amid a congeries of harmonies, his leisure fingers stroll listlessly over the keys, but in the moment of the mind's concentration in the proposition of an execution they descend in a harmonic crash! so, too, when the mental element has in any other department of thought become concentrated into an active purpose, the executive mental force is precipitated upon the required groups, and the action becomes strongly differentiated and pronounced. It will be seen, also, that at that time of mental concentration there is a corresponding absence of diffused phenomena throughout the organism.

In this connection it may also be incidentally noted as a fact of no small importance, that when the electrodes are applied only general movements of the affected parts are elicited. There is seen no detailing of movement with reference to a purpose—there is no specializing that would be necessary to certifying to the presence of a mental cause. Hence, two facts, at least, must be conceded: First, that the brain, as an instrument, is, comparatively, a simple one,—in device is not of the versatility that is necessary for an intellectual aspect of movement, in which fact we are again reminded that it is impossible for the mind to be the result of this physical organization; and, second, that the mental fabric—the individual mind—holds an external relation with the brain analogous somewhat to that which the electrodes themselves sustain to it; and that as in telegraphy many unlike messages pass over the same wire, so over one brain mass of nerve wires are discharged innumerable dissimilar forms and measures of mental impulses from its similarly adjacent mental operator.

It is, also, to be still further noted from these citations of facts that this mind is a *unit* of *parts* or functions and therefore exists in some manner of *form* and embodiment in this adjacent and separate relation, as the ideas and resolutions brought to bear upon the brain are fully formed and energized before being precipitated on the cell and nerve arrangement. And it comes to be seen again from this point of view that the mind, as such—on its own part—exists and does its work without a physical brain at all—that for ideation it has not even recourse to the much talked about gray matter. It is as the operator who first executes the idea and the purpose to do so within himself, before rattling it off on the wires!

This same principle is still further illustrated in the fact that this individual mind is capable of sending the same mental dispatch—the same purpose to be effected —over various and dissimilar departments of nerve wire. If one set of these wires is down, pre-occupied, or from other cause unavailable, it dispatches over another set. For example, when an object is to be removed the mental impulse will descend upon the group affecting the hand, but if the hand is not at liberty the mind changes the impellent force over to the group affecting the foot, perhaps ; and soon. However, the *idea*—the *message* or *purpose* in the transaction—is identically the same, by whichever member accomplished,—over whichever nerve wires transmitted. Hence, neither is the *operator* nor the *idea*, that are witnessed in the rational transaction, identified with the organism, nor dependent on it more than for a means of transaction.

Similar to this is that often seen in cases of approaching death, where the vital machinery is so depleted by the erosions and waste of disease as to be wholly unserviceable to the restorative vital forces, where deep lesions and extensive paralysis with confusion of interfallen fiber incident to the collapse of the mass, have necessarily taken place, the whole mind—the complete sentient self with all the sweet thoughtful affections re-appears in the countenance and on the lisping tongue. The fact is so common as to be not at all wonderful. It has often been remarked upon in cases of chronic insanity—where brain lesions have remained incurable. In these cases the recurrence to the normal state is not so gradual as to denote the restoration of the organism to wholeness and health, but comparatively instantaneous. It is Self re-appearing above the wreck, independent of breaks and wide disconnections of its former channels, seizing, independently of these, the remote centers directly and re-erecting them for this moment's use in the transmission of a greeting by the same loved one from practically beyond the tomb.

And, here it is to be further noted, as a matter of still further interest to the subject, that this recurrence to consciousness and to sentience cannot be entirely the result of vital reaction, from the fact that such a reaction is dependent on unbroken tissue. Reactions are the repairing forces, and do not thus suddenly rebuild or span over breaks. The marvelous fact is more readily understood by considering that it is from a mental effort, more or less intense, made by the departing self, *favored* by the reactive flow of the vital forces in the parts actuated. Similar impulses of mental force are on other occasions seen to be more or less effective in overcoming physical dormancies, as in some forms of alarming dreams wherein we remember having struggled immensely to regain control of our physical powers.

And when it was regained it was, at times, with such force as to cause a smart rebound of the body.

In cases of catalepsy the same fact is at times illustrated. A somewhat remarkable case of this character has been reported from Newark, N. J., of a young lady of that place in November, 1880. During her cataleptic trance of five weeks, she was without the power of recognizing or speaking. She lay painless and quiet, with little movement save "a slow twitching of the eyelids." "The severest electric shocks caused not even the twitch of a muscle. On her recovery, she stated that she had been conscious, but had but the one thought—the terrible one that her physicians might pronounce her dead and she be buried alive!" The agonizing thought could not have been without the greatest volitional effort. But "in vain did she try to speak. She could not move her lips." Without avail did the operator in her complete Self hammer the keys of the fallen wires to send out the infinitely important message that life was not yet departed and might be recalled to external consciousness. This, then, may indicate the straining effort by which the mental force, under such intense solicitude, may over-leap the breaks in nerves, or immediately seize upon the more external centers themselves and actuate the organs of sense or of sight, hearing and speech for the brief moment's parting salutation.

And when now we thus see that when the organism is so extensively broken down and so much of it actually carried away wholly beyond the bodily limits, without detriment to the wholeness of this sentient Self, is it not sufficiently apparent that the accomplishment of the little remaining work of decomposition—separation or death—of the body will likewise be a matter of indifference to the individual's survival in this same completeness? We note that up to this state of the procedure, disorganization has had only the effect to liberate the Self without in any respect having diminished or disqualified it. So, while the remaining shreds of organization by which its slight adherence to the external state are continued, are *but the same* in nature and character as the ones destroyed, the further progress and the final end of the work of death would be only of like effect—its further liberation and finally entire separation from the body, and the beginning of the career that awaits it in the region beyond.

Dr. Beale, in seeing the force of this same class of facts that I have here adduced, has very properly submitted from his first-class eminence as a physiologist, the challenge to mineralists: "Since all forms of vital power are transferable, is it not going farther than is warranted by reason to affirm, that no vital power can, under any circumstances, be freed from the material, and yet be?"

DREAMS AND SOMNAMBULISM.

We come now to consider the evidence of yet another class of facts—facts that are incidental to dreams and somnambulism or sleep-walking. In sleep, while the brain is much less active, the mind is known to be at times more efficient than in waking. In such cases the strongest and most accurate thinking transpires with little or no use of the brain; harmonizing with what has already been observed, that the conception of the thought and the impulse to its execution take place apart from the brain and prior to being delivered upon it. Indeed, there is no necessity of seeing that all thoughts go to the brain; but that even of the greatest, some may never appear upon that organ at all. While of some only the *remembrance* of them goes to the brain. Miss H. Martineau, of England, reports the case "of a congenital idiot who had lost his mother when he was under two years old, and who could not have subsequently been made cognizant of anything relating to her; and who yet when dying at the age of thirty, suddenly turned his head, looked bright and sensible, and exclaimed in a tone never heard from him before, 'Oh, my mother! how beautiful!' and sunk round again—dead" (Household Words, vol. 9, p. 200). The case is cited by Prof. Carpenter in his Mental Physiology, and seems to show conclusively that the mind underwent *enlargement* without the ordinary use of the brain,—that mind may have resources of development from a state unconnected with the brain.

In the case of this idiot, there occurred the momentary, unmistakable manifestation of a measure of appreciation and affection that is inseparable from a state of lucid reason, though without a corresponding brain, and is conclusive proof that the movements and conceptions, and, hence, enlargements of mind *may* take place with little or no regard to a brain substance. The enlargement in this example took place while on the dream side of his life—while the dwarfed, defective brain, with its darkening and disordering reactions on the mind, was harmlessly down in sleep.

Instances of extraordinary mental achievements during sleep, are of quite frequent occurrence. A few well authenticated examples will illustrate. On the authority of Prof. Wm. B. Carpenter, I here insert a narrative by the Rev. John de Liefde, taken from the experience of a fellow clergyman. The clergyman was, at the time referred to, a student of mathematics in the Mennonite Seminary of Amsterdam, under Prof. Von Swinden. A banking-house had given the professor a severe problem requiring very skillful figuring, upon which he had already made some unsuccessful attempts. Finally he selected from his students a number to whom he in turn submitted it, one of whom was this young student himself, who says:

"My ambition did not allow me any delay. I set to work the same evening, but without success. Another evening was sacrificed to my undertaking, but fruitlessly. At last I bent myself over my figures for the third evening. It was winter and I calculated till half-past one in the morning—all to no purpose! The product was erroneous. Low at heart, I threw down my pencil, which already by that time had beciphered three slates. I hesitated whether I would toil the night through, and begin my calculation anew; as I knew the professor wanted an answer the very same morning. But, lo! my candle was already burning in the socket; and, also, the persons with whom I lived had long gone to rest.

Then I also went to bed; my head filled with ciphers; and tired in mind, I fell asleep. In the morning, I awoke just early enough to dress and prepare myself to go to the lecture; vexed at heart at not having been able to solve the question and at having to disappoint my teacher. But, O wonder! as I approach my writing table, I find on it a paper, with figures in my own hand, and (think of my astonishment!) the whole problem upon it solved quite aright, and without a single blunder. I wanted to ask my *hospita* whether any one had been in my room; but was stopped by my own writing. *

* * Thus I must have calculated the problem in my sleep, and in the dark to boot; and what is most remarkable, the computation was so succinct, that what I saw now before me on a single folio sheet had required three slatefuls closely beciphered on both sides during my waking state. Prof. Von Swinden was quite amazed at the event, and declared to me that whilst calculating the problem himself, he had never once thought of a solution so simple and concise" (Mental Phys., pp. 593, 594).

Of the same class of phenomena is a circumstance referred to by Prof. Haven in his Mental Philosophy. Speaking of a school for young ladies where a prize had been offered for the best paintings, he says:

"Among the competitors was a young and timid girl, who was conscious of her inferiority in the art, yet strongly desirous of success. For a time, she was quite dissatisfied with the progress of her work; but by and by began to notice as she resumed her pencil in the morning that something had been added to the work since she last touched it. * * * The additions were evidently by a superior hand, far excelling her own in skill and workmanship. Her companions denied, each and severally, all knowledge of the matter. She placed articles of furniture against her door in such a way that any one entering would be sure to awaken her. They were undisturbed; but still the mysterious additions continued to be made. At last her companions concluded to watch without and make sure that no one entered her apartment during the night; but still the work went on. At length it occurred to them to watch her movements; and now the mystery was explained. They saw her, evidently in sound sleep, rise, dress, take her place at the table, and commence her work. It was her own hand that, unconsciously to herself, had executed the work in a style which in her waking moments she could not approach, and which quite surpassed all competition."

Another case, similar in character, is taken from Dr. Abercrombie, who relates respecting an eminent lawyer of Scotland, who had been consulted in respect to a case of much importance and of great difficulty,—that he had been studying it with intense interest and application. The doctor goes on to say:

"After several days had been occupied in this manner, he was observed by his wife to rise from his bed in the night and go to a writing-desk which stood in the bedroom. He then sat down and wrote a long paper which he carefully put in his desk, and returned to bed. The following morning he told his wife that he had had a most interesting dream;—that he had dreamt of delivering a clear and luminous opinion respecting a case which had exceedingly perplexed him; and that he would give any thing to recover the train of thought which had passed before him in his dream. She then directed him to the writing-desk, where he found the opinion clearly and fully written out; and this was afterward found to be perfectly correct" (Intellectual Powers, 5th Ed., p. 306).

Dr. Hammond seeks to parry the force of this example by suggesting that the man must have been awake while executing the work—that waking transactions are, at times, recalled as having been dreams. But the example he submits is not at all a parallel case. One, truly, *may passively* view a fire or hear a story told and in time recalling it, be uncertain as to whether it was a real transaction or only a dream. But hardly so of a matter of such deliberate straining effort, wherein the co-ordinations of the surrounding state—determining whether one was waking or sleeping—become most definitely impressed.

He remembered the great lucid effort as co-ordinating with the *dreaming* state, and the equally laborious, but less successful, as with the waking state. And in no case imaginable is memory more worthy of entire reliance.

These cases are somnambulistic dreams. They are "acted dreams," as Prof. Carpenter rightly denominates somnambulisms. In dreams of this character, the mind attains control of some of the nerves of motion, and at times, to some extent, also, those of the senses; and but for this last stated means of external manifestation and record of the passing thought, if recalled at all, it would be recalled as merely a dream. But somnambulists more commonly remember nothing of their somnambulic transactions,—not even recalling that they have *dreamed* correspondingly with the acts alleged of them in that state, or dreamed at all. So, but for the matter of mere accident, in these examples, their most successful thinking—their strongest and most sane achievements of mind, would in the one case have been vaguely recalled as only a dream; and in the other two, the artist girl and the young mathematician, not even the hint from a dream thereof remained to them of their mind's successful work in the dream-land. Nothing respecting themselves, for that time, could have been known but that they had been pursuing common sleep—sleep like any other sleep. And what achievements of like efficiency and sanity may not, then, have transpired to these people at *other* times, and to other people as well, that have remained utterly unknown to the waking side? And who with these facts before him shall say that such is not more or less common to human life all the time?

Grotesque as ordinary dreams represent its movements to have been, there are thus instances that show consistent, connected and systematic thinking to have been pursued by the mind during sleep. And because the more perfect of these are commonly not recalled after waking, but are known by having been somnambulistically acted out, we are led to see that the more *sane* transactions of *mind* in the sleeping state take place when the sleep is the *most complete!* This, also, is assured by the fact that in the waking state the apprehending powers of the mind are, according to the extent of the waking, diverted and employed by the brain forces, objectively upon the external or waking facts; which, in their glaring realness to the open senses, necessarily obscure the impressions of past mental movements in proportion that they have been less connected with the brain. Hence, the deepest dreams, ordinarily, are most forgotten. Besides a state of partial or divided consciousness is necessarily incompatible with clear thought. And so the most grotesque dreams are best remembered.

And from this it would also be quite natural to infer that when sleep again ensued, the mind might recover the forgotten transaction and possibly proceed again in respect to it, taking up the thread of the previous dream, specially so if the sleep were of the same degree of soundness.

And here, too, there are corroborations at hand. Prof. Hamilton, who says, "whether we recollect our dreams or not, we always dream," states touching this principle, "I have always observed that when suddenly awakening from sleep (and to ascertain the fact I have caused myself to be roused at different seasons of the night) I have always been enabled to observe that I was always in the middle of a dream" (Metaphysics, p. 225). Only part of the mind's transaction in that state was he able to recall. But what he recalled was in such *form* as to enable him to know that where it was discontinued to his memory, was only where it went under cover of some obscuring circumstance, and was not the beginning nor ending thereof. This is a very common fact in respect to dreams.

Then, again, there occur what seem to be "*serial dreams.*" Those who have been in the habit of taking account of their dreams have at times noted this peculiarity, that the mind in its wanderings has undergone a quite sensible reaction as of the surprise of suddenly arriving upon a matter of thought previously engaged upon, or upon a scenic display—a landscape or city, possibly—previously looked upon, and having an aspect of great familiarity, and yet in the waking state be able to recall of it little or nothing but the fact of a strong impression of that character having taken place. That such recoveries of prior trains of thought and scenic pictures, after the lapse of a period of waking, are matters of fact, is frequently shown in the transactions of somnambulists, of which a case given by Prof. Carpenter will serve to illustrate; though he cites it for a different purpose. The subject was a young lady of very sensitive organization and who had undergone a long and severe illness. Her illusion was in respect to an only brother who had died some years before. In her somnambulistic dreams she saw him and conversed with him, evincing the deepest emotions with extravagant forms of speech. On one occasion, he observes:

"It happened that when she passed into this condition, her sister, who was present, was wearing a locket containing some of their deceased brother's hair.

As soon as she perceived this locket, she made a violent snatch at it, and would not be satisfied until she got it into her possession, when she began to talk to it in the most endearing and extravagant terms. Her feelings were so strongly excited on this subject, that it was judged prudent to check them; and as she was inaccessible to all entreaties for the relinquishment of the locket, force was employed to obtain it from her. She was so determined, however, not to give it up, and was so angry at the gentle violence used that it was found necessary to abandon the attempt; and having become calmer, after a time, she passed off into ordinary sleep. Before going to sleep, however, she placed the locket under her pillow, remarking, 'Now I have hid it safely, and they shall not take it from me.' On awaking in the morning, she had not the slightest consciousness of what had passed, but the impression of the excited feelings still remained, for she remarked to her sister, 'I cannot tell what it is that makes me feel so; but every time that S— comes near me I have a kind of shuddering sensation,' the individual named being a servant whose constant attention to her had given rise to a feeling of strong attachment on the side of the invalid, but who had been the chief actor in the scene of the previous evening. This feeling wore off in the course of a day or two.

"A few days afterward, the somnambulism again recurred; and the patient, being upon the bed at the time, immediately began to search for the locket under her pillow. In consequence of its having been removed in the interval (in order that she might not, by accidentally finding it there, be led to inquire into the cause of its presence, of which it was thought better to keep her in ignorance) she was unable to find it; at which she expressed great disappointment, and continued searching for it, with the remark, 'It *must* be there; I put it there a few minutes ago, and no one can have taken it away' " (Mental Phys., pp. 597, 598).

Though here on waking there was no remembrance of what had thus transpired—not even of the careful hiding of the locket, when she re-entered the deep somnambulistic sleep, immediately the same train of thought and the same feelings and scenes, were recurred to and entered upon as if they had taken place but the previous moment, though several days of waking had intervened; giving evidence that not alone is the mind in that state capable, spasmodically, of individual unconnected efforts, but of *serial*, systematic chains of thought, though broken in upon and sundered by the diverting power of the waking state.

We have room for only a few, but citations of examples of the above character from the most unquestionable authorities, might be indefinitely prolonged. I have referred to them for the purpose of showing what the mind can do with little or no relation with the brain.

STATE OF THE BRAIN DURING SLEEP.

In sleep the brain reposes—is to a large extent or wholly without activity and the use of its function. "In profound ordinary sleep, the cerebrum with the sensory ganglia, is in a state of complete functional inactivity" (Carpenter's Phys., p. 610). Experiments invariably show the brain in a state of sleep to have receded from the cranium and to have assumed a state of comparative rest. Blumenbach and Dendy, severally referred to by Dr. Hammond, Ex-Surgeon General, U. S. Army, report cases in illustration of this fact. The former reports an instance of a young man having fallen and fractured his skull on the right side of the coronal suture. "After recovery took place a hiatus remained, covered only by the integument. While the young man was awake this chasm was quite superficial, but as soon as sleep ensued it became very deep. The change was due to the fact that during sleep the brain was in a collapsed condition" (Sleep and its Derangements, p. 30). The latter "states that there was, in 1821, at Montpellier, a woman who had lost part of her skull, and the brain and its membranes lay bare. When she was in deep sleep the brain remained motionless beneath the crest of the cranial bones; when she was dreaming, it became somewhat elevated; and when she was awake it was protruded through the fissures of the skull" (ibid).

Dr. Hammond has pursued this investigation on his own part by performing numerous operations on lower animals, finding always that during sleep the brain in like manner receded, and rose again upon waking. He observes, giving the process in full:

"Since the chapter on the Physiology of Sleep was written, I have, by additional experiments, satisfied myself that the theory then enunciated is correct in every particular.

"By means of an instrument adapted to show the extent of cerebral pressure, and which I first described nearly two years ago, I have been enabled to arrive at very positive results. In every instance the pressure was lessened during sleep and was increased during wakefulness. The experiments were performed upon dogs and rabbits. Briefly, the instrument consists of a brass tube, which is screwed into a round hole made in the skull by a trephine. Both ends of this tube are open, but into the upper is screwed another brass tube, the lower end of which is closed by a piece of very thin sheet of India rubber, and the upper end with a brass cap, into which is fastened a glass tube. This inner arrangement contains colored water, and to the glass tube a scale is affixed.

"This second brass tube is screwed into the first, till the thin rubber presses upon the dura mater and the level of the colored water stands at 0, which is the middle of the scale. Now, when the animal goes to sleep, the liquid falls in the tube, showing that the cerebral pressure has been diminished,—an event which can only take place in consequence of a reduction of the quantity of blood circulating through the brain. As soon as the animal awakes, the liquid arises at once. Nothing can exceed the conclusiveness of experiments of this character. No mere theorizing can avail against them" (pp. 317, 318). Trephining the skull and rendering a section of the brain bare to view, is so simple and convenient a way of observing this phenomena that the experiments are quite common.

He attributes this collapsing of the brain to the withdrawal of the circulation. Others are in doubt whether it is not the reverse. It, indeed, is more probable that the brain ceasing, from some other cause, to act and to require this nourishment, is why, in natural sleep, it is discontinued. The blood is only the repair material. It is not the repairer. It delivers its freight only to the bioplasts. From thence the cell building force takes and applies it. However, as also without the building material the artisan must stop, the interception of the circulation would cause a collapse. Certain it is that brain without blood would be deprived of its function. And this is the state of the brain when in natural sleep.

What he observed of it when in this collapsed state during sleep, was that it was bloodless. Referring to an experiment made by him in 1860, he says:

"A medium-sized dog was trephined over the left parietal bone, close to the sagittal suture, having previously been placed under the full anæsthetic influence of ether. The opening made by the trephine was enlarged with a pair of strong bone-forceps, so as to expose the dura mater to the extent of a full square inch. The membrane was then cut away and the brain brought to view. It was sunk below the inner surface of the skull, and but few vessels were visible. Those which could be perceived, however, evidently conveyed dark blood, and the whole exposed surface of the brain was of a purple color. As the anæsthetic influence passed off the circulation of the blood in the brain became more active. The purple hue faded away, and numerous small vessels fillled with red blood became visible; at the same time the volume of the brain increased, and when the animal became fully aroused, the organ protruded through the opening in the skull to such an extent that, at the most prominent part, its surface was more than a quarter of an inch above the external surface of the cranium. While the dog continued awake, the condition and position of the brain remained unchanged. After the lapse of half an hour, sleep ensued. While this was coming on, I watched the brain very attentively. Its volume slowly decreased; many of its smaller blood-vessels became invisible, and finally it was so much contracted that its surface, pale and apparently deprived of blood, was far below the level of the cranial wall" (pp. 38, 39).

Similar results followed the experiments of Mr. Durham, also cited by Dr. Hammond, performed on a dog about the same time, of which he says:

"As the effects of this agent (chloroform) passed off, the animal sank into a natural sleep, and then the condition of the brain was materially changed. Its surface became pale and sank down below the level of the bone; the veins ceased to be distended, and many which had been full of dark blood could no longer be distinguished. When the animal was roused, the surface of the brain became suffused with a red blush, and it ascended through the opening of the skull. As the mental excitement increased, the brain became more and more turgid with blood, and innumerable vessels sprang into sight. The circulation was also increased in rapidity. After being fed, the animal fell asleep, and the brain again became contracted and pale" (ibid, p. 34).

Dr. Hughlings Jackson examined the retina of the eye, by means of an opthalmoscope with a view to observing its condition during sleep, and found that it was paler and its arteries more contracted than in the waking state (see Royal Lond. Opthalm. Hos. Reports). This coating of nerve substance or mesh of nerve filaments, is quite the same order of tissue as that of the optic ganglion, of which, practically, it is a continuance, and would be characterized in sleep somewhat as the brain is. And we find, then, this examination of nerves closely identified with the brain substance itself, by the specially favorable circumstance of a transparent eye to look through, down in upon it in all its quiet naturalness, revealing the same state of facts.

Thus, then, is the brain functionless in the state of profound sleep. And though absolute sleep—a state of entire inaction of the brain—may not occur in life, it is functionless to the extent that sleep prevails; and to the same extent it is parted from the mind or Self; like as the paralyzed limb is parted from the will,—essentially as in death. Then what thinking in sleep transpires in the mind previously in the waking state joined with that brain, takes place, substantially, *in the state of death!*

Thus have we seen that of the transactions of the mind in sleep, the more efficient take place in the deeper sleep—in the more extended inaction of the brain—in the nearest approach to death.

If, then, the stronger and more sane thinking is possible with *less* brain contact (and our examples have shown that in sleep mind has achieved successes beyond the ability of its waking state), it is plainly conclusive, not alone that thinking goes on after all connection therewith is wholly sundered, but that in its entire freedom from it it will attain to greater strength and efficiency and wider range.

THE MIND'S RAPID MOVEMENT AND SOMETIMES KEEN APPREHENSION DURING DREAMS.

In the conclusion, thus arrived at, we have an explanation, also, why in dreams the mind is seen to execute its movements more rapidly than in waking, and why at times it displays such extraordinary attainment during sleep. Prof. Carpenter says, "One of the most remarkable of all the peculiarities in the state of dreaming, is the *rapidity* with which trains of thought pass through the mind; for a dream in which a long series of events has seemed to occur, and a multitude of images has been successively raised up, has been often certainly known to have occupied only a few minutes, or even seconds, although whole years may seem to the dreamer to have elapsed" (Mental Phys., p. 588). Dr. Hammond, referring to the same matter, supplies an incident from the *Revue de Paris* related by Lavalette, as occurring to him while in prison:

"One night, while I was asleep, the clock of the Palais de Justice struck twelve and awoke me. I heard the gate open to relieve the sentry, but I fell asleep again immediately. In this sleep I dreamt that I was standing in the Rue St. Honore. * * * All of a sudden, I perceived at the bottom of the street and advancing toward me, a troop of cavalry,—the men and horses, however, all flayed. The men held torches in their hands, the red flames of which illuminated faces without skin, and bloody muscles. Their hollow eyes rolled fearfully in their sockets, their mouths open from ear to ear, and helmets of hanging flesh covered their hideous heads. The horses dragged along their own skins in the kennels which overflowed with blood on all sides. Pale and disheveled women appeared and disappeared at the windows in dismal silence; low, inarticulate groans filled the air, and I remained in the street alone petrified with horror, and deprived of strength sufficient to seek my safety in flight. This horrible troop continued to pass along rapidly in a gallop, and casting frightful looks upon me. Their march continued, I thought, for five hours, and they were followed by an immense number of artillery wagons full of bleeding corpses, whose limbs still quivered; a disgusting smell of blood and bitumen almost choked me. At length the iron gates of the prison, shutting with great force, awoke me again. I made my repeater strike; it was no more than midnight, so that the horrible phantasmagoria lasted no more than two or three minutes—that is to say, the time necessary for relieving the sentry and closing the gate. The cold was severe and the watchword short. The next day the turnkey confirmed my calculations. I, nevertheless, do not remember any thing of my life, the duration of which I have been able more exactly to calculate, of which the details are deeper engraven on my memory, and of which I preserve a more perfect consciousness " (Sleep and its Derangements, pp. 79, 80).

Though the mind in this instance must have been near the waking state, and more hampered and distorted from brain influence than in deeper sleep, it yet detailed this series of impressions in a few minutes that would have required hours in the waking state.

So, also, there sometimes occur certain forms of extraordinary attainment,—of language speaking, and music rendering, etc., developed in trance and hypnotic or mesmeric subjects, exciting great astonishment, and often rendering a resort to spiritualistic theories of interpretations the only way out. A case of this character is also referred to by Prof. Carpenter, who relates it as follows:

"When Jenny Lind was singing in Manchester, she was invited by Mr. Braid to hear the performance of one of his hypnotized subjects, an illiterate factory girl, who had an excellent voice and ear, but whose musical powers had received scarcely any cultivation. This girl in the hypnotic state followed the Swedish nightingale's songs in different languages both instantaneously and correctly; and when in order to test her powers, Mdlle. Lind extemporized a long and elaborate chromatic exercise, she imitated this with no less precision, though unable in her waking state even to attempt anything of the sort. 'She caught the sounds so promptly,' says Mr. Braid, 'and gave both words and music so simultaneously and correctly, that several persons present could not discriminate whether there were two voices or only one'" (Mesmerism, Spiritualism, etc., pp. 19, 20).

In this case the rapidity of mental activity during sleep is also very forcibly exemplified. Scarcely a perceptible interval of time transpired between Miss Lind's utterances and their repetition by the girl. Besides there is seen to have been a corresponding and surpassing activity of the apprehending powers necessary to a proper vocalization of both the music and the unknown tongue; all evincing an accomplishment that in the waking state might have required years of laborious training. We are not to understand by the facts here given that the hypnotized subject at the time rationalized the music or the language.

Still another example of this class of facts, though referring to a different phase of mental activity, is cited by Dr. Hammond as having occurred in the course of his practice. He says:

"A young girl, recently under my professional care, was cataleptic on an average once a week, and epileptic twice or three times in the intervals. Five years previously she had spent six months in France, but had not acquired more than a very slight knowledge of the language, scarcely, in fact, sufficient to enable her to ask for what she wanted at her meals. Immediately before her cataleptic seizure, she went into a state of ecstacy, during which she recited poetry in French, and delivered harangues about virtue and godliness in the same language. She pronounced at these times exceedingly well, and seemed never at a loss for a word. To all surrounding influences she was apparently dead. But she sat bolt upright in her chair, her eyes staring at vacancy, and her organs of speech in constant action. Gradually she passed into the cataleptic paroxysm. She was an excellent example of what Mrs. Hardinge calls a 'trance medium.' The materialistic influence of bromide of potassium, however, cured her catalepsy and epilepsy, destroyed her knowledge of the French tongue and made her corporeal structure so gross that the spirits refused to make any further use of it for their manifestations" (Nervous Derangement, p. 117).

In this case the same imitative or repeative phase of mind is joined with the memory in its extraordinary activity; and that which was at some time a special tax on that faculty, or was from novelty or from some other occasion of interest peculiarly impressed, naturally became the theme of this activity; as is always to be expected. It is possible, though not probable, that the girl deliberately conversed in French. The wonderful achievement was a feat of the memory joined with the reflexive or imitative power.

A very similar case is referred to by Prof. Hamilton in his celebrated Lectures on Metaphysics. It is cited from Coleridge:

"A young woman of four or five and twenty, who could neither read nor write, was seized with a nervous fever; during which, according to the asseverations of all the priests and monks of the neighborhood, she became possessed, and, as it appeared, by a very learned devil. She continued incessantly talking Latin, Greek and Hebrew, in very pompous tones, and with most distinct enunciation. * * * The case had attracted the particular attention of a young physician, and by his statements many eminent physiologists and psychologists visited the town and cross-examined the case on the spot. Sheets full of her ravings were taken down from her own mouth, and were found to consist of sentences, coherent and intelligible each for itself, but with little or no connection with each other. Of the Hebrew, a small portion alone could be traced to the Bible, the remainder seemed to be in the rabbinical dialect. All trick or conspiracy was out of the question. * * * The young physician, however, determined to trace her past life step by step; for the patient was incapable of returning a rational answer. He at length succeeded in discovering the place where her parents had lived; traveling thither, found them dead, but an uncle surviving; and from him learned that the patient had been charitably taken by an old Protestant pastor at nine years old; had remained with him some years. * * With great difficulty, and after much search, our young medical philosopher discovered a niece of the pastor's, who lived with him as his housekeeper. * * * She remembered the girl. * * Anxious inquiries were then, of course, made concerning the pastor's habits; and the solution of the phenomenon was soon obtained. For it appeared that it had been the old man's custom, for years, to walk up and down a passage of his house into which the kitchen-door opened, and to read to himself, with a loud voice, out of his favorite books. A considerable number of these were still in the niece's possession. *

* Among the books were found a collection of the rabbinical writings, together with several of the Greek and Latin fathers; the physician succeeded in identifying so many passages with those taken down at the young woman's bedside, that no doubt could remain in any rational mind concerning the origin of the impressions made on her nervous system" (Lectures on

Metaphysics, pp. 239, 240).

Fortunately, through the sagacity and persevering energy of this young physician, definite light is thrown on this class of phenomena. Speaking in unknown languages in this case, including good pronunciation, is clearly seen to have been the work of *memory*, joined, as in the previous case, with the imitative faculty, and during a state of great activity and strength of both. She was, however, able to recall only the pastor's vocalizations of those tongues (that would naturally have produced a very *peculiar* impression on her) in entirety so far as to full sentences; while the ecstacy was not complete enough to properly bridge over the breaks between sentences and take the next in order.

Phenomena of this character, that have been greatly puzzling from ordinary standpoints of consideration, become very simple in the light of the fact thus developed, that mind in its own sphere and relieved to its own nature and away from physical contact, is of greater efficiency in its functions. And when Dr. Hammond, in the case of the epileptic French-speaking girl referred to, with sober good will heaves a bomb-shell over at the spiritualist, it turns out to be a boomerang. When he speaks of the bromide of potassium having cured her catalepsy and epilepsy, and so destroyed her knowledge of the French tongue, he is testifying against his own mineralism by submitting the fact that on the restoration of health the mind was again subjected to the restrictions the brain places upon it, and that it is in this state less efficient. Instead of the mind or ideation being merely "the clash of atoms," we see that the atoms are unable to clash nearly as fast as the mind would have them do.

We find, then, that this customary realization of self residing *apart from* the body, is not an *illusion* but a matter thoroughly sustained from scientific data.

WORDS IN CONCLUSION OF THIS CHAPTER.

To pass from existence in one state of realizing life into like existence in another, such as leaving our bodies at death implies, is certainly nothing more wonderful than is our evolving at birth from the senses and self of another to the senses and self of our own—a phenomenon that is an utterly impenetrable mystery; and yet it is *the very first fact* in the order of *our own existence*. The brain is of service in the economy of life in supplying it with some valuable form of subsistence from the physical side of being—impressions, perhaps, that are needful or indispensable to mind in the early state, though it is not at the present important to state what is the character of this need. So, too, is the umbilicus of the unborn child valuable to its pre-natal life in connecting it with a source of subsistence that in that state is indispensable. But the umbilicus is not a permanent necessity. Neither is the continuance of this tie joining it with the mother, determined by any very closely fixed period in the child's development. The child may be born—the tie sundered—before full maturity, and yet live and do well. So, likewise, may not the brain —the tie with the external world—be discontinued, the individual being be safely liberated, without regard to any special time of life after *Self* shall have been fully established?

And, yet further; as birth *must* take place—the umbilicus *must* be sundered in the course of time—to give to the growing man a larger liberty and wider range of action, so must the growing mind—the Self—in time outgrow the need of the brain ligature to the external world, to enter upon the yet greater liberty and yet wider range provided in the spiritual realm—the beyond of death.

CHAPTER XIV.

Man's Proper Immortality Affirmed by the Organic Law of His Being.

CONSIDERING the future life of man as an ascertained fact,—that at death he is merely divested of the body and still lives, it needs to be further settled that he will thence live always—is properly immortal.

DETERMINING DURATION.

The extent of the duration of an individual's existence, is, in all cases, to be estimated mainly by ascertaining what its adaptations are; as an adaptation may not be supposed to exist without an objective reality. Nature is in no instance so lacking as to produce an aimless creation; or to create uses and not also the object of their application. Everywhere the means and the end are conjoined; and the one is no more a fixed verity than is the other. The principle applies to all living nature. The webbed foot is made for service in the water; but its existence is no more a certainty than is that of the water which its peculiarity indicates. Indeed, the existence of the water may be said to be the *prior* fact—the fact that determined the conformation of the foot. So, too, the wing was constructed with reference to locomotion on the air; the fin, through the water; the foot, on solid ground; the eye was made to operate in properties that are peculiar to the light; the ear, to sound. But without the equal existence of these objective realities, air, water, earth, light and sound, these peculiar conformations of limbs and organs would not be called for, and would have no existence.

Furthermore, this principle is universally recognized. The naturalist, seeing a bird with webbed feet, says, It is aquatic—it is adapted to swimming; and there must be water hereabout. When the feet are prehensile, he says, This animal is adapted to climbing or digging and lives on trees or in the earth. When he takes up a tooth of required form he decides it to be from the carnivora—the flesh-eaters,—that the animal was hostile, and that in its age animals preyed upon each other. Its construction implies an adaptation—a use, and, as well, the *object* of the use.

These are of the more simple instances wherein the principle is illustrated. Let us now proceed to consider another, one of a somewhat different class. A seed germinated—a plant was born, which, completing its orbit of being, reached maturity and ripened its fruit. Now, although natural history is not sufficiently matured to enable the naturalist, from any philosophy of the mode of the plant's life and form to see that it is adapted to fruit,—the kind of fruit and the manner of its bearing, yet that its mode did from the first unfailingly point to it, no naturalist can doubt. The plant in its conception comprised its entire history; and the ending was as truly a factor thereof as the beginning.

What from the beginning was its future was as truly a fact thereof as was its present. Its future was but its *untranspired* fact. Its feebleness may not in all instances admit of all the facts in the conception transpiring. The progress of the plant may be intercepted by some accident befalling it—it may be crushed or its supply cut off, and thus not suffered to come to maturity, while still the destiny in its conception remains the same.

It required the existence of the *conditions* for the *ending* state as much as for those for the *beginning* state, to constitute for it the mode of its being. The plan rested as heavily on the *conditions* of the *ending* as on those of the *beginning* state of its life.

When, therefore, we have the life *adaptations* of an order of being, we have with equal certainty its future —as unequivocally as that one and one are two. In some instances they seem hopelessly obscure, as in the plant in its early state, or in the butterfly in the larval state. In other instances they are, however, very simple, and readily apparent.

Then to determine the term of duration after death, whether of man or beast, or any other type of life, it requires to be ascertained what is the function of its life, and thence what is the orbit of its movement that its destiny is to describe.

And here, before entering upon the solution of the problem of man's term of duration in the next life, we may as well at once attend upon the question that will inevitably arise in the mind of the reader, Is the brute not also immortal in case the man is?

Life in animals below man is characterized in many respects as in man himself. Their organisms are operated substantially in the same way. Their bodily movements are in obedience to impingements of force residing apart from the body. And these impingements indicate this force as more or less intelligent. In them, as in man, the nervous system is but an instrument.

And judging by what is known at the present time, this principle holds good down to the lowest limit of the kingdom. The animal element, in all its phases of individual being, holds, as does the human, an existence apart from the mineral embodiment which it animates. That, then, the *death of its body* does not bar the continuance of its individual existence, is necessarily to be conceded. And if there are no *after* death adverse conditions, its continuance might well be endless.

Of these, however, there is a possibility. Life in one aspect is identical with force however peculiar and wonderful it otherwise is. It is characterized by the laws of force. On its concentration it attains to increased activity and intensity, and often makes new disclosures of properties and develops to view new attributes or wider range of old ones. This we see, for example, in man. Straining efforts in study bring the mind out into clearer vision of principles. Straining of life under burdens of heavy sorrow has brought to realization the greater depths and breadths of affection. That which is a passive ether, may, by being focalized, become an effective agent. Physics affords numerous illustrations of this character. The rays of light converged through a lens become more luminous and more hot. The same fact is also illustrated in the electric light. Then that which must be conceded as a zo-ether—the animal element in primary diffusion (as to all elements such a state belongs)—is likewise susceptible of this kind of mutation, whose instances of focalization, or nuclii, are its individual forms; these being multiplied by the ordinary processes of generic propagation. The male and female factors in generation are frequently spoken of as the positive and negative states of the same element. And from their mutual ardor in copulation, originates the new individual, or nucleus, endowed with all the life and attributes of its kind.

A knowledge, in minutia, of these facts, is not at present attainable. We can speak only of the possibilities that are apparent from the general principle that is known. But the individuals thus derived—born—if not from their natures permanently continuous, would but be expected at the consummation of their period to lapse again into re-diffusion with their several elements.

Now instinct, the order of mentality residing in the brute, as has been seen (see Chap. 9), is not originative—is incapable of devising within itself and issuing from itself new modes, or to dis-establish itself from old ones. It is restricted to merely the power to *reflect* devices. It serves for their *echo*; not for their origin. Its indications are more those of an instrument than of a proprietor. And its functions being thus to merely *serve*, we may not know what, its individual forms may only be temporary.

And though these lower animals seem to possess both will and choice operating by the impulses of pleasure and pain, it admits of doubt that the merely auxiliary mental element of which their existences are constituted is capable of the conditions of a proper *Self*—anything more than a *sub*-Self, analogous to that kind of *self* that is constituted in every special sense, and that resides in its own special head or brain or sub-brain—the adjacent ganglion,—as for example the optic ganglion situated adjacent to the eye in the optic nerve rendering it a self-sentient member, as experiment proves it to be.

A passing word, in respect to the moral aspect of this view to the general reader, seems called for in this place. From customary observation of those beautiful beasts of domestication, so intimately and agreeably associated with man, and arrayed in those same senses in which he himself is, to say that this is all that there is of those lives, can hardly fail to impress one disagreeably; at first suggestion at least. But we recall that facts are altogether inexorable, and loyalty to them is ever to be preferred over any other consideration, however pleasing. Besides, to recognize all that is commonly seen in their existence, and to bestow all the consideration of love and sympathy and care that may be bestowed upon them, is fully justified by this view. It can cause no diminution of feeling interest in their welfare. At the same time to *themselves*, merely, their dissolution could not partake of the character of a calamity,—a disappointment or an injustice; as without reason, such an event could hardly be realized, and certainly not valued.

It would follow, only, that at the termination of their round of being, whatever length of duration that might require, and by whatever law might apply in the case, the power (whatever it should be) that so held their constituent mental elements in these concentrated, individualized forms, would, by change of conditions induced by the special character of their own properties, disappear; and the individual lives would lapse into re-distribution with the general tides of their original elements; possibly to be re-gathered and re-represented in other instances of individual life, in connection with *this* existence, or, also, possibly amid the scenes surrounding man in his immortal home.

It remains, however, to be said, that, should it prove that the beast is constituted with the element of reason *in latency*, that might under some form of coming circumstances in another state, become *active*, and so would become endowed with that high order of sentience, it, too, would be immortal,—and *human* as *well*. But of it, at present, there is no trace nor hope of a trace.

IN THE CASE OF MAN THE ESSENTIAL FACTS ARE ENTIRELY DIFFERENT.

In the living forms below man we find mind restricted to the level of mere instinct, and hampered with conditions that at best forebode their end. But the reverse of these conditions we find in the estate of the human mind. It possesses the elements of reason. And an analysis of this great order of mind leads at once to the discovery that its continuance is endless.

We first note that its adaptation (which is seen to be inexorable law) shows that the mission it is ordained to fulfill is such as to require endless time. It devises new modes, and dis-establishes itself from old ones, when they cease to answer its requirements. The transactions in the history of our arts and sciences are, in a limited way, a standing illustration of this truth. New devices—new modes—are incessantly appearing in every department of our activities, while old ones are being discontinued, as our sense of convenience calls for. From this fact in its nature its existence is not determined by one class of circumstances. On being brought into relation with new conditions incident to the line of its being, it would by this facility in its nature attain to new conditions of adjustment, dis-establishing itself from the old. New worlds of altogether new substances might thus be passed into and through, becoming as dead to the worlds left behind.

Endless contingencies would then seem to be provided for by the endlessly versatile genius of this order of mind; and from this aspect of the case it is adapted to an endless existence.

Then, added to this, we come to consider the next item of adaptation—that the reasoning element is an endlessly progressive sentience. And here we must stop to anticipate a probable criticism. The form of mind below it, too, is adapted to perceive on a plane that is of endless variety and extent. The adaptation is, however, to but the same state and to essentially the same thing, whether the object be one on a neighboring planet or immediately before it. Consistency with what is to be said does not require, therefore, that the mere animal must exist till it has seen the last thing in physical nature. The last object on the remotest star in the universe might as well be first seen as last. The mission of the representative of this order of mind, is in this respect, fulfilled in the very first act of its perception. Neither does it require priority in the order of what it sees. It requires not that a tree must be seen before there is ability to see a horse.

It is not so with the reasoning sentience of man. When he has perceived *one* and *one* in combination as *two* he has perceived but a single and simple principle —the additive. The multiplicative is founded on this, but is attainable only by additional mental acquirement —further enlargement and greater grasp of mind. And many a brain-weary pupil who has unraveled the usually prescribed course, principle by principle, will testify that the remotest fact of mathematical attainment is not perceived by the same low power that the first is, nor grasped by the same feeble fabric. But from these utterly simple beginnings, rises this principle of science to infinite enlargement and infinite variety. That the plan of the reasoning being—the appointment of its destiny—included the last and highest as certainly as the first and lowest element of this science, admits of no doubt whatever.

And that it was ordained to consummate the *first*, is a fact as commonly conceded as that the eye was formed to utilize the light. But the attainment from the first to the last is but the process of the mind's evolution along this line of principles. It is but unfolding the innate plan of its destiny; as the plant does when throwing out leaf after leaf in its progress toward bloom and fruit. No one suspects that of this great principle of science the last fact is in, and that the last knowable is known. No one, on reflection, questions that the knowable applies to the whole infinite extent of these principles,—to all the unknown as well as to those known. Hence, the reasoning mind, indisputably adapted to their attainment—by its essence and mechanism being ordained to verify all these in their order—one following upon another—makes the mission of man unendingly prolonged.

I have referred only to mathematics in the illustrations thus given. It will readily occur that the subjects of mental pursuit are numerous beyond calculation, and that the same observations will apply to each. In each the mind achieves its attainments by evolving its nature along the lines of its endless paths; the achievement of each principle giving it width and strength to reach and grasp the next. And on each his mission allots him the same unending career.

Again, in these facts of the ever enlarging and strengthening sentience we have the very opposite of termination. Truly the ox also for a time passes through an enlarging process, and yet is seen to attain to a limit prior to appropriating all the universal extent of assimilable elements. But, as before explained, the facts are not parallel. The stages in the development of the ox are all accomplished without passing on to a new form or state of elements. The last mouthful of grass at the end of his twenty years run of life is in no respect unlike the first. And the level of attainment made in the last was fully made in the first. All subsequent ones were but repetitions. The enlargement of the reasoning sentience is of an altogether different class of facts. The nature of these facts make it that the more knowing and seeing that transpire to it, the more is it set on to see and to know, and the larger are its qualifications to know and to see.

It is so related with existence that constantly recurring new mental scenery—new developments of principles—must arise to view, with their ever fresh inducements. The monotony of all the time continuing in *one* impression, tends to sometime destroy all desire in respect to it. But here each new achievement begets a new zest. The last achievement is then always the point where self is the most assured of its continuance. And this fact must so continue so long as the infinite mazes of the knowable unknown shall supply food for the ever more and more hungry mind. Thus do the very essence and mechanism of the reasoning element of which man is the finite embodiment, again indicate for him this destiny.

THE EVIDENCE OF PRESCIENCE.

In nature, everywhere, individual presentiments are taken as exponents of destiny. To some extent the individual is possessed of a prescience of its future. It is presciently affected by its destiny. In some this is stronger than in others. And parts only of destiny, usually, are impressed with sufficient clearness to be plainly noted. Neither are these at all times equally or even at all apparent to mere human discernment. But the pregnant dam, realizing that she is tending toward progeny, seeks for it appropriate seclusion. The bird, on arrival of the breeding season, from presciencing a brood, proceeds to build a requisite nest in anticipation of their requirements. Besides, the principle is here seen to extend to even the unconscious states of existence. In the ovulating process in the cavity of the bird, independent of her own volitions, an order of prescience, foreseeing the character of the dependence of the coming bird's pre-natal state incased in the shell away from the mother, stores under that shell, for its use during that period, the exact quality and quantity of the nutriment it shall require. The fly, too, deposits her eggs with reference to the sustenance of her larvæ. It sometimes happens that the same conditions are suited to her own wants, though more frequently not. The *Ichneumonidæ*, a large family, deposit their eggs in the larvæ, the pupæ and even the eggs, of other insects, on which their larvæ immediately feed. The *Urocerata* bore holes in trees in which they deposit their eggs, their larvæ being borers and subsisting on the juices of the wood. There is, then, the same principle of prescience to be seen present down in this lower kingdom that we see in the dam and the bird. And if possessed of the right means of apprehending, the principle were, doubtless, to be found of universal extent.

In other instances animals have a strong prescience of themselves as existing in a future period, seen in the fact that they lay away stores and make other provision for life's necessities with which to meet that coming time. For that purpose the squirrel is busy laying in supplies during the nutting season; the bee is filling its galleries with honey in the time when nature's laboratories are busily sending it forth; the beaver is raising its dam, and the muskrat is building its house.

The larva, at the requisite maturity of its nature for the incoming change, presciences itself as existing not only in a coming period but in a different mode of being, and in some instances, in different elements—in another world. It proceeds to place itself in suitable surroundings, with a view to the safety and promotion of its transformation. When the ordinary state of surrounding nature incidentally furnishes those conditions, the principle will be less, if at all, apparent. When the act consists in simply burrowing in the earth for lodgment during the chrysalis state, the fact is not prominently suggestive; unless we stop to notice that certain rules respecting depth are observed. We then see that there is a prescience of need as to measures of warmth, moisture, light, and air for self while undergoing the change. And when, as at times is seen, the arrangements include special shape and size of the chamber of transformation, a prescience of the new shape and mode of being, also, is forcibly suggested.

In some cases, however, the ordinary state of surrounding nature is very foreign to the needs of the insect. In the large family of the *Lepidoptera*, with the generality the transformation requires such particularity and delicacy of circumstance as that the most elaborate encasing and sealing in away from the ordinary influences of the elements, is indispensable. This may be conveniently seen in the construction of the silk cocoon. Of extraordinary care and diligence bestowed upon the construction of this wonderful tomb-cradle, we have an example in that important worm—the beneficent exuder of the silk of commerce. Figuier, in detailing its behaviour and mode of procedure, observes that up to the time of its maturity "the worm had never tried to leave its litter. It lived a sedentary life and never thought of wandering away from its food. Now it is seized with an important desire for changing its quarters. It gets up, it roams about and moves its head in all directions to find some place to cling on to. It walks over everything within its reach, particularly over those obstacles which are placed vertically. It aspires, not to descend, like the heroes of classic tragedy, but to rise.

* * It now looks for a convenient place in which to establish its cocoon. Every one has remarked how the animal sets to work to accomplish its task. It begins by throwing from different sides threads destined for fixing the cocoon. * * The proper space having been circumscribed by this means, the worm begins to unwind its thread. * * Folded upon itself almost like a horse-shoe, its back within, its legs without, the worm arranges its thread all around its body, describing ovals with its head. * * As long as the cocoon is not very thick one can watch it through the meshes of the web applying and fixing its thread, still to a certain degree soft, in such a manner as to make it adhere closely to the parts already formed" (The Insect World, p. 224). Upon the task it bestows seventy hours, as an average, of this kind of toil, weaving about itself, into the space of an inch and a half, over a thousand yards of silk fiber.

The first weaving is of floss silk closely matted, and forms an excellent protection from rain. Next beneath is spun the finer quality of silk in the manner referred to, up and down and crosswise in all directions about the body. Lastly, within this, and of still more delicate silk, and glued firmly together, is formed the last and innermost layer immediately surrounding it. The whole constitutes a chamber wall well calculated to exclude water, air, and cold, and what might be of no less importance, to break, by its most delicate elasticity, the force of rude jostlings.

To all these wise provisions—these elaborate arrangements—the little animal is moved by a prescience, however irrational, of not alone itself and its needs in the transforming state, but scarcely less also of itself as a being transformed—the objective fact which all these arrangements and proceedings include.

From the family of the *Neuroptera*, the larva of the widely prevalent and well-known dragon-fly, constitutes a fair subject for a still further illustration of this principle. On account of its sharply defined habits, it has been a favorite subject of remark by naturalists. Of it Figuier, the French naturalist above cited, appropriately says:

"The female lays her eggs in the water, from which emerge larvæ, which remind one somewhat of the form of the insect, only their body is more compact and their head flattened. The larvæ and pupæ inhabit the bottom of ponds and streams, where, keeping out of sight in the mud, they seek for insects, mollusks, small fish, etc. If any prey passes within their reach, they dart forward, like a spring, a very singular arm, which represents the under lip. * * * To effect its metamorphosis, it drags itself out of the water, where it has lived for nearly a year, climbs slowly to some neighboring plant, and hangs itself there. Very soon the sun dries and hardens its skin, which, all of a sudden, becomes crisp, and cracks. The dragon-fly then sets free its head and its thorax and its legs; its wings, still soft and wanting in vigor, gain strength by coming in contact with the air, and after a few hours they have attained their full development. Immediately the insect abandons, like a worn-out suit, the dull, slimy skin which had covered it so long, and which still preserves its shape, and dashes off in quest of prey" (The Insect World, pp. 420, 422).

From its birth it breathed water only, for which it was provided with gills. It lived exclusively at the bottom in the slime and mud; and its great vivacity is evidence that for the time it was well suited with that state. It evinced as complete an absence of relation with the atmospheric world above as did the fish. Yet on arrival of the requisite maturity, it was seized by a controlling impulse to leave its surrounding and to rise —to proceed in a direction hitherto unrecognized—to fix itself upon a *means* of ascent for existence in an element unexperienced and practically unknown. That the insects referred to employ their customary intelligence in these deportments cannot be questioned. And though they may not be said to follow their external senses in their choices severally of manner of deportment, they follow, *to the last*, a sentiment that is equivalent to sight in its power over the volitions. It *is* sight,—an *order* of sight whose apprehending qualities admit of its being thrown forward through time to seize upon and, with some measure of accuracy and fullness, define the facts of untranspired existence.

It hence follows that generic impressions, however obscure,—impressions that characterize a whole order or family of beings—are as fully to be relied on as evidence of the existence of the facts of being to which they point, as that a web-foot is evidence of water or an eye determines the existence of light.

Then, as still another fact in evidence of the endlessness of his future existence, it may be stated that man, too, is characterized by this same law of prescience, by which, however obscurely and without the details of mode and circumstances, he foresees himself as surviving without limit—to be always in a state intent on advancing to the attainment of the next fact of principle; and so onward throughout the endless knowable unknown. And, whatever his theoretical acquirements may lead him to *reason* out contrary to this, it is doubtful whether this sentiment of continued future existence *can* be *educated* into complete silence in any instance. Education may do much toward *obscuring*, but it can do nothing toward eliminating this constituent principle of his being. That he presciences himself in a survival of death, is evident from the race-wide impression that in some form the dead are still living on. Every land has at least its superstition respecting this—that that which would occur to all as the most probable time when his final ending should take place—physical death, has not so terminated him and does not. Neither would it be of consequence to claim the fact to be a superstition. Then the principle of this prescience would be necessary in turn to explain the presence of the superstition. Therefore in *this* form the impression were as valuable as a matter of evidence, as though it were found formulated in the most lucid terms of his reason. The phenomenon is plainly due to the prompting of a sense having an adequate power over the volitions; and, being common to the race, it cannot be otherwise regarded than a generic function; and points to an endless life as truly as to simply existence beyond the grave. It is necessarily founded on those provisions in the constitution of his nature which determine the mode and the extent of his continuance in being—the requirements and destiny of a reasoning mind. And, however unrealizing of it, this prescience cannot have reference to less than all of future life—an undefined vision of Self in all its coming history.

From the nature of the case the force of this prescience would be less realized in a mind pre-occupied by the luminous visions of reason tending to obscure it. It is, hence, more difficult to draw man's attention rightly upon it in his own case than in the case of the insects, etc. It is not readily detected, nor is its important bearing on this subject readily seen without careful inquiry into the nature and cause of those eager movements of mind, in its healthy state, toward achievements that lie extended out infinitely, along which, to be sure—along all this endless attaining—the existence of self is always the *prior* fact. These facts when seen and comprehended, become evidence quite conclusive and unquestionable. And the naturalist apprehending them rightly would say of the possessor of these peculiarly marked activities of mind, "This being is one destined, in some form, to survive always." He would say it upon the same principle that would be his authority for asserting of the insect that he sees weaving its cocoon, "This is a creature of a twofold life;" or of the one which, in opposition to all the custom of its previous life of adhering exclusively to the bottom of the pool, he now saw crawling toward the air above, "Its existence extends into another order of elements—into another world."

This principle of presciencing self in a future may be safely considered as present throughout all living nature. It is not necessary that we see it equally or even at all illustrated in each of the families, nor in *all* the *individuals* of the same family to yet be fully assured of its existence there. We need not be able to sense heat in the greatest cold attainable in order to know that heat still is there.

THE MAIN OBJECTIONS TO THIS THEORY CONSIDERED.

But here it may occur that still a serious flaw exists in this part of the argument. That plant whose nature included its future period of fruit—whose mode of development was evidence of its fruit-bearing destiny—whose last act of principle was as truly a fact of its being as its first—may have the fatal foot descend upon it; and that untranspired fact of its history may after all never transpire, and its existence be terminated short of this indicated destiny. The silk-worm weaving its cocoon for the use of its future self which it foresees, may be suddenly cut short by the proprietor choosing to utilize that cocoon in his crop of silk. The squirrel may fall a victim to the sportsman's shot before he shall have arrived in that future wherein he has prescienced himself in the enjoyment of his hoard of nuts. Then the man, too, it is objected, though presciencing himself of an endless continuance in life may suffer a similar disappointment.

But at most this objection could avail but in part, as the disappointment in no case applies to all of the same order or family. Always of each, some, at least, attain to the prescienced end, or have done so. And but for modifying accidents *all* would, beyond a doubt. But it has in substance been already said that the prescience is general and not specific in character, and is more or less obscure. Besides, though the individual does so foresee itself, the perception is by the generic law represented in it. Its prescience is of the family nature and the family destiny, and may be illustrated in a regiment of troops ordered to take a position. The order having been promulgated, the individual member anticipates himself in the appointed position, and deports himself accordingly. Yet by accident he may be prevented from attaining his anticipations; though in the regiment they will be fulfilled. By the general order necessarily represented in his individual case he has seen of himself what transpired only of his regiment. Bating only insuperable accidents it would also have transpired in his own case. So, too, the untranspired fact of principle in the plant is properly of its genus. The untranspired existence of the larva in the fly state in the air and by wings, did transpire in its genus, and was actually prescienced by it in respect to itself as *included* in the *nature* bearing that destiny; though it fell a prey to the fish before gaining the top of the water. And, also, but for the overmastering accident, it, too, would infallibly have attained to that end. And so the prescience was not in error.

But for accidents of surroundings there probably would be no variations as to features, size or destiny among the individuals of any family of plant or animal.

Still further, we have seen that the visible part of the plant is but the mineral structure of its embodiment—really its tool or its house, on which its existence is not finally dependent, and that the same is true of the body of the animal, of whatever order or family. Then who can say that the plant whose unfinished body was crushed, may not on its own side of nature, attain the same prescienced end of reproduction by a means not requiring the visible embodiment of germs? And may not the squirrel too, and the bee, in some form in a separate state of life, realize a supply of some character toward which their prescience vaguely led them, though it be not a physical aliment?

From the plain fact, however, that *the most favored* plant *always* attains to fruit,—*the most favored* caterpillar *always* attains to the state of the fly, etc., the objection wholly loses its force. The prescience after all, is *infallible*. It establishes the state and sets forth what manner of future the *genera* attains, in all cases. And as to the argument, it is a matter of entire indifference whether *individual exceptions* are referred to or not, more than to say that but for adequate hindrances no exceptions were possible; and, also, that whether there really *are* any such exceptions or not, in any order of life, is finally unknown.

But in the essential nature of man, altogether differing from the lower forms of life, there are facts to be seen why all individuals thereof must attain to the generic destiny. It is of a devisive volitience, capable not alone of apprehending the rationale in creation, but of creating—of originating ideals and embodying them; being thus co-ordinate *in substance* with the supreme essence embodying the supreme prerogatives; and is distinguished therefrom alone by the ever-abiding infinite difference that the infinite and the finite capacities and prerogatives must constitute.

Then the human individual being thus generically supreme above them, all lower elements must ultimately yield to its requirements, and are without a possibility to contravene its tendency to destiny, however inferior on the scale the representative may be found.

CONCLUDING OBSERVATIONS ON THIS CHAPTER.

It is not expected, that at first reading at least, in all instances where the reader is unaccustomed to the principles brought forward, these presentations will be wholly clear and satisfactory. Much will depend on the ready facility for perceiving the force there is in the universal law of tendencies. That trait of mind that will readily perceive that an object liberated before a major force at once becomes a projectile, and that without modifications derived from outlying modes of resistance, or from its own properties, it will continue the character of motion derived from the impulse (a fundamental law recognized in all mechanics, and that is the basis of all astronomical calculations) may be safely hoped to have little difficulty in following the argument and attaining its conclusions.

Yet still another difficulty is foreseen, even with this class of readers. The one unhabituated to continuing the mental vision of man as uninterruptedly passing on through death, will require time for the adjustment of his mental senses to that fact; as when one in order to see clearly an object portrayed in a stereoscope needs at the instrument to await awhile a certain adjustment of the eyes.

Only when one doubts that the plant that bore fruit was definitely actuated to that end by a tendency that resided in it in its beginning, and that was identical with it throughout its entire history, and on the contrary considers it, in each case, as having merely happened so, may he consistently doubt for the self of man an endless career.

It is true that mind has not in any instance been *seen* to have fulfilled this destiny, and may not so be seen. But does the thinker hesitate on this account? Has he seen the mind achieving the unknown achievements yet of the future? Does he know of any one who has? Certainly not. And does he doubt that the mind will attain to them?—that further principles *will* be known that are not yet known? Has he seen his approaching harvest in its golden maturity? Has any one seen it? Does he believe it possible that any one has seen it? It is impossible. Without admitting this same principle that in man establishes his immortal destiny, it is of no consequence to his purpose that he says, "Other harvests have been seen to mature;" for then it could no longer follow from *that* ripening that ripening would in *this* instance take place, though no hindrances whatever occurred! The sun, including the solar system, is known to accomplish an orbit. Has any one seen it accomplished? Has any one in the history of our race seen an instance of its accomplishment? No, neither has been seen. How then is it known? In its *deportment* a *tendency* to that effect is seen. And on the strength of this evidence *alone*, no astronomer doubts its truth. It is entirely sufficient that it is *seen* fulfilling! The same philosophy sees in man's deportment the tendency of this destiny, and likewise its fulfillment, which is evidence much less fallible than men require for their daily business transactions.

CHAPTER XV.

QUESTIONS RESPECTING THE RELATION OF THE TWO WORLDS.—THE LAWS AND MODES OF MENTAL INTERCOURSE OR THE TRANSMISSION OF THOUGHT.—INSPIRATION.

THE conclusions attained in the foregoing chapters would naturally and properly be followed by a desire to know to what extent the survivors in that inner and superior world may have the ability to know of us and our affairs in this; and also to what extent influences may be derived from them.

With a view to answering alone from the standpoint of natural facts, we first look to see what means of intercourse these facts supply. And first in order the present chapter is devoted to considering the mode by which one mind or self operates upon another mind or self,—how one observes another, and how thought and sympathy are transmitted. It being a fact that over all obstacles, individuals have to some extent intercourse with each other. All lament, however, that the means of intercourse are so incomplete and the intercourse is so imperfect. With the most expert ones there constantly is a mistaking of meaning, even on the same levels of attainment and on subjects of a common understanding. This is true of the highest circles of letters and of science. But it is particularly noticeable in the intercourse between men of science, where an accurate understanding is more imperatively necessary. How much misleading there has been over the terms "development" and "protoplasm," for example, in respect to which it is very uncertain even now whether any two are exactly understanding each other. Much of the debate over them is due to mutual misunderstandings.

With the more common class the deficiency is still greater. The field of thought upon which a clear, mutual understanding may take place with people of ordinary attainments is surprisingly limited. Only upon matters of very commonplace experience, in which all are largely participating, can understandings be relied upon with anything like mathematical certainty. Perplexed minds, who are painfully conscious of the imperfection of their linguistic arrangements for delivering their thoughts to others, are often heard to exclaim: "Oh, if I could only express myself!" It indicates the strait to which, in some measure, every mind is subject; while indeed many are so poor in language as to be mainly cut off from being understood, or known as to their mental status, save what may be seen in their general deportment.

RESPECTING THE MODE OF MENTAL INTERCOURSE.

The mode of mental intercourse in the present state of being is mainly by means of certain external signs of gestures and sounds, conventionally adopted, and addressed to the senses. These devices of communication are so obvious and pronounced as to almost wholly obscure certain other phenomena of a psychological character that are incident to human beings. Yet back of all artificial modes of speech, and quite independent of them, is a means of intercourse as to the *general character* of thought and feeling, that is quite universally intelligible, whereby a neighbor's sentiments may be obtained in some measure of fullness, of whose conventional language we are ignorant; whereby even the dumb brute may be understood and may also understand. The modulating impulses of thought and of passion, of pain and of pleasure, are often so pronounced as to be unmistakable by the most unskillful beholders, as to their general character, without the specialties and details that are incident to them. A physician of many years' practice once said, "I would rather trust my diagnosis of an infant than of the average adult. Its feelings without language are more easily and perfectly communicated than are those of the adult who undertakes to supplement the natural language of pain by verbal statements that are as likely to mislead as otherwise."

There is the blush that rises on the face from the abashed feelings, or from the feelings of shame. And there is the pale blench that comes from cringing fear. The eye glares forth the lurid gleams of frantic hatred or vengeance, terrifying to intercept. Or from it may fall, remotely opposite from this, the tender, glowing ardor of impassioned love, quite as impossible to resist as the other is to endure. Then from it will sparkle forth the humor of capricious wit, or gleam the earnestness of determined argument. Or its quiet, steady flame will plainly tell of laboring, straining evolutions of thought going on privately within.

It is to be remembered that beholding a being in life thus, is mainly the beholding of life itself,—the composite state of innumerable varieties of actuations that at every point of time are taking place within, and are both voluntarily and involuntarily reacting upon the organism. On a moment's reflection, the object of our contemplation, when thus looking on a fellow being, is not the mineral compound of flesh and blood, etc., that our senses lodge against; it is the inner self beyond, to the impulses of which the mobile, delicately pliant mineral aggregate yields expression, by means of the interlying elements of nerve forces. But these movements are the unconventional ones. They are not those artificially produced and mutually agreed upon to be used as "the signs of ideas." Upon reaching us through the medium of our senses, they rhythmically excite like impulses in ourselves, which is the basis of this common understanding by means of them. The sight of tears excites us to tears; the sight of smiles, to smiles; which is in no sense conventional, but is by sympathy or sameness of life, which in all instances under equal conditions yields the same phenomena, and by the phenomena, alternately, is excited the same impulse; as the string sharing the same chord of harmony with a neighboring string, when singing, awakens in the other the vibrations of the same song, and in turn when song is sounding forth from the other, is prompted to corresponding vibrations.

It is seen, then, that the transmission of thought, as ordinarily seen to occur, is by means of the law which enables the mind to impress intelligently modulated forces upon its own adjacent substances, voluntarily projecting the conventional sounds and gestures forth upon the neighboring senses of sight and hearing of another; and by which, too, still further, the *states* of feeling and of thought are involuntarily portrayed through upon the external features of Self to be observed by another.

But one more method, one less familiar to the general mind, should, properly, be here considered. The individual life, by the very conditions of its individuality, is, in its proper selfhood, impermeable and indiffusible by even its own element, somewhat as the crystallized part of a fluid does not admit into its personal limits the adjacent fluid, nor enter into diffusion therewith. Yet over an ever present co-equal ether of its own nature and plane, and infinitely abounding, and adequate to receive and transmit any grade of mental conception, and of sentiment and passion, on its plane, its impulses of thought and of feeling extend abroad to the limits of another individual, there to await the properly matured apprehending powers—the suitably refined and disciplined sensibilities, and the discriminating judgment, to be received and conveyed inward upon the register of consciousness of the neighboring individual.

From the obscureness of the elements involved in this statement, it naturally becomes more difficult to verify to the average undertanding. And for the purpose I refer to but a few classes of facts. In the order of nature each individual of whatever kingdom, is surrounded by an atmosphere or an ether of more or less density, consisting of its own order of substance under unlike conditions, and more or less stable. Our earth—a mineral ball—is enveloped in an atmosphere, which is of the mineral state, and hence is also mineral. This atmosphere, quite dense upon the surface, grows more rare as it widens out from the center to join the atmospheres of neighboring planets; and from the solar system, in yet greater rarity, it proceeds till it joins that of neighboring systems, and so on, overspreading infinity. When the steel-faced forge-hammer rebounds from a bar of cold steel with such a piercing ring, atoms themselves have not touched. The concussion was only upon their atmospheres in which they, themselves, remained all the while suspended. The *force*, however, was mainly effective upon the centers—the individuals—themselves, causing a change of their aggregates. The bar of steel and the face of the hammer were not quite the same after the stroke. It was, after all, a communication of individuals with each other, by way of their common atmospheres, which render their flexible, centripetal and centrifugal forces possible.

The same is true of planetary relations. They communicate with each other sympathetically, individual with individual, by means of the interlying ethers or atmospheres affording embodiment for the passage of forces and their modulations, of whatever kind. The electrical agitation of the sun is at once discernible upon the electric element of the earth, and, without doubt, in like manner affects other planetary centers. And so reciprocally. Beyond the reach of our physical perception, save in extreme instances, the measureless fields of spaces are strung in infinite variety of ways, by the lines of planetary and stellar intercourse.

Finding this fact prevalent throughout the mineral domain, and rigidly the law in respect to all its forms and phases, it is to be judged possible, at least, that an analogous relation is sustained between the individuals of the living and mental element. The two orders of existence, though never the same, are seen to be so far in harmony with each other as to have the law of force in common; and there subsists between the individuals of each, the fact of sympathy. The sympathy in each domain is in respect to properties of being, according to which their several elements deport themselves and develop their phenomena. In the mineral it is manifest mainly in the induction of chemical changes by varying the measures of force, which results in more or less influence on the general aspect of nature. But the spectroscope reveals the fact that even the special forms of substances are communicated on this plane. In the living and mental, the distinguishing properties are of thought and of feeling, in the wide use of these terms. At least the main bond of sympathy between intelligent individuals is in respect to these properties. When intelligence and feeling are absent from an object, our sympathy with it is quite impossible. Besides, for the individual who is the embodiment of these properties, there is a substantial attachment—an actual drawing force,—as literally as is that which impels one magnet upon another.

That this affection is not in respect to the external body, is duly apparent in the fact that when the body has generally fallen away, and what of it remains is an object of disgust and wholly repellent, the sympathy not alone but even the affection remains in full strength, and often attains to increased ardor. The attractive powers of the physical person are but of the real being within portrayed through it, to whom it is an instrument of more or less pleasing finish and graceful pliability. The exciting influence—the real magnet drawing upon Self, directing the attention upon the external form on which the realizing senses are lodged—is *within* the casket, *beyond the sensuous domain*.

The mental element, though by interlying forces joined therewith, as prominently seen in the union of body and mind, while not being identical with the mineral, is still by this common law of force, impossible to be without a reciprocal relation of its individual centers, by way of its own special substance in atmosphere, and wholly unconnected with external means of intercourse. And this reciprocity or intercourse can be only of the evolution of its functional properties, which mainly, if not wholly, consist of thoughts and feelings. It is, then, unavoidable, where confidence is placed in the fixedness and

300   CONSOLATIONS OF SCIENCE.

unity of natural law throughout its several systems of being, that independent of the customary avenues of external intercourse, there is some measure of intercourse or communication of states of mind and of feeling taking place between individual lives. But the overpowering glare of *external* realization, from the very nature of it, tends to divert from the use of this mode of intercourse and to obscure the realization of it when taking place.

Expectant attention, monopolizing the main energies of the mind devoted to intercourse, is constantly employed in receiving and sending dispatches by this route. When an impulse of the mind takes place in respect to another, it is, as the most practical way, at once dispatched through the organism. But a small percentage of thought is by impulse directed to the abstract mind of another in the manner that occurs, for example, in mental prayer. And were it done with a force quite sufficient to excite recognition in an adjacent mind in a quiescent state and expectant of it, such conditions are rarely found in a state where the senses are at all times so overpowered by glaring external phenomena as is common to man's earthly life.

ATTITUDE OF SCIENTIFIC MEN.

So difficult does this appear, and so unlike common phenomena, that usually the most conservative and safe of scientific men are found discrediting the claim of mind directly influencing mind independent of the organism. And here, on account of the reading public being more generally familiar with his works, and being at the same time first-class authority of many years' standing among the highest professional men, I again limit my references mainly to Prof. Wm. B. Carpenter, not forgetting that others are equally worthy. The experimental evidence is usually put under the head of Mesmerism or Hypnotism. In his recent work on Mental Physiology, he makes this strong statement, which he rigidly adheres to throughout:

"The writer does not hesitate to express the conviction, based on long, protracted, and careful examination of the evidence adduced to prove the existence of a mesmeric force acting independently of the consciousness of the 'subject,' that there is none that possesses the least claim to acceptance as scientific truth. * *
It has been repeatedly found that mesmerizers who had no hesitation in asserting that they could send particular individuals to sleep, or affect them in other ways by an effort of 'silent will,' have altogether failed to do so *when the subjects were carefully kept from any suspicion that such will was being exercised;* whilst, on the other hand, sensitive subjects have repeatedly gone to sleep *under the impression that they were being mesmerized from a distance,* when the supposed mesmerizer was not even thinking of them" (p. 619).

These statements he has fortified by a variety of careful, thorough and fair meaning tests which resulted in the failures he speaks of. But in some of these experiments there was possibly a violation of at least one proper and very important condition. The case he cites from the trial investigations of Dr. Noble, of Manchester, as being an example of the proper precaution to be taken, and the one he places foremost as such, is faulty in this very particular. The experiment by Dr. Noble, narrated by himself, is as follows:

"An intelligent and well-educated friend had a female servant, whom he had repeatedly thrown into a sleep-waking state, and on whom he had tried a variety of experiments, many of which we ourselves witnessed. We were at length informed that he had succeeded in magnetizing her from another room, and without her knowledge; that he had paralyzed particular limbs by a fixed gaze, unseen by the patient; and we hardly know what besides. These things were circumstantially related to us by many eye-witnesses; amongst others, by the medical attendant of the family, a most respectable and intelligent friend of our own. We were yet unsatisfied; we considered that these experiments were so constantly going on, that the presence of a visitor, or the occurrence of anything unusual, was sure to excite expectation of some mesmeric process. We were invited to come and judge for ourselves, and to propose whatever test we pleased. Now, had we visited the house, we should have felt dissatisfied with the result; we, therefore, proposed that the experiment should be carried out at our own residence; and it was made under the following circumstances:—The gentleman early one evening wrote a note, as if on business, directing it to ourselves. He thereupon summoned the female servant (the mesmeric subject), requesting her to convey the note to its destination, and wait for an answer. The gentleman himself, in her hearing, ordered a cab, stating that if any one called he was going to a place named, but was expected to return by a certain hour. Whilst the female servant was dressing for her errand, the master placed himself in the vehicle, and rapidly arrived at our dwelling. In about ten minutes afterward the note arrived, the gentleman in the meantime being secreted in an adjoining apartment. We requested the young woman, who had been shown into our study, to take a seat whilst we wrote the answer; at the same time placing the chair with its back to the door leading into the next room, which was left ajar. It had been agreed that after the admission of the girl into the place where we were, the magnetizer, approaching the door in silence on the other side, should commence operations. There, then, was the patient, or 'subject' placed within two feet of her magnetizer,—a door only intervening, and that but partially closed,—but she, all the while, perfectly free from all idea of what was going on. We were careful to avoid any unnecessary conversation with the girl, or even to look toward her, lest we should raise some suspicion in her own mind. We wrote our letter (as if in answer) for nearly a quarter of an hour, once or twice only making an indifferent remark; and on leaving the room for a light to read the supposed letter, we beckoned the operator away. No effect, whatever, had been produced, although we had been told that two or three minutes were sufficient, even when mesmerizing from the drawing-room, through walls and apartments, into the kitchen. In our own experiment the intervening distance had been very much less, and only one solid substance interposed, and that not complete; but here we suspect was the difference—*the 'subject' was unconscious of the magnetism and suspected nothing*" (Mental Physiology, pp. 619, 620).

Not all temperaments are influenced alike by the same circumstances. The Dr. himself (and so Prof. Carpenter) may have seen an applicant for promotion become non-plused and utterly fail in the presence of a severely critical and exacting examining committee, who under casual circumstances would have promptly succeeded in every test. The tendency of such circumstances as those above given, with the average individual as operator or as subject, would be to impair or to destroy about the first requisite condition of mind on which the successful operation depended,—in the operator that of *undiverted* strong concentration of purpose, and on the part of the subject, *undiverted* indifference or expectancy. The influence of mind immediately upon mind is, by the nature of the case, more difficult than by way of the open senses; and the excitement of operating under a critical test and under conditions of special anxiety, as seems evident in this case, *might* have been so much to the operator's disadvantage as to cause his failure *there*, when the same effort made under passive surroundings might have been promptly successful. The subject, too, was under less favorable conditions than in her familiar and unconstrained surroundings at home. One sick away at the residence of a most kind and freehearted neighbor, will, for the same reason, not do as well as at home, though of less comfortable appointment. While, therefore, the precautionary arrangements were truly well calculated to insure *failure*, they were equally well calculated to defeat the real ends of science. And these gentlemen of eminence, Dr. Noble in exacting these conditions and Prof. Carpenter in endorsing them, were therein unscientific. The same objection applies to many of the tests reported by Mr. Carpenter, Mr. Braid, Mr. Noble and others. A fair test will have great care to respect *mental* conditions. It is not to be conducted as one of physical mechanism or of mere bone and muscle, without regard to sensitiveness.

May not, then, this "intelligent and well-educated friend" have been defeated unfairly; and possibly without himself knowing to what the failure was due? And may not what he and others reported as examples of mesmerizing through intervening walls and apartments, after all, have really been as claimed? From the account it is to be judged that essentially the same precautions against giving the subject an occasion to expect anything, were taken at home. His qualification is endorsed, and the veracity of the "friend" is to be assumed. And so, probably, after all, the professor gives us real cases of mind operating on mind independent of the senses, in the illustrations set forth in opposition to the theory.

IMPORTANT INSTANCES OF MIND IMPRESSING MIND.

But the same persons are not always equally available for the phenomena, under the same circumstance, any more than that one should always be in the same state of health. Neither are races alike in this respect, as also in many others. Among Europeans it is only here and there one who is prominently a subject, while among the Orientals the subjects are much more numerous and much more susceptible—available for more profound depths of mesmeric sleep, being more sensitive to mental impressions. In India, for example, this temperamental state is much more prevalent and pronounced, and the illustrations are more extraordinary. Among Europeans now and then a case is reported of surgery without pain, under mesmerism, prior to the introduction of ether. In 1829, M. Cloquet, one of the most eminent surgeons of Paris, performed a severe operation on a female patient who had been thrown by mesmerism into a state of somnambulism. In the operation she showed herself entirely insensible to pain, whilst "of all that took place in it she had subsequently no recollection." In addition to this, Prof. Carpenter observes that about twelve years afterward two amputations were performed in England, one in Nottinghamshire and the other in Leicestershire, "upon mesmerized patients, who showed no other sign of consciousness than an almost inaudible moaning; both of them exhibiting an uninterrupted placidity of countenance; both of them declaring, when brought back to their ordinary state, that they were utterly unaware of what had been done to them during their sleep." (Mesmerism and Spiritualism, p. 14). About the same time, while a few cases thus here and there were reported in Europe and England, Dr. Esdaile, a surgeon of the British service in Calcutta, was employing it upon Indian patients with about the regularity that ether is now employed; in consideration of which the governor-general conferred upon him the rank of presidency-surgeon.

Under the influence of mesmerism he performed some of the most severe operations in the history of surgery, during which the patients were entirely unconscious. One of these, the removal of a tumor from the face of a peasant, forty years old, he relates as follows:

"In half an hour, the man was catalepsed. * * I put a long knife in at the corner of the mouth, and brought the point out over the cheek bone, dividing the parts between; from this, I pushed it through the skin at the inner corner of the eye and dissected the cheek back to the nose. The pressure of the tumor had caused the absorption of the anterior wall of the antrum, and pressing my fingers between it and the bones, it burst, and a shocking gush of blood and brain-like matter followed. The tumor extended as far as my fingers could reach under the orbit and cheek bone, and passed into the gullet—having destroyed the bones and partition of the nose. No one touched the man, and I turned his head into any position I desired, without resistance, and there it remained till I wished to move it again: when the blood accumulated I bent his head forward, and it ran from his mouth as if from a leaden spout. The man never moved nor showed any signs of life, except an occasional indistinct moan; but when I threw back his head, and passed my fingers into his throat to detach the mass in that direction, the stream of blood was directed into his windpipe, and some instinctive effort became necessary for existence; he therefore coughed, and leaned forward, to get rid of the blood; and I supposed that he then awoke. The operation was by this time finished, and he was laid on the floor to have his face sewed up, and while this was

doing, he, for the first time, opened his eyes. * *
The man declares by the most emphatic pantomime, that he felt no pain while in the chair, and that when he awoke I was sewing up his face on the floor" (Mesmerism in India, pp. 147, 148).

Not only is the availability of this race for mesmerism well shown in the experiences of this celebrated surgeon, but it is related, on good authority, that some of their fakirs, by a process of self-mesmerism, are enabled to so completely suspend the vital forces as to safely allow of being buried for weeks, and then be exhumed and restored. Prof. Carpenter relates, on the authority of Mr. Braid of Manchester, who obtained his information directly from British officers, who had been eye-witnesses of them in India, several instances, as follows:

"In one of these, vouched for by Sir Claude H. Wade (formerly political agent at the court of Runjeet Singh), the fakir was buried in an underground cell, under strict guardianship, for *six weeks;* the body had been twice dug up by Runjeet Singh during the period of interment, and had been found in the same position as when first buried.

"In the other case, narrated by Lieut. Boileau, in his 'Narrative of a Journey in Rajwarra,' in 1835, the man had been buried for ten days, in a grave lined with masonry and covered with large slabs of stone, and strictly guarded; and he assured Lieut. Boileau, that he was ready to submit to an interment of twelve months' duration, if desired. In the third case, narrated by Mr. Braid, the trial was made under the direct superintendence of a British officer, a period of nine days having been stipulated for on the part of the devotee; but this was shortened to three at the desire of the officer, who feared lest he should incur blame if the result was fatal. The appearance of the body when first disinterred, is described in all instances as having been quite corpse-like, and no pulsation could be detected in the heart or in the arteries" (Pin. Human Phys. pp. 868, 869).

A writer in Scribner's Monthly for Dec. 1880, gives a very full and interesting account of these death-like sleeps achieved by self-mesmerism, which are rarely, if ever, achieved by any other people. With them it is of traditional antiquity.

Dr. Esdaile derived from his experience with this people the fact that the mesmeric influence can be transmitted through the air for a considerable distance, and even pass through dense materials. An experiment of this kind was made substantially as follows:

A blind prisoner who was barely able to distinguish light from darkness was the subject. Operating upon him for ten minutes from without through the window, he was rendered insensible and slept for more than two hours. At another time, at a distance of twenty yards from him, wholly unknown by him as to his presence, after operating on him for fifteen minutes he was overpowered and fell from his seat unconscious,—was carried to his bed and slept three hours, at the end of which wondering how he came there. At another time he directed his sub-assistant surgeon to proceed to the jail and place the man with his face toward the wall, but not touching it, and take care not to excite his attention to the matter, and keep him engaged in conversation. Dr. Esdaile placed himself opposite to him on the other side of the wall, leaning his forehead against it, and after several attempts, at the end of seventeen minutes the subject ceased to reply in conversation and presently fell back like one dead.

Now if we may place reliance on these statements (and if we may not, on what statements may we?) made by competent and careful men, who share our largest confidence as men of learning and candor, what disposition is to be made of these facts? It is to be remembered, also, that claims of observation of like facts, by people of superior attainment and unquestionable veracity, could, in considerable numbers, be added to these, from various sources. The only solution that seems legitimate is that a mind projected its impulses upon a neighboring mind, by a medium not recognized by the external senses, and that the impulses were susceptible of being directed separately upon a line or route to the object mentally indicated, and upon leaving the mind did not become indiscriminately diffused upon all surrounding objects. The subject intended, alone, and not any of his associates, was thus affected. The facts supply sensuous proof of the most unquestionable character, that, as already seen by other facts, individual minds are related and hold some measure of correspondence by means of an interlying, passive, mental medium; upon quite the same principle, that one magnet, by means of a passive ether of essentially the same element, exerts force upon another. Now, in the exertion of force by one magnet upon another, intervening substances may be directly or sympathetically affected by the passing current, and, so far as they are identical in substance with the magnets themselves, become its vehicle. The gleam that under favorable circumstances is seen emitted between poles, the partial visibility of the earth's magnetic phenomena, in what are known as "northern lights," caused by impingement of plying forces upon suitable elements of the adjacent atmosphere, may be suggested as examples of the working of this law. Yet no one will fail to see that, primarily, the plying force is purely between and relative to the magnets themselves.

So in the correspondence between minds, in this independent manner, though inferior elements between, including those of the bodily organisms, may be influenced thereby, and be made instruments of achieving the mesmeric state, it will be apparent still that the force is primarily and purely that of mind upon mind, in the so-called mesmeric phenomena.

INSPIRATION.

Being founded on a law of mind that cannot be less than universally operative, this mode of intercourse, subject to weakening, aberrating, and obscuring influences, as we have observed in the case of our present existence, must be found in vogue with mind of the same order or in so far as the order is the same, in whatever mode or altitude of being. And from what has been to some extent seen, all intervening conditions are permeable by it with more or less effectiveness. The mind of the blind man was forcibly impressed by a neighboring mind of whose presence he had no knowledge whatever. And the operator had set aside all his own senses, save that of hearing, which was of but indirect service, by interposing a wall, at the time of delivering the impression. There is, then, very little difference to be accounted for between this state of things and what would have been if one of them had been out of the body and the other in or only partly in, or where neither had been in the body. The operator had a slight external means—rather a suggestion—by which to direct the impression,—a reverberation of the subject's voice and a confident memory of his position as seen previous to operating, and these were probably of no real necessity, more than to stimulate assurance. It is not stated and is not likely, that exact measurements were taken so that the mentally erected line should rest directly on the subject. The place of the subject was only approximately known. The direction was evidently secured by some form of sympathy attained from previous personal knowledge, or by a mental definition of the characteristics of the subject; as when while we think of a person we unconsciously picture him to mind. The mode is unknown and only a matter of curiosity. The fact of the transmitted control in these conditions, alone is important, and goes far, if not conclusively, to prove, by external means, that minds need not reside in the same order of senses nor in the same world, to be impressible, though vaguely it may be, one by the other.

It also is seen to be a feature of this law that the greater the attainment of the mind—the greater its altitude—the more influence may it exert and the more control may it assume, directly or indirectly. The refined and otherwise highly attained mind may not for the hour visibly wield a control over the wild, unthinking masses, equal to that of the more coarse and low, but in the years its power will be seen to have been the greater,—more strong and enduring, and hence more achieving.

The influence of the more attained mind upon lower minds, in this way, is not only more strong than that which may be returned upon it from them, but it seizes with a stronger grasp and transforms more rapidly the physical materials employed in its organism. It erects more lines of brain and other nerve fiber, and breaks more down. With the greater wear and tear of the organism, the average life-time of the higher intellect is yet longer than that of the lower; which is another instance illustrating the law that with the more exalted minds and realms of mind, is the major control and the more wide-reaching influence.

SEAT OF INFINITE POWER AND INFLUENCE.

And thus may we prolong the vision upward, elevation over elevation, till in the supremely exalted mind of the Deity himself we see vested the final supremacy of power, and the prerogative of an infinitely extended influence upon all the realms of being, down to their last details. The descent of this influence must be supposed to take place by essentially the same law which, from this Mind proceeding, animates all others of rational and moral qualities. It would, also, be from the promptings to good, incident to a feeling, rational intelligence; which promptings would always be characterized by the absolutely perfect wisdom that can belong to that state and being alone. Then, in case the state of finite beings might be truly requiring acts of direct correspondence from Him, such as consciously or unconsciously imparting elements of wisdom, or of foresight, or by temporal interpositions of any kind, no fact in nature would be more probable, more reasonable and scientific than that such inspiration or interposition should take place.

To what extent like inspirations between finite fellow beings may be taking place throughout the infinite ranges, is at present unimportant. But as in all states or worlds finite beings necessarily exist embodied in organisms of external senses, suited to surrounding nature, it may always be, as here, the less common mode of intercourse.

LIFE IS FILLED WITH INSTANCES OF PECULIAR IMPRESSIONS.

The obscuration of this mode of intercourse by the glaring realities of the sensuous state, has been referred to. Still life is more or less filled with peculiar impressions, sometimes of great importance, that are unaccounted for by ordinary facts—even by recourse to spasmodic brain movements. For example, there are impressions more or less common of some coming external matter of interest, which in due time transpires. At least there is a correspondence of particulars between the impression and what subsequently comes to pass. This could not well be the result of brain action. Is it not, indeed, necessary that such should be referred to this mode of intercourse, from a mind situated so as to see farther into cause and effect? And if these, then may not others also; though their explanation might be possible by another theory. If we were obliged to sense our experiences more closely, resulting in greater acuteness and discrimination, we might expect a proportionate accumulation of this kind of evidence,—from the faint glimmer of a detached, peculiar sensation of thought to the glaring, overpowering inspiration of a Hebrew prophet.

PEOPLE VARY IN AVAILABILITY FOR THIS PHENOMENA.

It has been observed that races are not alike susceptible in all things. The same class of facts pertaining to human nature we might find less common and less prominent in one nationality than in another. Races of equal attainment are not abreast in poetry, history, in science, and in art. One would be regarded as unwise to study sculpture or painting from the German schools; or chemistry from the Italian; or history from the French; or fine arts from the English. So he should not be expected to study the principles of architecture from the Jewish race, nor those of inspiration from the

European. And yet in the study of this subject by a European, nothing were more probable than that *his own* race, and perhaps his own experiences, would be the chief source from which to collect his facts—a race in whose entire history from barbarism up, less phenomena of this character has been alleged than has been alleged of any other people. But from what is authentically known of them, it is safe to judge that if the facts of individual life experiences of the great *Hebrew* race could be recovered in essential particulars as they occurred, it would be found a field immensely rich in instances of most striking illustrations of the law of inspiration as here set forth. No race has displayed to historic view evidence of as much and as unquestionable *inspirational phenomena* as has this, at one time for twenty consecutive centuries the most pure and influential race on the planet.

CHAPTER XVI.

QUESTIONS CONCERNING THE RELATION OF THE TWO WORLDS, CONTINUED.—DIFFICULTIES NECESSARILY ATTENDING THE TRANSMISSION OF THOUGHT.—THEY BECOME MORE FORMIDABLE BETWEEN RESIDENTS OF THE TWO WORLDS.

THE difficulties attending the transmission of thought, though numerous in detail, are few in class. They arise mainly out of individual obliquity from unequal development of functional forces, resulting in unintelligible constructions of thought; or, if it be the recipient, in defective modes of their apprehension. Or they arise out of individual unlikeness, one to another; out of unlikeness of their surroundings; or out of the unavailability of intervening substances, as to their properties or state of arrangement. These causes, of course, combine in endless variety of ways. Probably no instance of misunderstanding is due to one cause alone.

We often find people having quite nearly the same general appearance. Yet a close inspection will always bring to view some striking differences. So, too, with minds, however nearly their views and abilities may be the same, we need not canvass long to find many particulars in which one is not like the other. It is often remarked with more meaning than is apprehended, that people do not see and think alike from the fact that themselves are not alike. Each difference in conformation of individual mental substance, or even of the physical related therewith, stands for a corresponding difference in the mental forces and in the results they enact.

Then let it be supposed that a thought is evolved—has been brought from merely nascent impressions into a definite mental statement—and is addressed to a neighboring mind. By the mind from which it is evolved it is now also being seen,—it has become to that mind itself an objective reality, prior to being delivered, as truly as though it consisted of a letter or a telegram. But the thought is seen by the apprehending powers of the originator as it stands constructed or influenced by the resident mental forces, and hence by a light more or less refracted, and possibly not as it really is—a more or less incorrect representation of fact. Indeed, in the process of its evolving it was advanced along these same aberrated lines of mental vision to this final state. Then between what Self sees it to mean, and what another sees it to mean, there may be quite a difference. Nothing is more common than that one sees the constructions of his own thoughts conveying different meanings at different times. Often when one comes to re-read with a rested mind the thoughts put down in the last hours of a day of hard toil, he finds them not appearing as they then did. The explanation is, that the weary powers, in irregular order, were sinking down to rest—to replenish overdrawn forces—when the conceptions recorded were taking place, adding at each time a new refraction. There is, then, trouble at what must necessarily be the very first step in the transmission of thought. For, though the construction might be clothed in a wording perfectly intelligible to both the issuing and receiving minds, a transmission of the sentiment intended were, by this state of facts, quite impossible; only so far as the construction were a true exponent thereof, could the transmission be approximated. And this, again, only in case the receiving mind were itself, functionally, in exact balance.

But if such a state of mind were indeed possible, it would be the most extremely rare. And, in the proposed transaction, adding to the mental obliquity of the party issuing the communication, that, also, of the receiving party, at the other end of the route, would, plainly, give us a still wider misunderstanding between the two.

Obliquity in the same degree and manner in both individuals, might in some instances contribute to the transfer of thought, provided surroundings were the same. They would misconceive in the same manner, and would likely have their aberrations coincide, and, thereby seeing upon essentially the same lines of vision, would be more successful in apprehending each other's meanings. From this, those who come together in a sect by a free following of their inclinations, whether in philosophy, politics or religion, are more likely to be able to transfer to each other their exact sentiments on those subjects. And to this fact the crystallization into these several orders of society is mainly due.

Hence, conversely, in the unlikeness of individuals to each other is found a large part of the explanation why they do not more fully succeed in a mutual understanding over these dividing lines. Not alone are they affected by obliquities of mind, but in their *obliquities* they are not alike.

Also, surroundings are rarely the same, to any considerable extent. Then, the excitants of functions not being the same in both, to some extent the same obliquity with respect to each other must follow that follows from representation of unlike functional developments. The very just observation is often made, based on this fact, that one may not be wholly able to judge of another who is not in the same circumstances with him. And it were, indeed, a happy thing to have this charity extended to other conditions of like inevitable misunderstandings, out of which for want of this charity so many alienations rise. With difficulties even as small as these in the way of fully receiving each other's meaning, and the readiness with which, by these difficulties, misunderstandings occur through the lassitude of thought that attaches to the much that is all the time being said, what breadths of charity are not indeed constantly being called for.

THE INTERLYING SUBSTANCES.

From this brief reference to the difficulties that are constituted in the very structures of the minds themselves, we proceed to consider those that are incidental to the substances intervening between minds. So far as relates to this state of existence, these substances are mainly the physical elements employed in the organisms of the external body. Plainly these organisms are *between* the individual minds. All this embodiment —all this brain, these nerves and organs of sense, constituted of the mineral kingdom and extremely foreign to the mental element, when made the medium of intercourse, it would seem, would be more a barrier to arrest intercourse than otherwise; as iron, wood or stone, when interposed between water and its destined end, arrests its flow.

It is not necessary to here again go over the ground to show that mind in its essential nature is an element separate from the body,—that the body is an instrument which it seizes hold of and lets go again, in a large part at its own election,—that in its devices the principles of the microscope, telegraph and telephone, etc., are so fully and literally employed as that these inventions could well have been suggested by an accurate understanding of the organism and the mode of its being operated. The fact to be borne in mind is that the substances so employed are in themselves of the mineral state, and as void of mind or of mental characteristics as is a line of copper wire, and serve the ends of their employment in quite the same manner as does the wire when placed in the circuit. Minds in approaching each other in intercourse by way of the external senses alone, can themselves come no farther than the bioplastic cells into which the nerve fibers dip. From there onward to the next mind, is *apparatus* alone, supplemented by the elements, atmospheric and otherwise, still further lying out between the organisms themselves.

By this route, then, no mind sees, hears, or otherwise knows of a neighboring mind, only as impressions come and go over these manifold nerve-wires in and out by the organs of sense. Let us suppose a case. Two individuals in full possession of their faculties are engaged in neighborly intercourse. They are casually sitting or standing in each other's presence. What is now taking place? Literally, there is a direction of the senses—one set upon another,—all very sensitively alert. Conventional sounds and gestures are proceeding, by a somewhat regular alternation, from each. A fluctuating demeanor of countenance is seen according to how the communication takes effect within, or as purposes mature and get into readiness for deliverance. The illustration will, perhaps, be rendered more forcible by recalling a scene of intercourse between people using a speech not known by ourselves, where we are brought to note more particularly the external demeanor.

This half pantomimic representation to sensuous view, is the physical organisms undergoing the process of intercourse between the two veiled minds within. Yet the realization of the fact of *intercourse*, rendered unquestionable by recognition of the many evidences of common thought and feeling, quite effectually obscures this mineral aspect of the case, and confounds the external person with the real self—renders, to casual observation, operator and apparatus indistinguishably the same.

The real facts transpiring are that these neighboring minds are from within operating their organisms in this manner in delivering messages to each other, mainly addressing them by the use of conventional sounds or oral speech, to the *hearing* department of sense; while others which may not be sent that way may, from the legible countenance and gesticulations, be directed by way of the light to the *seeing* department. The process, with all facilities in full operation, is at best a tedious and slow drill. When the conception is of some length, often much of what in the order of transmission comes last, is forgotten in substance or in the arrangement, while what goes before is being rattled off. The flight of an impression along a nerve is said to be not as rapid as that of the eagle. And as has been seen, the mind operates much more rapidly in dreams, when less encumbered by the organism, than in the waking state.

But this organism, like any other apparatus or instrument, is, to a considerable extent, liable to be faulty and to do its work imperfectly. The materials thereof, as when employed in more simple mechanisms, are subject to wear and tear, and, in time, to yield their hold and break down, causing a corresponding diversion of the forces to which they supplied a vehicle or a bridge. In this repect, mechanically considered, its liability to get out of *true* working order is not equaled by any other instrument. The nervous arrangement alone is much more extensive and complicated than is seen of any other device of art or of nature, though the system is one of simplicity.

Allowing, then, for the great superiority of the mental forces, and of the vital forces largely at their command, and their adaptability, like a good economist, to rendering substitutes for deficiencies, it is hardly possible that at any time, with the most favored individual, there are not many derangements large enough to cause, in its transit, important variations to the idea dispatched.

MIND IN THE PROCESSES OF INSANITY.

In illustration of how thought becomes arrested, aberrated and tangled in its passage through the organism, conditions of mind in cases where the organism is diseased, may be cited. What is manifest in respect to it then is but an exaggeration of the perversions that to some extent always prevail, even when at the best. In recognized instances of insanity—in the instances of those wonderful misworkings of the mind, the nervous system is invariably found in a state of corresponding disorder. Most people, from some one or more of the numerous causes, have been, to some extent, insane in one or more of the numerous forms of pronounced insanity; to say nothing of the trivial moody states about which the mind is generally fluctuating. In most countries people are liable to extensive malarial disturbances, usually characterized by delirious fevers. To become "flighty" is very common; while at times—frequent enough to have been seen by most every one—the aberration rises to frenzy, fretting the vision with the most strange and terrifying fancies, and apprehending nothing in its real state of fact. The poison of alcohol, so deplorably prevalent, is a yet more efficient means to the same end. Following its havoc with the nervous machinery, when imbibed to the extent that is often seen, comes not alone greater perversion to transpiring thought, but a corresponding perversion of the æsthetical and moral senses, together with (in many cases) a *reversing* of the normal current of sympathy and affection. In consequence of it, not alone are ideas obscured and entangled, but there is a descent from refinement to coarseness and vulgarity; from a relish of virtue there is a change to the relish of vice; instead of affection, hatred is cherished toward the dearest friends; while promptings to acts of affection are converted to desires for the infliction of injury. Instances of insanity—from other causes, however, in some examples partake of this same character. Even at times when the judgment is healthy and ordinarily sane, the impulse to vice and crime becomes overmastering. At the rising of the impulse, the patient is at times terrified with the spectacle of crime into the execution of which these impulses are dragging him over his prostrate will, and he sounds with most anxious solicitude the note of alarm, begging that the intended victim fly for safety.

Though cases of insanity of this character are not rare and may readily be recalled by most people from their own knowledge, a few examples cited by Prof. Maudsley of London, a well-known authority on brain disease, are well to the point. The first he gives on the authority of the eminent Dr. Pinel of France, and is in substance as follows:

"A man who had previously followed a mechanical occupation, but was afterward confined at Bicetre, experienced *at regular intervals*, fits of rage, ushered in by the following symptoms: At first he experienced a sensation of burning heat in the bowels, with an intense thirst and obstinate constipation; this sense of heat spread by degrees over the breast, neck, and face, with a bright color; sometimes it became still more intense, and produced violent and frequent pulsations in the arteries of those parts, as if they were going to burst; at last the nervous affection reached the brain and then the patient was seized with an irresistible sanguinary propensity; and if he could lay hold of any sharp instrument, he was ready to sacrifice the first person that came in his way. In other respects he enjoyed the free exercise of his reason; even during the fits he replied directly to questions put to him, and showed no kind of incoherence in his ideas, no sign of delirium; he even felt deeply all the horror of his situation, and was often penetrated with remorse, as if he was responsible for his mad propensity. Before his confinement at Bicetre a fit of madness seized him in his own house; he immediately warned his wife of it, to whom he was much attached; and he had only time to cry out to her to run away lest he should put her to a violent death. * *
This internal combat between a sane reason in opposition to sanguinary cruelty reduced him to the brink of despair" (Responsibility in Mental Disease, pp. 141, 142).

A somewhat similar case he relates from Dr. Jean

Esquirol, a French physician of great note who died in 1840, and who with Pinel was also greatly interested in the study and care of the insane. It is of a country gentleman who was of good health and circumstances, and of the age of forty-five, who came to consult him about his case. Of his case the doctor says:

"There was no indication of the slightest disorder of reason in him; he answered with precision all my questions which were numerous. * * Nevertheless in the night he awoke suddenly with the thought of killing his wife, who was lying by his side. He left his bed, and walked up and down the room for an hour, after which, feeling no more disquietude, he lay down and went to sleep; three weeks afterward the same idea occurred on three occasions, always in the night. During the day he took plenty of exercise, occupied himself with his numerous affairs, and had only the remembrance of what he had felt in the night. He had been married twenty years, had always enjoyed health, *

* had never had the least disagreement with his wife, to whom he was attached. * * He is sad and troubled about his condition; has left his wife from fear that he might yield to his propensity" (ibid, pp. 147, 148).

Another case which he cites is that of a gentleman fifty years of age, who came to consult him about his condition, being much disturbed by homicidal impulses. They were so constantly and strongly impressed upon his mind that (though a man of great energy and self control) "he was compelled to live away from his family, wandering from hotel to hotel, lest he should become a murderer" (ibid, p. 144). Another case is that of a lady quite advanced in years, who "was afflicted with recurring paroxysms of convulsive excitement, in which she always made desperate attempts to strangle her daughter, who was very kind and attentive to her, and to whom she was much attached" (ibid, p. 145). Still another case he cites as follows:

"A man at fifty-five years, sober and industrious, had suffered from an attack of cerebral hemorrhage, a year ago, and remained hemiplegic. His intelligence was sound and he followed his usual occupation. But his character was changed: he felt weary of life; he had become morose and irritable; and he complained that at times the *blood rose to his head*, when vertigo, noises in the ears, and flashes before the eyes occurred. These attacks became periodic. During them his heart beat violently, his eyes were injected, the face flushed, the fingers of paralyzed side contracted, the arteries of neck throbbed; he was unspeakably dejected, wept, said he was lost, and became furious, throwing himself upon wife and children" (ibid, p. 170).

Not alone are the promptings to suicide and homicide, but to the entire list of crimes and vices common to mankind. Nothing is more common than vulgarity and profanity. And in the long years ago the poet philosopher Lucretius, terrified by the strong promptings to lewdness, realized in paroxysms of insanity, raised his hand against his own life to prevent its falling a prey to these vile impulses of his diseased brain. Commonly these take place in exact reverse of the character when sane. Or, probably, where any trait of mind or of feeling is cherished with some special measure of *interest*, the reversing of it takes place; so that not only is the one loved now being hated, but the one hated is being loved. If the patient previously had been specially cherishing piety, the disorder will likely have rendered him profane, particularly so if the disturbance has become acute.

Prof. Maudsley himself very truly observes in respect to one phase of this order of insanity as follows:

"The symptoms are chiefly those of disorder of the moral sentiments, and the two conditions of excitement and depression vary in degree and intensity in different cases. In the state of excitement the sufferer is very much like a person who is half intoxicated—loquacious, boastful, aggressive, never weary of talking of himself and of the wonderful things which he can do. And he does things which he would never have dreamed of doing in his sober senses—engages in projects of social or political reform, or launches into commercial speculations quite foreign to his natural character and habits. His morals undergo a sad degeneration: heretofore modest, truthful, and chaste, he is now full of self-glorification, disregardful of truth, and given to excesses; he displays a complete indifference to the feelings of those who are related to him, frequents low company, tramples upon social and domestic proprieties, and is angrily impatient of the slightest remonstrance or interference" (ibid, pp. 176, 177).

Of another phase, the epileptic, he continues:

"Nothing can be more striking than the abrupt and extreme change in moral character which is witnessed sometimes in asylum epileptics before or after an outbreak of epilepsy. Hitherto industrious, attentive, and docile, the disposition and conduct undergo a sudden change. They become negligent, lazy, indolent, forget very simple things, will not do their work, pass their time in inaction or wander about aimlessly; their disposition, too, becomes evil—they are for the time liars, thieves, suspicious, discontented and irritable, and on the slightest pretexts, or without actual provocation, yield to sudden outbreaks of violence" (ibid, p. 178).

In these instances of "moral insanity" it is often the case that not alone does the mind itself remain sane and strong to judge of the misdemeanors toward which they are impelled, as other people do, but there is also the same *repugnance* thereto that others have. They abhor and deplore in the very midst of the proceedings. In such cases it is, then, plain that not the entire principle of the moral sense is intercepted by the state of disorder in the organism to which the painful perversion is due,—that indeed *back* of the organism the moral sense itself is sane; upon the principle set forth by St. Paul as to his own experience, "When I would do good, evil is present with me," and which to the same limited but important extent, is true of the best while in the flesh.

While, therefore, there must be differences between individuals as to the rectitude and strength of the moral sense itself, wholly back of the organism, its transmission over the organism is liable to be very imperfect, to exactly reverse it, as seen in these insanities. "Assuredly," says Mr. Maudsley, "moral insanity is disorder of mind produced by disorder of brain. In examining the conditions of its occurrence, we have seen how plainly it follows the recognized causes of insanity; how it may precede for a time the outbreaks of various forms of unequivocal general alienation; how it accompanies intellectual insanity in most of its varieties; how it may follow other forms of general insanity; how it may precede or follow epilepsy or occur as a masked epilepsy " (ibid, p. 182).

What has been said of "moral insanity" is of course, in principle, applicable to mental insanity, which surely is no less prevalent. It is found that however weak and unbalanced the purely mental functions themselves may be, there is an exact correspondence between the tangled, meaningless or misleading expressions of thought and the manner of an existing brain disorder—its broken state, or its unserviceableness from some other fact,—brain lesions, its over-pressure of blood or the deficiency of its supply. Dr. Carpenter attributes much of its impairment brought on by "an impairment of nutrition." The causes are numberless when we go into detail.

Aside from contending with the disorders and imperfections within the brain mechanism itself, there are sometimes defects at the very beginning of the transmission of thought by this route. It is sometimes difficult to get the forces of the mind at all delivered upon the instrument. The mind finds it at times difficult to get hold of the requisite part of this living mechanism, from the absence of requisite means of connection. Many may from their own experience recall difficulties, on a smaller scale, like the following cases cited from Sir Robert Christison, by Prof. Carpenter:

"*a.* 'The first was that of a gentleman who frequently could not carry out what he *wished* to perform. Often on endeavoring to undress, he was two hours before he could get off his coat, all his mental faculties, volition excepted, being perfect. On one occasion having ordered a glass of water, it was presented to him on a tray, but he could not take it, though anxious to do so; and he kept the servant standing before him half an hour, when the obstruction was overcome.

"*b.* 'In the other case the peculiarity was limited. If, when walking in the street this individual came to a gap in the line of houses, his will suddenly became inoperative, and he could not proceed. An unbuilt-on space in the street was sure to stop him. Crossing a street also was very difficult; and on going in or out of a door, he was always arrested for some minutes. Both of these gentlemen graphically described their feelings to be 'As if another person had taken possession of their will'" (Mental Physiology, p. 385).

The sensation of these gentlemen referred to in the words, "As if another person, had possession of their will," could only have been of the fact that their wills were not *effective*. The fact of these somewhat singular phenomena or extreme exemplification of a more or less common difficulty, was that to that extent there was an inability on the part of the mind to get hold of the right nerves, which, when it got to them worked well enough.

The *will* itself was not "paralyzed," it was actively trying to command the organism. And it persisted till "the obstruction was overcome." It was somewhat like when one in an alarming dream seeks desperately to move, and for a time is unable; or as when one in stammering or stuttering, mentally strains and is for a time unable to gain possession of the nerve centers controlling the organs of speech.

Another kind of derangement of the organism, and of frequent occurrence, is that seen in certain forms of *Aphasia*, where the patient, though he be wholly rational and the organs of speech healthy and entire, and at his command, is powerless to seize the right word, when endeavoring to speak. When the mind orders the word, one of quite opposite meaning is produced. A professional gentleman of high standing, upon my remarking this fact to him, answered me that the difficulty had at several times occurred to himself with sufficient force to attract his attention. As for example when he was intending to say "east" the word "west" was uttered.

Prof. Carpenter reports a very pronounced case of a gentleman of considerable scientific attainment, a life-long acquaintance, who became very seriously troubled in this way. He had attained to over seventy years of age, but retained an unusual degree of bodily vigor. In his case, however, the malady took a wider range than simply the want of power to obtain the proper word. He was come to be more forgetful of words than usual, and sometimes failed to grasp their meaning, and to recognize people when seen in unusual places. Mr.

Carpenter, in speaking of him, makes the following statement:

"The want of memory of words then showed itself more conspicuously; one word being substituted for another, sometimes in a manner that showed the chain of association to be (as it were) bent or distorted, but sometimes without any recognizable relation. Thus on calling one day at the writer's residence, and finding neither him nor Mrs. C. at home, he asked his son (then quite a lad) 'how his *wife* was,' meaning, of course, his *mother*. But about the same time he told a friend that he 'had had his umbrella washed,' the meaning of which was gradually discovered to be, that he had his hair cut" (Mental Physiology, p. 445).

THE PATHOLOGY OR PHILOSOPHY.

In the pathology of this a partial insight may be had as to why the mind becomes so adversely affected while traversing an impaired organism, so far as pertains to recent impairments. Every brain track or nerve line, by use becomes to some extent automatic, and in consequence, is disposed to impart its quality of action to any impulse that passes upon it; much after what is seen in the use of a musical instrument—a horn or a violin. It will, by use, become accustomed to qualities of tone till it comes to automatically *favor* those qualities, and with greater difficulty yields to rendering others. When an arm is excited to action, its first impulse is to execute its own special movements. However, it may be induced to perform the function of the leg. The principle holds good in respect to bodily activities generally, and is a physiological law.

And though by the conditions of the argument no explanation is called for as to the mode of operation or mis-operation, by which the messages of thought become perverted within the organism, this simple law may suggest all, and the facts may be considered as being well and truly stated by Prof. Maudsley when he says:

"When injury or disease has destroyed that part of the brain which ministers to the expression of ideas in speech, as in the condition of disease known as aphasia, the person must slowly learn again to talk his own language; he is like a child learning to speak, or like one who is learning to talk a foreign language; he must educate another portion of brain to do the work which the damaged portion can no longer do" (Responsibility in Mental Diseases, p. 19).

To the reactions that must take place with such innovations and usurpations incident to establishing these new routes for the mind, might well be ascribed all the strange phenomena of the insane; though we have no means of verifying in detail or to understand anything of the *mechanical* aspect of the case.

The few only of the great world of human beings are so badly deranged as to be pronounced insane. How much of this unsoundness is prevalent with those who are denominated the sane people of which we see communities made up, were hard to even approximate. Perhaps none are without physical defects in the form of disease, the disturbance of which must, to some extent, affect the so-called state of mind, and render its manifestation or transmission of thought incomplete and incorrect; while, without regard to disease, there are the healthy irregularities and unbalanced conditions that are not possible to be without their corresponding aberrations. And there are the instances where the perversions by disease—the deformities by this cause—have, unfortunately, *in that form*, settled into healthy fiber, remaining in the organism as healthy gnarls, knots and cavities, the seats of former injuries, continue in the tree; or as the healthy crooked limb remains on the body, the healthy sightless orb in the socket, or the healthy soundless drum in the ear, to give their lameness and cast their shadow and their silence where what these defects withhold is vital to the full execution of the organism's work.

Then, again, when we come to consider that there are *two* organisms to be traversed by each dispatch between minds—that correctly *apprehending* is quite as necessary as correctly *revealing* ideas, and is as dependent on the good state of the organism of the receiver as correct dispatching is on that of the *sender*, and that it is as liable to the same imperfections—we see that the obstacles to transmission seen in the *one* organism, as above, are always to be multiplied by *two*. And then when we come to add to this what must in part be the result of this same organic deficiency, and part that of its imperfect development, the deficiency of the instrument of language, upon which so large a part of the transfer of ideas depends, we may judge of the limited extent to which we are able to understand one another in life. But a few are able to converse understandingly upon unfamiliar topics; topics that are not the embodiments of mutual and often repeated experiences. In attempting to introduce wholly new ideas or experiences, how soon do we discover our insular situation of mind. How we strike out and grasp, vainly, at this or that word or figure of speech by which to make ourselves understood. People, though they have a very gratifying measure of mutual understanding, are also, many of them, painfully realizing that for much of the inner thought—the newer and often higher and more valuable—there are no means to communicate.

THE DIFFICULTIES OF TRANSMITTING THOUGHT ENLARGE BETWEEN RESIDENTS OF THE TWO WORLDS.

But while, in this manner, between minds residing in them, these embodying elements place such obscurity and effect such perversion, it is also a fact that by means of them a large and satisfying measure of intercourse becomes possible and is constantly transpiring. From them is supplied a system of external senses that is common to all minds resident in the sensuous state. And these, co-ordinating in the attainment of the same common facts of nature, in this proxy way supply a bridge over which mind may hold commerce with mind. Imperfectly as they serve us, they are still the means of directly *knowing* much of each other, who are living on this same side or in this same aspect of being; which must be also true of the residents of any other world. From this fact residents in elements so unlike as not to afford senses in common, must necessarily be of very limited measures of intercourse; and the fact of such dissimilarity of elements in the two states is itself sufficient cause why we have so little special knowledge of those living in the land beyond death.

What they may see and know of *us* may well be more than what we see and know of *them*. In life, as in all other respects, the superior comprehends more of attainment than the inferior. In them, therefore, the mental modes of perception not alone, are to be considered as more effective in discerning neighboring lives, regardless of dissimilarity of embodiment, but it is to be considered that the same higher order of attainment would afford them also wider range of power over adjacent elements; to utilize them—those that are in freedom drifting, or those (as the ancients believed) which are wrought into organisms in the embodiments of their kindred yet surviving in the mortal land—to some extent as means of perception and of impression.

But with all these possibilities and probabilities, while we see little and know little practically of them, their knowledge of us is necessarily, also, more restricted and uncertain than is ours of each other, or theirs of one another on their own side of existence.

CHAPTER XVII.

QUESTIONS RESPECTING THE RELATION OF THE TWO WORLDS, CONTINUED.—FACTS ESTABLISHING THE POSSIBILITY OF INTERCOURSE BETWEEN MINDS WITHIN THE FLESH AND THOSE BEYOND.—CONDITIONS OF LUCID INTERCOURSE EXTREMELY RARE.—SPECIAL DEVICES FOR THE ATTAINMENT OF INTERCOURSE, IMPRACTICABLE AND ENDANGERING TO MIND AND MORALS.

FROM the fact of the continuance of life into the region beyond death it does not follow that between that world and this there should be any means of intercourse whatever. Neither, when otherwise sufficiently assured of their existence, is the intercourse with the departed of greatest importance. In some respects we see that good might come of it; especially so if that world were seen to be superior to this in the gratifications it would afford to the better part of life; and provided the intercourse were so complete and true as to rightly represent the facts pertaining to that life.

Yet, too, we can see how that in instances quite common, it would be detrimental. It is not always the case that people who do the most visiting—who, socially, are all the time lying in each other's bosoms, are doing as well by their own lives and by a needy world, as if it were otherwise; especially so where the friendship is exclusive—limited to a small coterie, to the home, to the family and kindred, perhaps. To a large part of the good in the world—the real comfort and happiness—hard, self-denying labor has been essential. And it is doubtful whether real good is not always so precious and rare as to be ever equally costly. And to the extent that habits detract from the interest to be taken in the general welfare, are they to be regarded as injurious to mankind.

The privilege of intercourse of this kind, then, while often it would be extremely gratifying and helpful, might after all, as a whole, be easily over-estimated; while upon the importance of an entire assurance that our departed are still living in all their essential wholeness, and are continuing under the same beneficent regulations of life (a fact that must follow from their survival), it were difficult to place an estimate adequately high.

But in the past, before the scientific attainments of our day, from such intercourse alone, or from phenomena that were that in appearance, the assurance of another life could have been derived in sufficient strength to have materially influenced the sentiments of the people—to have been the strong incentive to mental development that its influence has averaged to the race.

The evidence as to the possibility of intercourse between the two worlds, must first be in respect to the part in it taken by the residents on the other side. We must first consider what possibilities are with them that would enable them to deliver messages through to the people of this world—by what means at their command they could make themselves understood by us, or impart influences upon us, of which we might or might not have an understanding, or be aware.

By the nature of the case, much of what should go into the answer to this inquiry, is matter that is exclusively vested in the limits of that world itself, and beyond our present means of ascertaining. Beyond those facts that are constitutionally essential to existence, or that necessarily follow from such facts, and must remain essentially the same in all worlds, we cannot presume to venture any statements. Of the details beyond what are thus facts arising purely from the necessities of being, we cannot be supposed to have anything very definite to say. However, it may quite safely be judged that they are more able on their part to overcome the intervening obstacles than are we—that possibly if the restrictions on our part were as well removed as on theirs, the measure of intercourse might be considerable.

From the facts brought to view concerning the forms of substance in this state—that in the higher there are properties with prerogatives not appearing in the lower —it is hardly to be doubted that in each separate higher state of being, the passive substances, corresponding to these of the *mineral* with us, likewise present properties not met with in the lower world; which might constitute them available means of achieving more of the desired ends of their occupants. Then, too, might this avail of power, more than what we in this state are privileged with, include a more extensive mastery of the elements between them and us.

Observe what new and wonderful means of intercourse have come to us in the last few years by means of more extended research in our higher and more subtile forms of substance. This intercourse transpires by means of ethers greatly condensed and crystallized and extended between parties over distances indefinitely great. But what are the facts in respect to this wire, doing telegraphic and telephonic service? We cut out a section and subject it to a not very high degree of heat, and it recedes from visibility. Continuing to be the same substance, the atmospheres of its atoms are so immeasurably extended as to render it invisibly rare, and altogether intangible. This dissolution has been but a process of its forces, induced by adjacent forces, and proves its own forces to be mainly the agents of its consolidation, not alone, but the parts, concerning itself, that constituted it the tractile medium for the dispatches.

By casual or unskilled observation, these facts are not being considered; but, on reflection, it is plain enough that in this medium of intercourse, we are operating but a series of *forces*, one incumbent upon and actuating the other, in obedience to the causative force leaping forth from the intelligent will of man.

And yet these forces, of which our explorers have learned but a few, and those imperfectly well, are constantly showing complications with other forces still more remote, the number, variety, and influence of which, none can tell. Probably to the ever rising intelligence they will only multiply and extend; as the enlarging telescope, instead of finding a boundary, only increases the number and the distance of stars. The remotest atom is a compound; and hence, too, every force, however remote, is a cluster, the whole surmounted by the Infinite Mind.

But only in their larger classification and more comprehensive grouping, can they be considered as appearing to the earlier understanding. And to the Infinite Mind alone, may they be open to view in their infinite detail of operation. These forces are largely, if not entirely, *represented* between the finite mind and the external aspect of the mineral state; which state seems, however, to be so conditioned that to life therein, the higher forces are not attainable in efficient measures; while the departed, by the sundering process of death, have risen into larger possession of them, and more away from the possession of the lower. And this seems to constitute the difference, as to state, between the two worlds we call the physical and the spiritual; however abrupt and wide that difference may be.

It cannot be certainly known how extensive sundering of relation with physical forces, this separation from the body includes. But from the fact that the departed are so completely unrecognizable by all the sensuous modes of recognition, it becomes quite certain that their abode and identification are with a world of substance essentially foreign to our own; and by their more extended requirements of being, it could only be of a corresponding higher order.

But the fact must constantly remain in view, that the minds of the physical and of the spiritual worlds are of the same mental substance and forces, with one another—that these forces, while in the body, are having the mineral at command, as we have amply seen and are all the time realizing. And that mind is not entirely dependent for its contact with external nature upon *exact* forms of organization, is definitely known in that in the body it shifts from one group of nerves to another, and at times, also, to those of lower forms; and that it repairs brain and even creates new brain, by the lower forces at its command. And, hence, it is a fact that it is provided with some form of force that supplies to it a means of laying hold of loose, unassimilated, mineral substance. And to this loose substance the otherwise embodied mind is disembodied. It is practically, to all intents and purposes, disembodied mind from the spirit world so far actuating and directing the mineral elements of this. Neither does this need to seem like drawing out the illustration to a "hair-splitting" fineness, or like a straining to make out a case. The fact is sufficiently bold to have become a matter of science, and is of a class of facts already cited. However, the principle is commonly referred to for other purposes than the one for which I am here employing it; which, notwithstanding, does not render it less useful in this connection. It is, then, not to be disputed that with the human mind in the other world, there is retained some measure of power to control mineral elements of this world.

EXPECTANT ATTENTION.

Appropriate to this may be cited a few facts of the class given in illustration of the law of "emotional excitement" or "expectant attention," as the principle is more commonly named. Prof. Carpenter in treating of this law makes use of the following illustrations:

"A lady, who was watching her little child at play, saw a heavy window-sash fall upon its hand, cutting off three of the fingers; and she was so much overcome by fright and distress, as to be unable to render it any assistance. A surgeon was speedily obtained, who, having dressed the wounds, turned himself to the mother, whom he found seated, moaning, and complaining of pain in her hand. On examination, three fingers, corresponding to those injured in the child, were discovered to be swollen and inflamed, although they had ailed nothing prior to the accident. In four-and-twenty hours, incisions were made into them, and pus was evacuated; sloughs were afterward discharged, and the wounds ultimately healed" (Mental Physiology, p. 682).

Again:

"A highly intelligent lady known to Dr. Tuke related to him that one day she was walking past a public institution and observed a child, in whom she was particularly interested, coming out through the iron gate. She saw that he let go the gate after opening it, and that it seemed likely to close upon him, and concluded that it would do so with such force as to crush his ankle;

however, this did not happen. 'It was impossible,' she says, 'by word or act to be quick enough to meet the supposed emergency; and, in fact, I found I could not move, for such intense pain came on in the ankle corresponding to the one which I thought the boy would have injured, that I could only put my hand on it to lessen its extreme painfulness. *I am sure I did not move so as to strain or sprain it.* The walk home—a distance of about a quarter of a mile—was very laborious, and in taking off my stocking I found *a circle round the ankle, as if it had been painted with red currant juice, with a large spot of the same on the outer part.* By morning the whole foot was inflamed, and I was a prisoner to my bed for many days'" (ibid).

Facts of this kind are not so uncommon as one not familiar with this class of reading might suppose. Mr. C. accounts for these by the theory of "*local* disorder of nutrition followed upon powerful emotion, determined as to their seat by the intense direction of the attention to a particular part of the body." While, in the main, this theory may be the true one, it does not sufficiently provide for the facts in the case that are of chief importance. That the effect should be so exclusively *local*, that the location should be so far from the seat of the disturbing cause—the mind, and that the disordered nutrition should be so instantaneously destructive of the tissue, are not made clear. The detonation of thunder will precipitate the oxidation of milk when drawn, and so disorder it; and the intense mental disturbance of the mother may render her milk fatally unfit for the child, as is sometimes the case, even so particularly impressing upon it the special form of the disturbance as that the disturbance will be, in effect, reproduced in the child; still the impression is general and not local. In these cases the effects are so very local, as to be denoted by exact bounds; and where nutrition could only be present in a state of assimilation. Besides the effects were not of the character of the famishing or diseasing of the fiber, but of their massive, mechanical crushing; upon which, in due time, disease followed; the same as if the crushing had been caused by external violence—by the falling sash or the closing gate.

We note, also, that the bruises were not on the *brain*, on which the mind ordinarily delivers its forces, nor was there any damage discovered along the nerves—the line of travel—leading from the brain to the wounded part; all of which *should* have been, if the mind, with its crushing force, had reached the spot by the usual way of the organism. Evidently the organism was little, if at all, employed in delivering this force on a remote member of the body. These powerful impulses of mind, so crushingly laying hold on the distant fiber, as by these facts, could only have reached their destination, sympathetically indicated, by having taken a route through matter practically external of the body.

But in the light of these facts, might not the principle that provided a condition that was in these cases so effective, provide, also, for mental force to be administered on external mineral nature in measures indefinitely greater?—to have entirely sundered the maternal fingers, and the ankle?

Also, we saw, in the instance of mesmerism, the power of the mind to concentrate forces upon a *line*, and upon special *points*, and *on* definite *objects*,—that not all adjacent minds were affected—only the one intended. So here we have, and in relation to another class of circumstances, yet another illustration of the same power. Though involuntarily and unconsciously executed, that there was a concentration of mental forces and whatever other forces were required, on the wounded part, is manifest beyond doubt. As to the mode by which the forces are combined and made available—how they are made to seize on objects, though questions to be expected, need not here be asked, nor answered. *How* the magnetic forces seize upon a fiber of metal and join it with another, or upon the elements constituting the fiber, bringing them into the needed density, while it would be interesting as a matter of knowledge, could have no bearing on the fact of intercourse by telegraphy. The present indications are that all the lower forces, *per se*, operate in circuits and actuate each other by the well-known law of induction. But when we decide to move an arm, we are merely conscious of sending an impulse upon it, and that, in accordance with the direction indicated in the impulse, the arm moves. We have no realization of *getting hold* of the arm. Were it paralyzed, the unavailing will-pressure being a more pronounced effort, might cause the sensation of an endeavor to seize it, by carefully noticing.

STIGMATIZATION.

In these instances the forces acting so instantaneously, would suggest that they are involuntary, and of no avail for the voluntary purposes of the mind. But the voluntary and involuntary processes so imperceptibly merge in each other as that these instances cannot be taken as conclusive. Indeed, we find, that under other conditions of essentially the same phenomena, the facts are of opposite indication. In illustration, more especially of the law of "expectant attention," Mr. C. cites one of those singular cases of stigmatization, sometimes met with in reports of intense religious emotion, taken from Macmillan's Magazine of April, 1871, and is as follows:

"The most recent case of this kind, that of Louise Lateau, has undergone a scrutiny so careful, on the part of medical men determined to find out the deceit, if such should exist, that there seems no adequate reason for doubting its genuineness. This young Belgian peasant had been the subject of an exhausting illness, from which she recovered rapidly after receiving the sacrament; a circumstance which obviously made a strong impression on her mind. Soon afterward, blood began to issue every Friday from a spot in her left side; in the course of a few months, similar bleeding spots established themselves on the front and back of each hand, and on the upper surface of each foot, while a circle of small spots formed on the forehead; and the hemorrhage from these recurred every Friday, sometimes to a considerable amount. About the same time, fits of 'ecstasy' began to occur, commencing every Friday between eight and nine A. M., and ending at about six P. M.; interrupting her in conversation, in prayer, or in manual occupations. This state seems to have been intermediate between that of the biologized and that of the hypnotized subject; for, whilst as unconscious as the latter of all sense impressions, she retained, like the former, a recollection of all that had passed through her mind during the 'ecstasy.' She described herself as suddenly plunged into a vast flood of bright light, from which more or less distinct forms soon began to evolve themselves; she then witnessed the several scenes of the passion successively passing before her. She minutely described the cross and the vestments, the wounds, the crown of thorns about the head of the Savior; and gave various details regarding the persons about the cross,— the disciples, holy women, Jews, and Roman soldiers. And the progress of her vision might be traced by the succession of actions she performed at different stages of it; most of these being movements expressive of her own emotions; whilst regularly, about three P. M., she extended her limbs in the form of a cross. The fit terminated with a state of extreme physical prostration: the pulse being scarcely perceptible, the breathing slow and feeble, and the whole surface bedewed with a cold perspiration. After this state had continued about ten minutes, a return to the normal condition rapidly took place. These last phenomena, which were paralleled to a certain degree in Mr. Braid's experiments, seem quite beyond the power of intentional simulation; while the tests applied to determine the possibility of the artificial production of the stigmata and of the issue of blood from them, appear no less conclusive as to their non-simulation" (Mental Phys., pp. 689, 690).

While the entire sanity of this and similar subjects may be questioned, the facts of the stigmatization and the ecstasy, which alone concern the principle under consideration, and are of any value whatever, are well authenticated. Her case (which is recent—she being born in 1850) was examined under all the advantages of modern science, by a commission sent for that purpose by the Royal Academy of Medicine of Belgium, who, after a most determined, painstaking and complete investigation, pronounced the stigmatization and ecstasies, real; but the physiological and pathological principles cited in explanation, fail to account for these special local transudations of blood. The general transudation of blood through the perspiratory ducts of the skin ("sweating blood") under conditions of great emotional excitement, is a well-known fact, and in the light of physiological principles may be readily conceded.

In this case the essential facts are not materially unlike those of the examples previously cited. In those the fiber was crushed in definite localities without affecting the surrounding parts, as in case of an ordinary bruise. In this, the fiber was so displaced as to allow the passage of the blood out through the skin, while, also, the surrounding part seemed unaffected. In the others, as in this, the wounds were extremely sensitive and sore. In the former, the injuries were inflicted by sudden intense mental impulses. Those impulses were directed on the parts painfully imagined or seen injured in others for whom tender affections were cherished; and the injury was in each case in the form of the injury imaginarily seen. In this case there was no sudden impulse of the mind—no startle or fright. But, instead, it is seen that the subject rapidly recovered from an exhausting illness, after having received the sacrament. Hence the subject of the sacrament must have made a much stronger impression on her mind than is usual. Besides, at about the same time occurred those *ecstasies*, in which the passion scene stood out before her, vividly displaying to her view the crucifixion—the transfixed condition of her passionately loved Savior—of which the overpowering impressions would not fail to be those blood-issuing, living wounds, suggesting terrific pains; which would not fail to be located on corresponding parts of her own person, causing intense concentration of the mental forces, and their seizing, breaking and sundering of the fiber.

Then here, too, as in the other named particulars, there is an exact parallel between this and the other examples: the injuries in her person, too, were, in location and in form, the same as those imaginarily seen on the person of another. And we may only point to one feature of difference, and this not at all a radical one. It is that in this case the means of voluntarily determining the direction and execution of these forces upon a definite object is more fully demonstrable. Notwithstanding the *ecstasy* was uncontrollable, the element of reason was represented, and in such relation as to constitute the stigmatization, essentially, an act of the will. Not directly so, but indirectly; being in position to determine the direction and the execution of the forces. We see that the dominant impressions produced the stigmata; that many other features of the general scene were also sorely impressive; but that among all these, reason (such as it was) drew the major attention to the wounds, upon which followed (upon their sympathetic seats in her own person) the concentration and precipitation of the forces in measure and manner adequate to produce these wounds. Truly, when the reasonableness of a proposed act greatly preponderates over that of another, the volition may indistinguishably merge into a necessity—at least into the appearance of necessity—when in *fact* it continues to be *volition*. The full agency of the mind remains in the transaction. So in this case.

Another illustration of the principle is seen in that the mental impulses of the mother extend with prominent effect to the person of the child while in the fetal state, though "there is no nervous communication" whatever between them. Mr. C's explanation is that as the child in that state is wholly nourished from the blood of the mother, the impression is received on her blood only, causing minute alterations in it, and being in this form transmitted would correspondingly influence the bodily formation of the child. The explanation would apply very satisfactorily but for the fact that the blood would be expected to affect the body of the mother in some measure the same as that of the child, seeing she derives all her own nourishment from the same fluid. But this is not seen. It could apply only by considering the impression to be made on the volume of the blood separately belonging to the child, which would make it necessary that it be delivered upon the blood only after it has entered the person of the child,—beyond all nerve connection with the mother,—in another individual; it mattering not whether on the blood or fiber.

But the blood, also, is without nerve connection. It is merely a train of supply material not yet incorporated, being propelled along the passages to its destination by mechanical appliances, and may have been brought through artificial tubes over from the veins of another and be in reality the blood of another individual. And, in any case, its seizure by the mental forces would be the mind seizing substances having no specific connection with any organism. And although by means of the more intimate blending of their vital forces while thus situated with respect to each other, and being more impressible during its early states of development, the mental forces of the mother are more effective on the child, *in utero,* than upon a person external; yet so seizing its blood or the fiber itself, is, in principle, *seizing and influencing the body of a neighbor.*

MIRACULOUS CURES.

Still further illustrations of this law are to be found among the many instances of wonderful cures cited in all ages. "Expectant Attention" will here go far to explain what is not fraud. We have place for but a few examples. The first is from Dr. Paris, cited by Dr. Hammond, and is specially important on account of the prominent part taken in it by Sir Humphrey Davy. Dr. Paris says:

"As soon as the powers of nitrous oxide gas were discovered, Dr. Beddoes at once concluded that it must necessarily be a specific for paralysis; a patient was selected for trial, and the management of it was entrusted to Sir Humphrey Davy. Previous to the administration of the gas, he inserted a small thermometer under the tongue of the patient, as he was accustomed to do upon such occasions, to ascertain the degree of animal temperature, with a view to future comparison. The paralytic man, wholly ignorant of the nature of the process to which he was to be submitted, but deeply impressed from the representations of Dr. Beddoes with the certainty of its success, no sooner felt the thermometer under his tongue than he concluded that the talisman was in full operation, and in a burst of enthusiasm declared that he already experienced the effect of its benign influence through his whole body. The opportunity was too tempting to be lost; Davy cast one intelligent glance at Coleridge, and desired his patient to visit him the following day, when the same ceremony was performed, and repeated every succeeding day for a fortnight; the patient gradually improving during that period when he was dismissed as cured, no other application having been used" (Nervous Derangement, p. 224).

The second is from Dr. Carpenter, and, though the event is of over two hundred years ago, is regarded as entirely reliable. The subject was a niece of Pascal, one of the first men of science of that time. The young girl was sorely afflicted with *fistula lachrymalis*.

It was at a time when the orders of the Jesuits and Jansenists were at the height of their hostility. The account proceeds as follows:

"The poor girl had been threatened with the 'actual cautery' by the eminent surgeon under whose care she was, as the only way of getting rid of the disease of the bones of the nose, which manifested itself in an intolerable fetor; and the day was fixed for its application. Two days previously, however, the patient walked in procession before a 'holy thorn,' which was being exhibited with great ceremony in the chapel of the convent; and was recommended by the nuns, as she passed before the altar, to apply the precious relic to her eye, and implore relief from the dreaded infliction. This she did, no doubt, with the most childlike confidence and heartfelt sincerity; and her faith was rewarded by the favorable change which took place within a few hours, and which had so far advanced by the time of the surgeon's next visit, that he wisely did not interfere, the cure in a short time becoming complete. Of course, this 'miracle' was vaunted by the Jansenist party as indicating the special favor of the Virgin, while the Jesuits could scarcely bring themselves to believe in its reality. A most careful enquiry was made by direction of the court; the testimony of the surgeons and others, who knew the exact conditions of the patient both before and after the 'miracle' (that condition being patent to their observation), was conclusive; and the reality of the cure could no longer be denied, though it remained inconceivable to the Jesuits that a miracle should have been worked in favor of their opponents" (Mental Phys., p. 685).

These cures occurred without any effects having been produced upon the fibers of the impaired structures but those by the mental forces. There was no virtue in the thorn itself, nor in anything attaching to it. A thorn from a neighboring field, if this should not have been such, if surrounded with the same holy mysteries in the mind of the girl, would have been equally efficacious. And so likewise the paralytic would have realized as much good from any simple object conveniently at hand, if unknown to him, thrust under his tongue or otherwise pretentiously applied, and supposed to be the great agent of the certain cure. To impulses of mind, made strong and persistent by expectant attention upon the cure that loomed above all doubt, was due whatever change to structure was necessary to restoration.

"Miracles" of this kind may at any time be expected to occur under conditions of this character, and without, after all, *being* miracles. And there is no reason to doubt that they are of frequent occurrence, and beyond the saintly limits of Lourdes and Knock, and without their being *necessarily* the works of any order of supernatural interference.

It is, then, seen that the very *quality* of the purpose becomes imparted to the substance. The expectance of an injury is followed by the appearance of the injury expected and imaginarily seen—the fiber is seized and disturbed in a way to correspond. In the expectance of the removal of an evil—the healing of an injured part, the fiber is seized in a way to produce restoration.

That *all* should be available for such phenomena to the extent even of it being merely perceivable, is not called for. People vary greatly in other respects, and why not in this? It is a matter of mind as well as of body, and largely of education. For the best of reasons, a skeptic or one of ordinary faith in historic Christianity, could not possibly be a subject of stigmata; while one of but ordinary faith in the talismanic virtues of relics, could not be the subject of the cure by the touch of the "holy thorn;" while, reversely, one mentally conditioned to be benefited in *this* way, would probably fail to realize the paralytic's cure under the direction of *merely men of science*. And whether with or without religious sentiments, one having but ordinary believing powers, would be expected to be without results in any case.

Science, then, as the state of human attainment now is, to find bold examples of the working of this law, would look more hopefully among the superstitious, where believing has attained to greater freedom from doubt, and to greater strength; and from this less cultured class of minds, for still more striking illustrations, would look forward to an age of *greater* culture than the present, wherein the power of believing, having greater appreciation, would be nurtured into greater prominence.

By these testimonials of science, *mind as mind*, is seen to have at its command, a means, from its own seat, apart from the interlying brain and other nerves, to move external substances at will,—however limited this means, or rare the requisite conditions for its employment; also, that it has the ability, to a great extent, to characterize those movements by its special purposes. And the essential conditions being in the mind itself, whose surrounding elements are, ever, to some extent, subservient to it, it could not be necessary that the mind should be a being of this world. It might be from the next, or of any superior world beyond.

And as these means are seen to exist, thus limited, or at all, in the use of minds so limited and hampered as those of the present state, it cannot fail to be seen that with minds of the greater attainment, to be met with in the region beyond the flesh, the principle might be employed to a greater extent—to the wielding of ponderous substances or gaining measurable or joint control of the organism of a fellow mind.

But merely the *existence of the means* of intercourse between the two worlds and not the extent and the frequency of the employment thereof, is here established. *That* is a subject for further consideration.

On recalling the facts we have developed, the possibility of intercourse would consist of

ABOUT TWO GENERAL MODES.

These would be, first, mind acting on mind directly, as seen in part in Dr. Esdaile's case of mesmerism, possibly inclusive of what is called clairvoyance; and second, external phenomena addressed to the senses in conventional signs, or any manner of external demonstration. This would include whatever pertains to movements of the organism or any signs in external nature. In the first instance, the impressions received and those returned, mentally, would be the exchange of sentiments, which would be intercourse. In the second place, the mind on the spiritual side would make itself understood by addressing the senses of the one on the mortal side, much after the manner of a fellow mortal, by some form of apparition. The answer returned to the spirit would be by its discernment of the thought transpiring in the mortal party, or possibly by some mode of personal sight of the physical phenomena used in replying.

From this it would appear that they of the other side would have less difficulty in receiving our sentiments than we theirs. *They* might be in possession of our dispatches and we without even the means of knowing of it.

From the nature of the facts governing in the matter, and they are of a very tangible character, instances that might be properly termed communications from the spirit world, could not, as the world of mankind now is, be numerous, however common might be the impressions of an intangible character derived from that source. What has been said of unlikeness in minds being a hindrance to the communication of thought, applies here. So, likewise, the difficulty of rendering impressions directly of mind upon mind, in the presence of a system of waking senses filling the mind with the glaring realities of an external world, which only the severest discipline, on the part of the most favored minds, can shut out or render passive, is almost wholly insurmountable. So that nearly every door of this, the best and most available route between the worlds, is, for the time, closed and barred.

Then, when we come to consider the seizing and the occupying of the organism of a fellow mind (after the fashion of a medium), we have to first consider that the resident mind itself continues to share it and in some measure at least divides the control, so that from this cause accuracy of work would be quite impossible. But supposing, for the sake of a case, that the organism were wholly vacated for the new incumbent, there would be the almost inevitable disparity between its provisions —its special forms, and measures of transmitting power, and the new-comer who is to use it. And this trouble being the main cause of aberrations, and always resulting in some form of mental derangement, in residents of *this* world, the results of such occupancy, or co-occupancy, could not be materially otherwise than to some extent insanities, and unsafe.

It would seem that the most sane effects of spirits upon physical substances would be such as might take place outside of the aberrating influences of the living organism, which would, by what we have seen, be hardly possible with ordinary minds in either world.

DIM REALIZATIONS OF ONE WORLD BY THE OTHER.

Also, it is to be noted that in proportion to this limited means of intercourse, there must be a corresponding insensibility of each other's state or world. Where there are no adapted senses to perceive, there must be darkness or the aspect of nothingness; which fact, in respect to this case, may in one way be viewed as a painful privation, and in another—to the innumerable uninformed and weak—as a great mercy. That *we* do not see the world of the departed is due to the fact that we are without requisite senses, and additionally, that we *have* a system of senses so inexorably fixing our mind on *this*, and against which our strong yearnings are of little or no avail. The same, to some extent (and with the average new arrival there, to a *large* extent), is necessarily true of the residents of the other world, where, the nature of the mind being the same, it requires the same or corresponding facilities—senses for communication with environments. The realness of that world to those residing there, would tend to lessen the chances of clear perceptions respecting this.

Our utter diminutiveness in everything—the total absence of attainment in anything, at birth, and with nothing in respect to us that is not directly descended *from our ancestry*, makes it absolutely certain that this world is our true beginning place—that we never existed in another, nor had prior existence in this—have then never been in the world of the departed, and have nothing to remember in respect to it, save those who from us have entered there. It is otherwise with them. They go from us enlarged, experienced, and full of memories of their previous life and world, now only veiled from sight; and hence with a stronger realization of its existence and the existence of the remaining ones, with their conditions and affairs, the efforts of the mind to seize enlightening means with respect to these, would be more successfully made. Hence, we and our world and our affairs, might well be better known to them than are they and theirs to us.

However, the thought often cherished in late years, that after death we may more completely behold the scenery of *this* world, that we shall be conditioned to go all over its broad face to see its many wonders and be intimately with the people yet residing in the mortal land, is without a probability. The presences of the departed, that may in some alleged instances well be believed in, are to be otherwise understood. The principles governing the conditions of this intercourse, provide amply that such may take place; and yet that they are not immediate, personal presences, that would involve a recognition of sensuous nature generally.

The nature of the presence may be measurably comprehended by a reference to telephonic communication. Prior to this device, the immediate intercourse of friends not personally present to each other, evinced not the slightest sign of a possibility, while to-day finds them, by means of a passive wire, whispering in each other's ears by use of literally the same sounds they would employ in the same room with one another, though physical nature, hundreds of miles in thickness, is lying between them. The identification of the friend might thus be complete; and so far as this simple transaction of talking is concerned, all this intervening distance and obstruction is annihilated and the presence has much of the nature of realness, and is quite satisfying.

But not so of the surrounding scenery. It continues utterly concealed by the interlying obstructions. At each end of the wire is located a bright world,—a house and a home and inmates. Between the worlds the forces incident to the wire, afford the only means of the perception of each other.

Similarly to this, as has been seen in various illustrations, are the mental forces available in conveying impressions between remote minds, quite independent of environing substance and external senses; and of being projected upon a line to a specific individual; rendering it plainly possible to excite the most confident and satisfactory realization of the immediate personal presence of a spiritual being, though the presence be not a fact. The principle may readily explain, when the range of its possibilities are all considered, all of what may be found to be real instances of visitation of the departed, even to bodily appearances, which might, all the way from the other world, be miraged upon the consciousness of the subject.

For numerous reasons, all means of intercourse must always be less with the minds of less attainment in that culture which includes the believing powers, while no limit is to be placed upon the extent to which power of this kind may be vested in spirits of the highest orders, who are ever worthy to be trusted with its wise administration.

SPECIAL DEVICES FOR THE ATTAINMENT OF INTERCOURSE IMPRACTICABLE, DANGEROUS, ETC.

From a purely practical point of view, a few words of caution may here be parenthetically placed in the closing of this chapter. In connection with the subject of intercourse between the two worlds, in which, at all times, many have been deeply interested, with varying good and ill, probably nothing has been more deplorable than the evil results of, by unwise means, seeking to facilitate it. The understanding generally has been, that the first step to be taken was toward becoming entirely passive to impressions—toward self-dispossession of all resistance to the ingress of foreign sentiments and agencies from the invisible side,—unwisely saying to unknown applicants, "Thy will be done."

This applies not alone to where foreign control over self was sought, but, as well, where, in a circle or society of people, for the purpose of intercourse with spirits, effort was being made. And such requirement is not without good reasons. With a view to attaining the results sought, these conditions become a necessity; on the same principle that when one wishes the full benefit of a teacher or leader he renders himself passive to his wish. But in these cases the trouble is that no definite principle or character of thought is made requisition for. In passively following a guide who is known as to his sentiments, a definite and exclusive purpose is maintained; and the mind retains in possession the elements of resistance and of aggression, and remains really as invulnerable to improper sentiments as at any time; while here it is materially otherwise. Without a knowledge or a concern, as is often the case (and what the end—impartial deliverance of messages to second parties—really calls for), as to what shall be the character of the principle transmitted, one is liable to attain to little or no choice of principles or motives; and in this state, for want of its exercise, will presently be without requisite power to hold to the higher principles, and in place, will accept and go into identification with, the lower.

There is not room to here go into detail, but the results, when rightly canvassed, may generally be found to harmonize with this conclusion. If the body undergoes deterioration under the unnatural nervous processes, as is generally seen, the evil effects on the mind and morals, are at least equally, and often still more, to be deplored.

IN CONCLUSION.

The illusions of mind are so abundant and versatile, that it were difficult to determine when we have an instance of real spirit intercourse. There often are phenomena reported that are inexplicable by any other theory. But whether the conditions were adequately seen, however conscientiously reported, may, again, at times, admit of doubt. In all cases it were safer to rely on the element of enlightened reason, than on sensuous observation of alleged facts of intercourse, for the proof of a future life. For while the most unsuggestive occurrence might be a real instance of the phenomena, a strongly suggestive one might contain nothing of it.

By the very nature of the case, the conditions of it are obscure, and it may mix with a long train of our most ordinary thoughts and transactions, and with many people may make a large part of their life experiences; while others, who may be overpoweringly impressed that they are habitually having intercourse with the departed, are simply suffering from nervous disorders.

CHAPTER XVIII.

CONSIDERATION OF THE CLAIMS OF INTERCOURSE BETWEEN THE TWO WORLDS.—THE PROBABLE AND IMPROBABLE.—ITS APPEARANCE IN THE BIBLE, ETC.

THE brief space allotted to this chapter will not admit the discussion to extend far into the details of theories, and to many of the alleged facts, of intercourse between the residents of the two worlds. It is only necessary to set forth the principles that apply from the facts already submitted, with a few more facts in which their still further working may be seen.

Man may be supposed to be attended in all ages by some measure and form of the phenomena of his entire nature, sufficiently distinct for recognition. This may be supposed to differ with the changes he is constantly undergoing; not only because change in himself would have a corresponding effect upon the phenomena, but no less because, in the judgment of the controlling mind or minds above him, his *needs* undergo change. In infancy, childhood, youth, maturity and old age, the same general nature appears, but, in passing through the range of these stages, at each, some habits and uses are laid off and others taken on, always toward more personal prerogatives and wider independence. At mature infancy the child leaves the mother's nipple and takes the spoon, while from the nourishment of milk it goes to the nourishment of bread. On entering youth it releases the parent from much of the care over its own person; to the perceptive habit of thought, which was the main feature of mind to be seen in childhood, it adds the reflective—takes up abstract studies, generalizes principles, and lays out for itself in the future. The parental government remaining over it, employs less sensuous means and more mental. On entering maturity the parental government is mostly discontinued, and the ability to govern and manage is so enlarged as to include the government and management of others. On arriving at the greater period of old age, the mind leaves more fully the narrow limits of selfishness—of local and self interest—and grows cosmopolitan. From the exclusive love of the *few*—the home, the state and the nation—it enlarges to include the *nations* and the entire race; and from the deferential esteem of human superiors, enlarges to include more fully the homage of the Infinite Mind.

He who has looked upon the progress of the race, during its historic period, will not fail to see in the history of the human mind, the same graduated scale—one stage and class of wants rising upon another, without any departure from the essential nature. In the earlier ages, with individual exceptions, the aggregate mind is distinctly seen to have been weak and fickle, as is generally true of childhood; at once bringing to view the small attainment of reflective powers. The form of mind present and employed, was chiefly the perceptive and sensuous, which could be evoked only by external appearances—by some sort of outward physical sensation. Government was possible, mainly, by reference to sensuous pain. In this way, mainly, could the people be made to see and have regard to limits placed by social law. And in respect to instruction of any character, the principles were necessary to be brought within reach of this means of knowing.

Then, to establish confidence in the existence of the spiritual state of being, so important to the stimulation of mental and moral growth, philosophy, without sufficient reasoning abilities, being inapplicable, resort could only be had to addressing phenomena of this character to the eye. And supposing that there was an adequate power at the time ministering to man's needs, wisely directing for him according to the means at hand, as we would do by a child, and as it is safe to say an interested superior state would have done, we would expect to find phenomena of a spiritual character to have been more abundant and striking, with people in those far-back ages, than at the present time. Besides, the feeble condition of the general mind, with a view to attaining mental and moral development, might well have rendered the impression of spiritual phenomena indispensable.

But, as to the prevalence of *alleged* phenomena of intercourse between the worlds, in proportion to the number of the people, one age may represent as much of it as another. And if there might be more found in one age than in others, it should be in that where nervous energy is undergoing the greatest tax. All kinds of nervous affections, with their modifying effects on mental actions, as a rule, are more frequent with people who are performing more brain labor.

However, in no age may this intercourse be found to have been as common as is generally claimed by believers. After counting out the frauds, and the instances of which the explanation may be readily found by reference to the laws governing the hallucinations of mind, what will be left, will, in most cases, be found but a small percentage. All ages have had their jugglers, outwitting the most shrewd of non-professionals, drawing public patronage by imposing claims of holding intercourse with the dead. And, as a rule, to which there may be honorable exceptions, on the ground of wide prevailing frauds of this kind, professionals are to be regarded as unsafe. By a credulity rendered doubly strong by keen desire for evidence of the survival of the beloved dead, on a large class of good, intelligent people, the claims of these jugglers are imposed without difficulty, and when it may seem to them that they have guarded with due care every point.

But there are incidents at times occurring where only the purest integrity could be ascribed, such as seeing the departed alive, face to face, and perhaps engaging them in conversation, which certainly would be very convincing to any ordinary person. The conversation might, likewise, disclose, on the part of the visitant, such knowledge, of private character, present or past, pertaining to the consulting individual, as would be of great additional force. The spiritualistic literature of our own day, with its unending variety and numbers of detailed incidents would hardly supply a really stronger example. And yet the apparition might be no more than a subjective experience,—either from a strongly excited imagination—the image-creating power—or from an intensely vivid memorization, or, still more likely, from the joint occurrence of both; but be no more really a second party or outside spiritual being, than is the artist's fancy sketch, standing in the canvas, a real person. Nor would the incidental conversation, with the substance thereof, be necessarily anything different in kind from an imaginary conversation, in which the responding words necessarily also appear conveying the thoughts imagined to be existing in the imaginary party.

Hallucinations of this kind, as well as of others, in endless variety, are known to result of physical derangement. Dr. Hammond says:

"Physical causes, calculated to increase the amount of blood in the brain or to alter its quality, may give rise to hallucinations of various kinds. A gentleman under the professional care of the writer, can always cause the appearance of images by tying a handkerchief moderately tight around his neck; and there is one form which is always the first to come and the last to disappear. It consists of a male figure clothed in costume worn in England three hundred years ago, and bearing a striking resemblance to the portraits of Sir Walter Raleigh. This figure not only imposes on the sight but also on the hearing; for questions put to it are answered promptly" (Nervous Derangement, p. 233).

The doctor in this same connection and place submits an instance related in Nicholson's Journal, which is as follows:

"I know a gentleman in the vigor of life, who, in my opinion, is not exceeded by any one in acquired knowledge and originality of deep research; and who for nine months in succession was always visited by a figure of the same man, threatening to destroy him, at the time of his going to rest. It appeared upon his lying down, and instantly disappeared when he resumed the erect position" (vol. 6., p. 166).

The explanation rendered is the very natural one, that "the recumbent position facilitated the flow of blood to the brain, and at the same time tended, in a measure, to retard its exit. Hence, the appearance of the figure was due to the resulting congestion. As soon as the gentleman rose from bed the reverse condition existed, the congestion disappeared and the apparition went with it."

Apparitions from this cause, at times, are accompanied with the sensation of their tangibility—with the ability to employ force, as sometimes occurs in dreams when one undergoes an act of force administered upon his person, possibly strong enough to wake him, and from which he may have sensations of soreness following into the waking state,—being the result of a specifically directed mental shock as in the case of the bruised fingers and ankle. And here is, opportunely, also, a case well illustrating this, though meant for a somewhat different purpose, cited by the same authority. He says:

"Mayo (in "Lessons on the Truths Contained in Popular Superstitions,") relates the case of a Herr von Baczko, already subject to hallucinations, his right side weak from paralysis, his right eye blind, and the vision of the left imperfect, who, while one evening engaged in translating a pamphlet into Polish, suddenly felt a poke in his back. He turned round and discovered that it proceeded from a negro or Egyptian boy, apparently about twelve years of age. Although convinced that the whole was an hallucination, he thought it best to knock the apparition down, when he felt that it afforded a sensible resistance. The boy then attacked him on the other side and gave his left arm a peculiarly disagreeable twist, when Baczko again pushed him off. The negro continued to visit him constantly during four months, preserving the same appearance and remaining tangible, then he came seldomer, and finally appearing as a brown colored apparition with an owl's head, he took his leave" (ibid, p. 234).

Whatever may be the causes of the physical disturbances, hallucinations of this character directly result from them; they come with them and with them also disappear.

However, apparitions of the dead, not alone, are reported, but also of the living; and why should they not? Mr. Robert Dale Owen, a spiritualist, and yet a very conservative, careful, and candid writer, in 1861 wrote a work that circulated largely among thoughtful readers of this country and England, in which we find the following statement, taken from a lady, then residing in Washington, and who was the daughter of a western clergyman of well-known reputation. In every respect it seems to be well authenticated. The lady relates two such apparitions having taken place in one day at her residence in Indiana, on the bank of the Ohio River:

"On the 15th day of September, 1845," said Mrs. D., "my younger sister, J., was married, and came with her husband, Mr. H. M., to pass a portion of the honeymoon in our pleasant retreat. On the 18th of the same month, we all went, by invitation, to spend the day at a friend's house about a mile distant. As twilight came on, finding my two little ones growing restless, we decided to return home. After waiting some time for my sister's husband, who had gone off to pay a visit in a neighboring village, saying he would return soon, we set out without him. Arrived at home, my sister, who occupied an upper room, telling me she would go and change her walking dress, proceeded up stairs, while I remained below to see my drowsy babes safe in bed. The moon, I remember, was shining brightly at the time. Suddenly, after a minute or two, my sister burst into the room, wringing her hands in despair, and weeping bitterly. 'Oh, sister, sister!' she exclaimed, 'I shall lose him, I know I shall! Hugh is going to die!' In the greatest astonishment, I inquired what was the matter; and then between sobs, she related to me the cause of her alarm as follows:

"As she ran up stairs to their room she saw her husband seated at the extremity of the upper veranda, his hat on, a cigar in his mouth, and his feet on the railing, apparently enjoying the cool river breeze. Supposing, of course, that he had returned before we did, she approached him, saying, 'Why, Hugh, when did you get here? Why did you not return and come with us?' As he made no reply, she went up to him, and bride-like, was about to put her arms around his neck, when, to her horror, the figure was gone and the chair empty. *

* * It was not till more than two hours afterward, when my brother-in-law actually returned, that she resumed her tranquillity.

"Previous to this, however,—namely, about an hour before Hugh's return,—while we were sitting in the parlor on the lower floor, I saw a boy, some sixteen years of age, look in at the door of the room. It was a lad whom my husband employed to work in the garden and about the house, and who, in his leisure hours, used to take great delight in amusing my little son Frank, of whom he was very fond. He was dressed as was his wont, in a suit of blue summer cloth, with an old palm-leaf hat without a band, and he advanced, in his usual bashful way, a step or two into the room, then stopped and looked around apparently in search of something. Supposing he was looking for the children, I said to him, 'Frank is in bed, Silas, and asleep long ago.' He did not reply, but, turning with a quiet smile that was common to him, left the room, and I noticed from the window, that he lingered near the outside door, walking backward and forward before it once or twice.

* * * Shortly after, my husband, coming in, said, 'I wonder where Silas is? He must be somewhere about.' I replied, 'He was here a few minutes since, and I spoke to him.' Thereupon Mr. D. went out and

called him, but no answer. He sought him all over the premises, then in his room, but in vain. * * * At breakfast he first made his appearance. 'Where have you been, Silas?' said Mr. D. The boy replied that he had been 'up on the island fishing.' 'But,' I said, 'you were here last night.' 'Oh, no,' he replied, with the simple accent of truth. 'Mr. D. gave me leave to go fishing yesterday; and I understood I need not return till this morning; so I stayed away all night. I have not been near here since yesterday morning.'

"I could not doubt the lad's word. He had no motive for deceiving us. The island, of which he spoke, was two miles distant from our house. * *

"It is proper I should add that my sister's impression that the apparition of her husband foreboded death did not prove true. He outlived her; and no misfortune which could in any way connect with the appearance happened in the family. Nor did Silas die; nor, so far as I know, did anything unusual happen to him" (Footfalls on the Boundary of Another World, pp. 321, 324.—Lippincott & Co., Publishers).

What was the physical condition of such unusual character, in which these sisters were for the time affected so nearly alike, may not be easily determined; but the representations were so perfect in all respects as to be indistinguishable from the real persons. No instance of spirit visitation would be more unquestionable. And yet that they were *subjective*, and not at all *objective*, impressions, is too plain to be doubted. The sister followed an illusion of her own mental creation. She had rushed toward an empty chair; and the said

Mrs. D. addressed her words to empty space. When in the shadowy evening the belated boy sees a stump or a stone transformed into a crouching beast, the super-added features there appearing to complete its form, are but subjective facts of his own mind.

But there is another feature to be here considered— one of no small importance to this whole matter—which is that the same mental specter may at the same time be apparent to quite a number. Dozens, hundreds, perhaps thousands, may be quite instantaneously affected in the same manner. The fact has variously been referred to, that mind to some extent acts directly on mind; that, as, by means of an element in common, magnets exert force on each other, so minds are related and partake in some measure of each other's conception of thought,—that the same mental image to which fancy might excite one mind, might at once become common; as all along the wire, to the open offices, the same dispatch is simultaneously rattled off. Then, where people are situated together in a humdrum, passive sort of way, or in a way to make their senses and feelings run together into a common channel, with some measure of the realization of exclusiveness therewith, as on ship-board, or in a military body, a long-continued one-sided meeting, or a mediumistic circle, such phenomena would be properly expected to occur. In this way, people of good minds might readily partake of a delusion of a very surprising character.

Facts of this character are not at all uncommon.

Dr. D. H. Tuke, eminently trustworthy, is authority for the following:

"A curious illustration of the influence of the imagination in magnifying the perceptions of sensorial impressions derived from the outer world, occurred during the conflagration of the Crystal Palace in the winter of 1866-7. When the animals were destroyed, it was supposed that the chimpanzee had succeeded in escaping from his cage. Attracted to the roof with this expectation in full force, men saw the unhappy animal holding on to it and writhing in agony to get astride one of the iron ribs. It need not be said that its struggles were watched by those below with breathless suspense, as the newspapers informed us, with 'sickening dread.' But there was no animal whatever there, and all this feeling was thrown away upon a tattered piece of blind, so torn as to resemble, to the eye of fancy, the body, arms and legs of an ape" (Illustrations of the Influence of the Mind upon the Body, etc., London, p. 44).

Another illustration is given in a fact cited by Dr. Hibbert, of Edinburgh. I quote it, also, from Dr. Hammond. It is from a statement by a sea captain of Newcastle-upon-Tyne, and is as follows:

"His cook," he said, "chanced to die on their passage homeward. The honest fellow having had one of his legs a little shorter than the other, used to walk in that way which our vulgar idiom calls 'up and down.' A few nights after his body had been committed to the deep, our captain was alarmed by his mate with an account that the cook was walking before the ship, and that all hands were on deck to see him. The captain after an oath or two for having been disturbed, ordered them to let him alone and try which, the ship or he, should first get to Newcastle. But turning out on further importunity, he honestly confessed that he had like to have caught the contagion, for, on seeing something move in a way so similar to that his old friend used, and withal having a cap on so like that he was wont to wear, he verily thought there was more in the report than he was at first willing to believe. A general panic diffused itself. He ordered the ship to be steered toward the object, but not a man would move the helm. Compelled to do this himself, he found on a nearer approach, that the ridiculous cause of all their terror was a part of a main-top, the remains of some wreck floating before them" (Nervous Derangements, pp. 237, 238)

An Italian writer relates the assembling of a crowd of people on the streets of Florence to see an angel hovering in the sky; which was found to be merely a gilded figure of an angel mounted above the dome of a church. A mist had somewhat obscured the dome itself, while above it the sun was reflecting on the image.

A similar and very remarkable event of this character is also given in this connection by Dr. Hammond, and credited to the celebrated French physician, M. Parent, who died in 1836. The account is taken from Laurent in his own words substantially as follows:

"The first battalion of the regiment of Latour d'Auvergne, of which I was surgeon-major, while in garrison at Palmi in Calabria, received orders to march at once

to Tropea in order to oppose the landing from a fleet which threatened that part of the country. * * *
When they reached Tropea they found their camp ready and their quarters prepared, but as the battalion had come from the farthest point and was the last to arrive, they were assigned the worst barracks, and thus eight hundred men were lodged in a place which, in ordinary times, would not have sufficed for half their number. They were crowded together on straw placed on the ground and, being without covering, were unable to undress. The building in which they were placed was an old, abandoned abbey, and the inhabitants had predicted that they would not be able to stay there all night in peace, as it was frequented by ghosts, which had disturbed other regiments quartered there. We laughed at their credulity; but what was our surprise to hear about midnight the most fearful cries proceeding from every corner of the abbey, and to see the soldiers rushing terrified from the building. I questioned them in regard to the cause of their alarm, and all replied that the devil lived in the building, and that they had seen him enter by an opening, into their room, under the figure of a very large dog with long black hair, and throwing himself upon their chests for an instant, had disappeared through another opening in the opposite side of the apartment. We laughed at their consternation, and endeavored to prove to them the phenomenon was due to a very simple and natural cause and was only the effect of their imagination; but we failed to convince them, nor could we persuade them to return to their barracks. They passed the night scattered along the sea-shore, and in various parts of the town.

In the morning I questioned anew the non-commissioned officers and some of the oldest soldiers. They assured me that they were not accessible to fear; that they did not believe in dreams or ghosts, but that they were fully persuaded that they had not been deceived in respect to the events of the preceding night. They said that they had not fallen asleep when the dog appeared, that they had obtained a good view of him, and that they were almost suffocated when he leaped on their breasts.

"We remained all day at Tropea, and the town being full of troops we were forced to retain the same barracks, but we could not make the soldiers sleep in them again without our promise that we would pass the night with them. I went there at half past eleven with the commanding officer; the other officers were, more for curiosity's sake than anything else, distributed in the several rooms. We scarcely expected to witness a repetition of the events of the preceding night, for the soldiers had gone to sleep reassured by the presence of their officers who remained awake. But at about one o'clock in all the rooms at the same time, the cries of the previous night were repeated, and again the soldiers rushed out to escape the suffocating embraces of the big black dog. We had all remained awake watching for what might happen, but, as may be supposed, had seen nothing" (Nervous Derangement, pp. 239, 240).

In this case the minds of the eight hundred, or nearly so, were merged into a oneness of mental sensibility—into a common medium of mental sense and activity, so that the same specter would be created, and alike deported, in all these minds in the same instant of time.

In *all* the departments of the house the dog was the *same*, and each man had the *same* horrible hug from him. In one instance when, as the men protested, they were awake, in the other when they were asleep; which, however, could be of no consequence. But the officers, who were socially separate and not included in this fusion of mind, were not hallucinated—did not see nor feel the dog. That it was a nightmare, as the doctors concluded, may be true enough so far as that definition goes; but the only fact of interest remains thereby unexplained, and may be explained only on the principle I have been setting forth, here and elsewhere, and of which it is a capital illustration.

This principle of hallucination, if the necessary facts could be obtained, would, with hardly a doubt, supply a ready explanation to many of the chief wonders of "physical phenomena" in alleged spirit intercourse; while, in the imposition of fraud, by parties capable of establishing its conditions, its application would often supply an indispensable help. Under proper conditions, (into which any one who is an honest investigator may drift, provided his temperamental make-up is of the requisite impressibility), without regard to education and integrity, it spares no one.

Mr. Robert Dale Owen, previously cited, a well-known American author and statesman, and a man of special integrity and of a careful, conservative nature, it will be remembered, was made a victim of delusion in the "Katie King" affair in Philadelphia a few years ago. A quite detailed report of these interviews with "Katie" was published in the Atlantic Monthly for January, 1875, over Mr. Owen's own signature. The interviews —"forty memorable sittings"—were held in the previous June and July, and were attended by his friend, Dr. Child, and quite a number of others. At these *seances*, many "materializations" besides those of "Katie" were exhibited from the cabinet; some of whom were immediately recognized by parties present. But always the same appearances were recognized by all in the same way, as in case of any ordinary exhibition. What transpired was, indeed, most marvelous. At one time, Mr. O. was invited by "Katie" to cut off a lock of her hair, which she had separated with her own fingers. In a short time, however, the ringlet so removed by Mr. O. dissolved from view. For the benefit of other parties, she, taking the scissors herself, cut bits from her dress and veil, whereof the openings presently disappeared and the garments were whole again. She repeatedly walked out of the cabinet in the presence of all; at times advancing and touching them, and imprinting a kiss. "Once," says Mr. Owen, —"and for the last time that evening—she emerged from the cabinet, came quietly close up to me, extending a hand. I passed my left arm gently round her, and sustained her left arm, bare from the elbow, in my right hand. To the touch her garments and person were exactly like those of an earthly creature."

Still further he says of another sitting: "This evening, having observed that 'Katie' delighted in flowers, I handed her a large calla lily. She smelt it, exclaiming:

'What a charming odor!' Each time that evening when she issued from the cabinet, she carried the flower in her hand. I begged her, if she could, to repeat for us the phenomenon of disappearance, and had placed myself so that I could see her entire person without the intervention of any part of the cabinet front. It is an era in one's life, when one witnesses, in perfection, this marvelous manifestation. 'Katie' stood on the very threshold of the cabinet, directly in front of me, and scarcely nine feet distant. I saw her, with absolute distinctness, from head to foot, during all the time she gradually faded out and re-appeared. The head disappeared a little before the rest of her form, and the feet and lower part of the drapery remained visible after the body and the cross she wore had vanished. But the lily was to be seen, suspended in the air, several seconds after the hand which held it was gone; then it vanished, last of all. When the figure re-appeared, that lily showed itself in advance of all else, at first like a bright crystal, about eighteen inches from the floor; but gradually rising and assuming the lily shape as the hand which held it, and the form to which that hand belonged, first shimmered and then brightened into view. In less than a minute after the re-appearance commenced, Katie issued from the cabinet in full beauty, bearing the lily in her right hand, with the cross on her bosom, and arrayed in the self-same costume previously worn; then, coming toward us, she saluted the circle with all her wonted grace. I am not sure whether we have on record, any account of the vanishing and re-appearance, in the light, of physical objects; at least any example where it was observed so closely and in such perfection as this. During the sitting of July 10, 'Katie' allowed us again to witness this phenomenon; and, on that occasion, a bouquet which she held in her hand vanished and re-appeared, as the lily and the cross had done."

Another feature of a no less interesting character was seen in a subsequent sitting, and related by Mr. O. as follows: "During this and the sitting of June 12, the re-appearance seemed to be effected in a somewhat modified way. The form came into view first as a sort of dwarfed or condensed Katie, not over eighteen inches high; then the figure appeared to be elongated, almost as a pocket telescope is drawn to its full length, till the veritable Katie, not a fold of her shining raiment disarranged, stood in full stature before us.   *   *   *

Another phenomenon, that of levitation, which we witnessed during the sitting of July 12, and on four or five other occasions, recalled some of the old paintings of the transfiguration. Within the cabinet, but in full view, we saw Katie's entire form—her graceful garments literally 'white as the light'—suspended in mid-air. I observed that she gently moved hands and feet, as a swimmer, upright in the water, might. She remained thus, each time, from ten to fifteen seconds."

These delectable pictures, by mere sensuous evidence of spirit intercourse unsurpassed, were, no doubt, of exquisite enjoyment; and would have been so, to many, though known to be delusions. After having written the article and forwarded it, Mr. Owen was made acquainted with the fact of a fraud being at the bottom of the performances, fully confessed; when, with proper integrity, he telegraphed the publishers to withhold it, and, being too late, sent a counter-statement to the public through the dailies.

If the delusions were most remarkable, it is to be remembered that the conditions, too, were extraordinarily favorable. Much of this time spent away from the common aspect of the world, with their continuously, for weeks, drifting more and more intimately into one idea, and expectant of the same general class of objective appearances, and in view of what is possible and more or less at all times transpiring, it is not at all surprising that these should have been subjectively impressed with the same images—should have seen the same "Katie," the same flowers, draperies and movements—heard the same voice and words, etc., etc.; as the Londoners saw the same distressed monkey; the Florentines, the same mid-heaven soaring angel; and the soldiers, the same spectral dog.

EVIL SPIRITS, ETC.

But these phenomena, however, derived from the same principle, are to be regarded as wholly different from that of inspiration or of mental intercourse; from the fact that their conditions place them beyond the direct control of the will. And it may here be added that to influences of this character—involuntary and unconscious emanations of mind, more or less necessary to all its activities, indifferently drifting off upon this adjacent mental atmosphere, and becoming lodged upon a mind with a physical organism, with the liability of being unadapted thereto, and thus being transformed in the organism into vicious insanities—might at times be due those peculiar disturbances that apparently imply the presence of an external vicious spirit, as demoniacal possession, and witchcrafts, of the past, and the possession of mediums by low spirits—as is often alleged—in our day;—there being at the same time, no external spirit directly concerned, while, too, the mind from whom the influence unconsciously drifted away, might be immaculately pure. But the principles of ordinary insanity sufficiently cover all such cases, without reference to agencies from another sphere.

TRANCE MEDIUMS.

And here, before closing under this head, a word at least requires to be said in respect to the claims of intercourse through trance-speaking mediums; though the trance medium and the somnambulist so commonly represent the same class of phenomena, as to rarely, if ever, require separate classification. That thoughts from the other world to this, may sometimes find favorable conditions of this character, is, of course, possible. But the occasional brilliancies displayed, that render the claim that these are influenced from the other world, plausible with some, are not worthy of reliance.

So far as I have seen, thought produced in that state is so aimless and little connected as to indicate epileptic brain actions. But, aside from the notoriety, little importance can be attached to such operations at best. The productions generally might well be inferior to those of their own sober efforts.

We have, however, seen that minds from the other world sustain such relation to those of this, that, with the average, as they live and die, there are conditions, though seldom, where tangible intercourse would be possible and to be expected; and it may mingle with the class of phenomena we have just been considering. Innumerable diamonds, in dimensions of dust, may be scattered throughout all the sand-fields of the globe; but of Kohinoors, the world exhumed, might not supply a dozen.

Profane history is not without instances, unavoidably told, of definite mental presentiments and counsels, of great interest, that to mere human means of discernment were quite impossible. The career of Joan of Arc, with the divinations of coming events in her military career against the English in France, her being directed by "voices" from minds of superior military ability, that she came to the field of war an unlettered peasant girl from the wild interior, are as truly matters of history as are the campaigns of Napoleon.

SPIRIT INTERCOURSE AS PERTAINING TO THE BIBLE.

In these manifestations, as they occur in the common course of human events, there is noticeably little unity of conception or of motive,—no general policy nor plan, nor common objective end. They mainly pertain to local and individual affairs and are of a temporal character, and not, therefore, attributable to any forecasting, general order of management, nor to any highly attained individual mind. The opposite of this is manifest in that which pertains to the Biblical record. Over those thousands of years the prophecies and teachings from this source, have maintained the most inflexible adherence to the same theology, anthropology, and ethics, the same motive and objective end. On those ever changeful human nature could make no impression. The last and the first of this long line of prophets, seers and apostles, were in essentials in strict accord as to their teaching and manner of life. To maintain this unity through all these ages, against continuous circumstances so strongly hostile, and when the best human elements of the times were mentally and morally so unequal to their appreciation, required an immense mental force of high order, to be continually applied. Besides, the principles which they taught and the spirit that mainly characterized those recognized on this roll, were such as are at this greatly advanced day, by our best minds, being pronounced unsurpassed.

Such, then, is plainly a phenomenon, and due to a corresponding cause—an agency of unlimited supremacy over both man and his environments, actuated by a vast motive of beneficence to the race; from earliest times maintaining a moral light and life-giving principle in the world that should unfold the civilization that now is and that which is to come. And that the means of intercourse, found in readiness existing in the nature of things, as we have seen, when they were or could be made sufficient therefor, should have been employed in all this, were more reasonable than to suppose special ones needlessly to have been extemporized. Hence, that indications of epilepsy, catalepsy, trance, etc., should be discovered to have characterized the deportment of even the most celebrated of these in their times of prophesying, etc., as scientific writers have claimed, were properly to be expected; and could detract nothing from the highest estimate placed upon their mission. Also, that certain alleged necromancies and divinations, then widely prevalent, were strictly forbidden by these, when they themselves held intercourse with angels, is no evidence of a purpose to monopolize the intercourse between the two worlds, but of the false character of these pretensions, and their tendency to evil in community.

And, lastly, there is really no call for belief that any of the angelic visitations recorded in the Bible, were in character such as not to come under the law that personal appearances or other demonstrations of spirit presence, are alone by mental impressions from that world, fixed upon the minds or physical substances of this world. However striking and real their appearance among men in the flesh, they could not have personally disappeared from their own world to which, necessarily, they are allied by senses as we are to this.

CHAPTER XIX.

Approximate Analysis of Real Life in the Land Immortal.—Changes that are Possible; that are Probable; that are Improbable; that are Impossible.—Bodily State and Advantages.—Death and "Old Age" Abolished.—Palpable Surroundings.—Recognitions, Reunions and Companionships.—Education and Worship.

AS to the first meaning of that wonderful word, "Self"—of the conditions, and their philosophy, that underlie and form into "Self," our ignorance, without the trace of a hope, must be as enduring as our existence. But happily *after* its institution, the laws that determine its qualities, necessities, possibilities and destinies, are as securely in hand as is the simplest principle in nature; and what parts of them our understanding has not yet fully traced, are, with a fixed certainty, of the ever interesting order of "*the knowable unknown.*"

In respect to the aspects of life in the coming existence, many of the details must remain unknown till those sceneries shall directly fall upon us through the new organs for our senses, which, taking the place of these now relating us with this existence, shall locate us in that. It must, also, be considered that on arriving there, all may realize, perhaps, prominent expectations unfulfilled.

CHANGES THAT ARE POSSIBLE.

As to changes that are possible in the next world, considered with respect to this, the general fact that has already been referred to, may be noted, that in the higher order of substance, passive elements may well reveal themselves in a greater variety of characters and uses. In this fact, mainly or alone, could we look for changes or the cause of changes that are not to be anticipated and defined from this state. And these, in class, can only be few, and without influence upon the radical nature of life itself. They are only of *environment*, over which life's own conservative laws are, throughout, finally supreme. The forces of those superior passive elements or environments might, if essentially the same, be still differently balanced, and correspondingly affect the mode and the aspect of their existence. For example, the densities and gravities might, by that means, vary from those of ours. And how soon a not very great change in respect to these in ours, might cause a material shifting in the modes of existence here below. Our mineral environment of the present state is as it is by the mere fact that the invested forces are, in just this way, balancing each other. The major part of it (so far at least as our world is concerned) is sufficiently dense to be relatively fixed and firm, of which forms derived from it are to quite an extent stable and continuous; which is a matter quite essential to the development of individual being; mentally as well as bodily. But much of it, too, is fluid; and much is volitant, to an unlimited extent. One part of these is rolling in the external cavities of the earth, too heavy and fixed to rise; another is drifting in the form of clouds, resting on the bosoms of atmospheric strata—mountain ranges, in a state of nebulæ. Other forms are constituting the atmosphere, with its burden of impalpable dusts and gases, extending over all one continuous envelope, and reaching out into the inaccessible ethers above.

With a not very great change of temperature modifying their forces, in some of these substances the change would be quite important. Let it be the water for example: and a not very great increase of the general heat would transform all the oceans into vapor; or if it were a decrease, they would be beds of ice-rock. Should, by some circumstance, the same relaxation to the forces of this element take place without the agency of heat, rendering essentially the same results, and, to many classes of animals, life would become impossible or their modes of being would be greatly changed, with transformations of their organisms. But suppose, on the same principle, that some fact of nature should transpire by which the gravity of atmospheric air would be increased to nearly equal that of water, what unthought-of changes might not then take place in the matter of locomotion; seemingly, without much inconveniencing any of the orders of life now existing? Water-breathing and air-breathing animals would, generally, be restricted to their several elements only so far as would be necessary for nourishment, or to suit the sense of congeniality. Man, himself, with little more effort than is required for his ascending the water, could, also, ascend the air.

While we can well see how in our world such an arrangement would be greatly inferior to the one existing, —that much greater would be the impurities of the atmosphere, and that less of inspiring beauties would be possible, we may safely judge that in a higher order of substance, through a more perfect adjustment of elements in normal relation with each other, the tendency would be to increase fixedness and to render the separation of extremes more wide and complete. Hence, there would be less antagonism and more reciprocity in the forces. And hence, with all the elements in greater purity and completeness of adjustment, there, also, would be a greater stability of their modes and greater freedom, by which they would be more available to the vital agents, and be subject to greater variety of arrangement of whatever character.

In these, then, we see indicated, though not specifically defined, not alone changes that are possible, but that are, also, probable. That is, in the very nature of these facts, as to substance, it becomes quite necessary to foresee modifications in the future body of nature, harmonizing with those provisions. And added to this, as a matter of course, must follow the consideration that the environment will carry its peculiarities into the appointments of the future body for man. Considering, again, for a moment, as to how the embodiment of self is effected here, we see that, first and last, it is achieved by assimilating forces working involuntarily and insensibly upon surrounding material substances, bringing them into the required combination. Reference to those forces, by way of consciousness, is had alone by the sense of hunger excited along the preliminary passages of food, calling for the substances they require. This hunger to appease, we place the desired aliment into the passages, out of which it is taken and placed in position.

Now, the assimilation of substances into requisite bodily form, is in any state unavoidable. But the same mode of access to the required substances may not be always necessary. Artificial arrangements for its procuring may not always be required. And the breaking of bulk by an internal chemistry is in some conceivable cases unnecessary. Water and salt, though of eminent service to the economy, undergo no digestion, but pass in required measures directly on to their destinations. Oxygen, in large quantities, is partaken of independently of the alimentary system, by the great endosmotic filter of the lungs, and by the same organ, exosmotically, is its effete product eliminated. And at times when the stomach is insufficient for its function, oleaginous food, in considerable amounts, is taken through the skin, by its being externally laid on; and through that organ in return, is much of the worn-out material cast away.

Apparently, then, it is from the low and unrefined order of the environing substance, that the spacious internal organs for receiving and dissolving massive aggregates, are called for, in our present embodiments.

Then, in so far as this, and in whatever is dependent thereon, change is probable in the appointments of the future body. And however there may be, in respect to minor matters, other changes in it, in no other respect is there any so probable as in that which concerns the means of subsisting it from its surrounding elements.

The same principle, too, might be expected to apply to individuals of lower forms of life, should they appear. This is rendered probable from the necessity of the existence of more direct and immediate adjustment, and the more ready subservience to adjacent higher forces on the part of elements of a higher order; as is foreseen of the elements of our present surrounding, when they shall be more advanced on the route to that ultimate harmony of their primal parts, toward which all their unceasing movements under our eyes are tending to finally bring them. Then, too, from this it would seem probable that bodily subsistence might be more by involuntary processes, and of less tax on time and the mental energies.

But, let the changes in the new condition be these or any others which this line of facts might legitimately suggest, there need be no regrets in their anticipation. In neither of the changes that our bodies have undergone in the natural way from childhood up, though quite numerous, has our estate of happiness suffered depreciation. From them has come no inconvenience, unless it has been from their worn-out condition in old age. In early infancy the thymus gland is a large, active and highly necessary organ, which with age wholly disappears, as the need of it is discontinued by the arrival of new conditions. But in parting with the old and entering upon the new form of organism, nothing is seen to indicate any change in the sense of sameness in-self or in the tenor of enjoyments.

CHANGES THAT ARE IMPROBABLE.

Under this head a few general facts will cover all that it will be of importance to refer to. It will be improbable that that existence will be changed from an essentially cosmical or world-like character and aspect. However widely sundered one order of substance may lie from another, from the requirements of its being, certain facts found in one must exist in respect to the other. To its parts there must be an underlying sameness, co-equality, and adherence, in order to have expression at the same plane of being. These facts in passive substance,—substance, which, for its special placement or direction, depends on the impingements of vitality in some form—will, necessarily, establish its extension in space, not alone, but also its gravitation, with oscillations occasioned by the diversity of the special elemental qualities or parts, comprehended by this underlying sameness. Then, densities, fixities, shapes and all the essential properties and habits of substances, seen in our world and determined by the same basic facts, are belonging to the next existence, also,—if passive substance of any form shall have representation there; which the presence of the ever-continuing rational mind, requiring this aspect of being for food, seemingly makes a necessity. As these are *mental requirements*, it is in the highest degree improbable that substance of this character should be discontinued from the mind in all its unending future. That we should, then, at any time in all our unending career in a spiritual existence, find our surroundings to impress us as materially unlike a body of nature—a world—a universe of worlds, is to be set down as highly improbable.

Besides, considerations of number, figure, relatively, etc., are inseparable from all forms of thought or mental procedure. And these can find no prompting expressions in a nature outside of the mind, but in substance of this character. Hence, the ever growing mind may never lay this book of nature aside.

We now come from this to the next general fact in order in considering the *im*probable in place of the probable: Again that of our embodiment in that world. A probable modification has been arrived at. But an essential *unlikeness* in form and feature the facts import as improbable. For substantial reasons, the organism as to form, uses, and aspect, cannot be expected to differ very essentially from that of this world, when here it is in its complete and normal state. Self is constituted in definitely characterized forces determining the type of being, which can be no less fixed and enduring in the character of their arrangement, than is the being itself. These forces, too, necessarily give character to form in harmony with that arrangement. And this type, as has been seen, is *prior* to the embodiment. It shapes the external body on the internal pattern.

In the lower forms of substance these forces are necessarily more hampered, and, in their results, more defective,—deviating into physical excesses in some parts and into deficiencies in others,—possibly into "mimic" developments in some instances, and in others where the circumstances call for such, into the formation of temporary organs. But as is seen of the vegetable, that the embodiment is more perfect where the conditions for its proper development are more fully present, what change of our bodily form would be occasioned by the presence of a higher order of elements, could only be to that which would be more pleasing—to more symmetry and harmony.

And still further, it is to be noted that the existing functions of the several senses will depend on embodiment in proper organs, to bring them into correspondence with that future body of nature,—that these must be from the elements of that nature itself, of which the similarity of properties might well render those organs faithful reminders of their earthly predecessors. Embodiment is, hence, not only a necessity, but at least a close, recognizable resemblance is equally a necessity. And among the improbabilities, in respect to that state, will be the loss of the bodily means of recognizing those previously known. In corroboration of this, we may further note that in the properties so determined upon in respect to that inner body of nature, are provided all the conditions that are known to us as necessary to sound, light, and heat—temperature. Then organs of vision and of hearing, as well as the organic arrangement for general sensibility, are called for,—to which we may safely add the remainder of the list of the sense arrangements pertaining to our present existence, as they, also, refer to material conditions embraced in the generalizations named.

As truly as the lobster puts forth a new claw in place of the one removed, the dog would replace the missing foot on the airy part at which he vainly licks, and the man would replace with a new one, the amputated arm, removed from the one he still feels is there, if these were as closely related with this order of passive substance as is the lobster. That not being the case, which can be the only reason, the forces of these sensations of the limbs still existing, subjective though they may be, as claimed by some, might well be expected to find the processes of reclothing themselves available in a higher order of substance.

CHANGES THAT ARE IMPOSSIBLE.

These, likewise, for the present, it will be sufficient to refer to in but a few particulars. It may well be believed that while passive substance is all the time shifting into new relations, change in the nature of the elements themselves is a permanent impossibility. And all existences that are continued into the next state, if they are favored with the same liberty, will acquit themselves of the same deportment. When, therefore, we have seen the rational mind in one world, we have seen it for all worlds wherein the liberty is the same.

In the world of most restraint we must see it in less of itself; while still by its shifting therein from one condition to another, it fails not to display its nature sufficiently well to be safely judged of in respect to its endowments, and its character and aspect when existing at its best, and which must be its final attainment.

Speaking of the rational mind, necessarily includes all its co-attributes of sentiment—the various affections, and the moral, reverential, and religious senses, which are found with that order of mind alone. And in the existence of these, as of mind, must be included their requirements and the essential modes of their gratification and enlargement. So that likewise when we see man with these in one world we see him so in all worlds wherein his nature has equal freedom.

In short, then, that man should appear in the next world, the embodiment of a nature that is not that of his present, with the sentiments and tendencies not the same, so far as the conditions might be the same, is, from a human standpoint of view, impossible. Should the conditions of that world be more favorable to his nature than are the present, then, too, would his best estate in this, the most completely represent his state in the next, and the dispositions and demeanors of life at its best in this world, would be the most perfect exhibition to be seen on earth, of what is his real life in the Land Immortal.

That the conditions of the next world are in advance of those pertaining to this, need not here be re-argued. That it lies in advance on the line of our progress—our mental and all sentient enlargement—and is placed to meet the needs of our coming growth, is sufficient. The thinking mind recognizes no requirement of proof more conclusive. Hence, the first general fact that strikes the realizing sense is that in all respects life is by the change raised to greater advantages and will display more of its real self. So, then, in proceeding to give an approximate view of life beyond the tomb, we have to proceed to answer the question as to what might be the indication of life at its best. The extreme classes of mankind point oppositely. The low barbarian regards his the favored class and state, and points with deep disdain to the civilized state of life, as one of wide departure from the simple and the true, while his more enlightened brother is deploring that state, and striving to raise him to his own. Generally there is an agreement of the civilized or partially civilized, that what is comporting with the Christianity of the gospel, is life at its best. At any rate, that which would be the most intelligent, just, benevolent, and refined would be regarded as such. If leaving unconsidered the adaptations to the spiritual, these would be agreed upon by less believing men of science, as life at its best.

But all nature sets forth that growth of all the constituent parts, in harmony, is necessary to attainment toward the perfected—the uppermost state. The ungrown plant is by none regarded at its best. Neither when growth has been confined to but a part of its structure, leaving others unmatured. To this principle, all must agree that man is no exception. But to this there is still another criterion to be added, which may be, besides, a help in determining when all of man is included in the growth—the enlargement.

Measures of force are to be consulted. With the *most* attainment, in whatever department of being, resides the most power,—from it proceeds the greater—the most overmastering—influence over the elements of its kind. From the less, in the given time, only less could proceed. Then in tracing the forces that have influenced, not the greatest number of individuals, but the greatest aggregate of mind, the clue will lead, necessarily, to the minds or mind of the greatest attainment. In our age the aggregate of mind is immense over all other ages; and its special development, and where it rises above all contrast with the remainder of the world, and completely overpowers it, is abruptly limited with the communities where the popular mind is brought most directly facing the open gospels,—where, by the minds holding chief control over the great mass, an almost universal deference is shown to the central character in those gospels. The control seen in this deference has not been attained, and is not continued without force of the requisite nature. If the force consists in purely ideas, then, as we know, ideas throughout have not the *same* measure of force; and the difference must be founded on a corresponding difference in the measures of power possessed by the minds issuing them; which would determine the most attained mind to be that of Jesus in the gospels. But deference is equally if not more to the *life*, than ideas of Jesus.

Then, again, the effect of this *life* is achieved by force of a requisite nature; and that from other lives equal effects are not following, is only from the fact that in measures of this force they are not his equals; and that, in attainment, the life of Jesus is in the same measure transcendent over theirs. He may be regarded as merely human or as superhuman, it is the same, so far as this law is concerned.

Next in reigning influence over the same lives, have been and are his immediate disciples—the Apostles—who are deferred to next to him. And always, circumstances being equal, the one who is the most nearly the Jesus type of life, is the one having the largest influence on the body of mankind. But so commonly are the operations of this force beneath the face of affairs, that, by the common mind, its magnitude is not seen. It is, however, ascertained, and, by the duly reflective, may not be doubted. What the influence of a superficial storm is to that of an ocean-deep tidal wave, is that of Cæsar to that of Paul, on the human world. And, always, influence is force, derived from adequate sources. The disparity of their effects but denotes the disparity of the *attainments* of these two great lives of history.

Then it were necessary to conclude that what Jesus and Paul in theory and life recognized as parts of the nature of self, requiring equal culture to bring man to his best, is of higher authority than would be the claims from lives of less attainment; and that worshiping and supplicating the Supreme Being is based on a part of our nature, and requires practice and culture as much as does the element of ethics or esthetics, or pure intellect. And now it being understood what are the elements in attainment in life at its best in this state, we have an outline view of the workings of life in the next,—upon what tendencies it is employed, seeking their fulfillment.

THE BODILY STATE.—DEATH ABOLISHED.

But before entering upon any details, some further reflections upon the personal state seem in place. Considerable has already been said concerning the embodiment, without referring to certain facts that bear upon its continuance—whether it is indefinite, or eternal, or terminates within a quite uniform limit of time, as is the case with our present bodies. What can have any bearing upon that with any certainty, is what may be derived from the facts of life itself, together with the conclusions that have been arrived at in respect to the cosmical substance of that state, and what are the facts concerning death in this existence. In brief, the separation from the body in this world, as generally understood, takes place by some disqualifying changes in the bodily substances,—as by way of accidents suddenly throwing them apart, sometimes very instantaneously and utterly; or, more commonly, by the intrusion of foreign agencies, as poisons or infusorial parasites, in one way or another, consuming or otherwise disqualifying the fiber; which may take but a few moments, or it may require many years. These intrusions are, of course, in the lower order of substance more easily made, as to the chemical poisons and the living germs, from the facts that *extremes* are more *intimate*, and the conservative forces are less vigorous to exclude. Also, from facts referred to, violences are more common and extreme in lower substances, adjustments of elements being less free and regular.

In the earlier states, life is less secure, though the organism is more free from disturbing agencies. The feebler self with its feebler forces, lays hold less strongly on the surrounding material. In the enlarged self the efficiency is increased, the adhesion is firmer, and the control is more complete. So much does this control increase with the attainment of life, that though the foreign elements must be much more abundant, and the destroying forces greatly increased, with sunderings and paralyzations much more extensive, what remains is held with a force never so great. Somewhat Phœnix-like, half successful effort is made at evoking a newness out of the old, by the partial restoration of sight, hearing, and other senses, as well as at times a partial replacing of the organism in other respects.

A professional friend of the writer has several times related to him the case of a lady of his acquaintance in Canada who had recovered sight, hearing, teeth, and hair from nearly a total loss of these, above the age of seventy.

Thus, then, in this world, life attains to the extent of maintaining a very sensible competition with these hostilities which in these substances are so specially strong and finally succeed wholly in demolishing the organism, revealing, distinctly, a principle that under more favorable conditions would result in the permanent embodiment of self.

Then, in the next, where, by the nature of the elements, as seen, such violent movements as here take place, could have no occasion and would be without occurrence, and where substances, by a more free and direct adjustment, would not drift so far into wrong relations, producing antagonisms, as here, and where with greater attainments, the pertaining forces of life would be more effective in their conservative efforts, bodily dissolution would have little visible cause. It is, to be sure, not claimed how much higher that order of substance is than this, nor how much higher is required for such a state of things; but it is to be remembered that it lies so remote as to be without a sensuous trace being discernible from this department of existence, and could hardly be so near as to involve the necessity of any more death. But that in rising time there should be no departures, farther inward, constituting entrances into still further invisible worlds of still higher relations of being, is not provided against by this conclusion. On the contrary, the line of facts that has governed all conclusions in this work, seems to strongly imply such changes. Not that the endless peopling, in any numbers imaginable, on the same plane of substance, could make any impression on the infinite space, and that over-crowded conditions would necessitate such departures, but that such might be incidental in the processes of endlessly attaining. To be sure, higher orders of substance might always occupy the same space simultaneously with the lower, without impinging, while *embodiments* only, might have sensible relation with space. But all this I would have regarded as problematical only, and in no sense as essential.

OLD AGE ABOLISHED.

And still further, with no death-producing causes remaining, manifestly there would be left none from which decrepitude could result to the accumulation of any measure of age. On the contrary, increase of age, in a general way, would stand for increase of attainments, whereof instead of more paralysis, wrinkles, and fadedness there would be greater perfection, and more vivacity and bloom. Intelligence, affection, moral, esthetical and religious senses, all in their several forms enlarged, involving higher qualities and more ardor in each, could only result in more commanding graces of life and correspondingly more charms to its embodiment. And though it is not to be understood that the power of life over life is from the condition of the body, but from life only, regardless of whether there is a body about or not, in the event of a body existing, perfections of the person are very desirable supplements. There is, then, satisfaction in anticipating, in the conditions that remedy, in the next life, the evils of old age in this, equally, relief from encumbering defects of body that harass so many of our beautiful lives here.

PALPABLE SURROUNDINGS.

From the order of facts we have followed, a tactile

relation with that external existence is a necessary conclusion,—to not alone look upon, and otherwise passively perceive it, but to impinge upon and devise with respect to it—to direct and shape it to ends. What these shapings may be like, is not to be said. The very first essay might be the most wide of the mark. But passive forms of substance, for their best state and results, await intelligent direction. Our world under the guiding hand of man, expresses beauties that were otherwise not to be expected. Save in the aspect of its vast, unwieldy developments, as mountains, rivers, seas, and the heavenly expanse, our most gratifying impressions from nature are those of its modification by art. The beautiful gardens and parks are not met with in the wild confusion of nature in its spontaneous states. Foliage and bloom, rich as at times they are in the state of undirected nature, do not there equal those which in their native regions are receiving the judicious care of man. The same is true of animals under domestication. Though their culture is at times eccentric, and in a sense against nature, from which they return at first opportunity, still, as impressing the intelligent eye, from the state of culture they are more pleasing and helpful than from the undirected and the unrestrained condition.

It is, therefore, hardly to be doubted that man, in the next state, will avail himself of his never failing superiority, for the larger gratification of his increasing desire for knowledge, and for his rising tastes, to direct the elements of that nature to higher achievements, and thus minister more largely to those wants than would result from their unaided efforts. It may be judged necessary that he should thus minister to his own bodily needs, possibly in ways approximating those of his ministry to those needs in this world, or it may not; but a nature, cultivated and wrought into uses above where spontaneity would carry it, would hardly fail to be found where man's dominion extends over it.

RECOGNITIONS.

As to the ability of merely recent acquaintances recognizing one another in the other world, the fact of it was referred to and substantially settled, while speaking of embodiments there. With continued likeness of person, of perceiving powers, and of judgment, there could be no failure about it. There could be little more difficulty in recognizing a friend whom, because of *death*, we have not seen for some years, than whom, by one of the many causes of separation in this life, we have not seen for the same time. From some considerations, the difficulty would not be as great. Let it be that the party to be recognized has been subjected to much sickness, or to disfiguring accident, which would not apply with respect to the next world, and the difficulty might be greater here than there. Here, sometimes, under such circumstances, it fails. In some cases the liabilities would be the same there. Let the separation have taken place many years previous in the early infancy of the party; or let the party have been subjected to the influences of a greatly changed mode of life for quite a term of years, the identification would be very difficult if not in some instances quite impossible, whether in this world, or in the next. A large part of the race die in tiny infancy and in early youth, before being is fully outlined. And this outlining—this extension of the figure to the full enlargement, and the completion of the person, might, in the coming state, as here, result in a loss of recognition. But, perhaps, little more would it occur from this cause than it would in a corresponding time from the enlargement and finish of life itself,—retaining, perhaps, little of the habits and manners of life in the previous state, on which to fix a recognition.

Such separations, as pertaining to parents and children, though rare, are now and then reported of our present world—babies being stolen or by other means taken from them, not to be rejoined with them till after many years. Sometimes, as in the early settlements of our country, such kidnappings are perpetrated by savages, and so far as the nature of the child will allow, it will be made into a savage, losing, if it had attained it, the mother tongue and the recollection of parents and kindred. Identification of such is necessarily difficult, if not impossible, in this life.

In cases of such complete separation, the evidences relied on for identification usually are permanent marks on the person, or the accents in speech, or other congenital traits. Where it has not extended beyond the usual means of recognition, family names, appearances, habits and events, with sometimes contemporary witnesses, are referred to. In these respects, the other world manifestly has advantages over this. To say nothing of the frequent possibilities of the departed reading the conditions and general character of the events incident to remaining friends, the constant stream of arrivals from the lower country might allow of no break in the chain of social evidence from the earliest to the latest comer. Besides, the family mental traits and tastes are usually so intimately interwoven with self, as to long survive under the strongest modifying influences. And, naturally, these would be by none more readily detected than by those of like nature. In a higher state, also, congenital traits would be more pronounced, while the ability to note them would be keener. We find it, then, possible to identify in the next world more reliably than in this; whatever unforeseeable facts might render recognition for a time less clear.

And these, taken together, namely: that there is an unbroken chain of eye-witnesses, extending even to parties separated and lost to each other in this world, and that peculiarities that are permanent, and consistent with the utmost goodness of character, are there more legible than here, what yearnings for recognition may not then in time be gratified?

REUNIONS.

The question of reunion, if not the very foremost in respect to the future, with enlightened minds, could hardly be less than second to existence itself. Few harder strains has human nature borne than those pertaining to yearnings for the departed; possibly little thinking how important may be those strains of longing as helps in preserving the very tie of interest on which the earlier coming together again depends—that there are conditions in which these yearnings are legible to some extent by the minds of the departed.

In considering the matter of reunion, philosophical inquiry might recall that physical nature exists in many grand divisions,—that there exist not only innumerable and immeasurable systems of worlds that might be supposed inhabited now or at some time, but that the same world, as ours, might be so conditioned as to practically bar one class of people in and another out; and that it might be substantially the same with the corresponding material of the spiritual universe. And certainly of divisions there, there is at least the greatest probability; but, evidently, not with restrictions in the same measures to its inhabitants that our state places about us, for reasons already referred to. However, supposing differences to exist, and with reference to suiting grades of spiritual development, the tendency from the lower to the higher life could not be permanently intercepted.

But though, in our world, cosmical conditions re-act upon human life—elevating or depressing it, and its influences have been so strong as to, in the long years, have broken up the family of man into races of great differences, yet in the same country, in the same neighborhood, and in the same house, may be found, at least may be *placed and continued* quite indefinitely, the lowest and the highest man of our planet. Hence, in a world or in a universe where elements are more equally balanced, differences of conditions in localities might well not be of sufficient consequence to make an important difference in the direction people should take from this existence to the next.

Also, differences in individuals, inclusive of our world, exist only in the measures and forms of their attainments, which are as various as the race is numerous, ranging from the highest intelligence to the lowest ignorance, and from the most lovely virtues to the most abhorrent vices and crimes. And for the universal good, the elevation of the lowest, too, is required; and the kind offices thereof being helpful to the elevation of the higher, the same higher order of environment might well be even the best place for the culture and discipline, of whatever character, needful to be administered; there being no difference in the constitutional nature and ultimate requirements in all the family of man.

It is then to be judged that while the several casts of life, from sameness of measures and forms of attainment, resulting in more nearly the same shades of thought and sentiment, would tend to gravitate toward communities and departments, there could no fixed, separate states result. Nor would arrivals and reunions be determined by affinities for such states alone, but, as well, by reasons of previously established interests. And while attachments from this cause may not be permanent in all coming time, those lives who have by any proper means become to each other objects of greatest interest, will, by the best reasons, be foremost to reunite. Such, by the facts cited in the remarks on recognition, will not have been really separated. To the survivor, it would be a separation more than to the departed, who, besides the more favored condition for, at times, reading impressions derived from the life below, has intelligence by arrivals ever continuing to be made, while none—certainly not with equal reliability—are returning below.

It is to be remembered, too, that the departed are in a state more favorable to ardor in love, in interest, in solicitude, that greater warmth, in that holier element, exists with the party above for the party below, than these heavy elements will allow to be cherished and returned. It would, then, be but in strict accordance with the established facts of nature, that the event of a loved one from below entering among the scenes of the next world, would be a theme of joy in the circle above, only mitigated by the sorrow of bereavement in the circle below,—that it would be anticipated by preparations made in the spirit in which friends make ready for the arrival of loved ones from abroad,—that when the departure here and the arrival there take place, the first objects upon which the new orbs would rest would be the faces and forms of the most intimately dear ones, perhaps, long associated with the dead.

COMPANIONSHIPS.

In a previous chapter it was shown that human life is no exception to nature in all the orders of it known, in that its individuals are in possession of a principle of mutual adherence. And not only is this adherence in aggregate, but it exists in special forms, as between attributes and qualities. That is, human life being human life, alone is cause of a certain general attachment to it by a human life—a drawing toward it as a magnet toward a magnet; that all things being equal, an artist is specially drawn toward an artist; and of these, again, by further specializing, a sculptor is drawn toward a sculptor, a painter toward a painter, a musician toward a musician. And thus might the illustration be indefinitely continued. The intelligent have attractions for the intelligent, the benevolent for those of benevolence, and the refined for those of refinement; and so also, though this needs qualifying, the ignorant, the selfish, and the coarse and vulgar, each is drawn to his kind. Strictly considered, it does not admit to be said that the ignorant and the low generally, are *drawn* together. That is, it cannot be said that the reverse of intelligence, which is neither a function nor a quality, but merely vacuity—nihility, can *draw*. And so of selfishness and coarseness, they denote *absences* rather than *entities*. That in such respects individuals stand for *nothing*, is the truth rather than that what so distinguishes them, is a *something*. Great ignorance is rather the name of a corresponding *lack* of intelligence, than the name of a *something*. So, too, of "great coarseness," "great vulgarity" or "great vice." It is, then, not possible that these conditions in themselves have drawing qualities; and the real fact in respect to what may seem so, more likely is this: That these, from inability to be allied with people of attainment in these respects, on account of the small interest they are able to supply, are in a sense ejected and *forced* upon their kind, to form communities with views and modes of life corresponding to those levels. Such aggregates of common sentiments and common causes breeding sympathies, become drawing forces in themselves; which constitutes an explanation of evil society and its seeming power to attract. But here, still, intelligence attracts intelligence, benevolence, benevolence, and virtue, virtue. Deference is bestowed upon the most shrewd and cunning; and he who is generous and disposed to deal fairly among their class, is regarded with distinction, etc.

We, then, here see the law of society crystallizations —of special friendships and companionships, above the general love and interest one feels for his fellows, as such. The law is, also, seen to be the result of principles that are permanently inseparable from life. And, moreover, instead of a tendency to more exclusiveness and greater remoteness from others, it becomes, in the wisdom that must in higher attainments characterize it, a most effective means to enlarge the love and interest for the general mass; as to all real culture the enlarged powers of appreciation render not only special friendships more intimately dear, but the outside relationships of life proportionately rise in interest—are more nearly approached and more included. As when we, with a larger and purer telescope, increase our means of seeing, we come not only nearer to the more immediate planets of our own system, but to the remoter ones therein, and to the farthest stars. Also, environment can never be wholly the same to two minds, from the fact that they must occupy separate standpoints, and that its features, in all times and places, are not the same, nor can be. Plainly, then, minds can never fall into sameness of balance, temperament, and taste, but diversity in these respects, like diversity in sounds of music, will always contribute its sweet impressions upon life.

Individuals, then, might, without special conditions of attachment—without considerations of necessary arbitrary bonds—drift away upon unlike currents, which, though rambling more or less apart, are never lost from the tide. But, again, arbitrary enactments from proper sources of authority, limiting and directing conduct, are a constant necessity to finite life. We are always in *our* modern day, with our unknown before us, with our nature less perfectly understood by ourselves than certain others understand it; with no means, but guardian authority, to direct us, and by which to find the best way. Then, too, error is ever *less* right than the truth, and less to the purposes of life; and to incur it is to incur at least a privation; and to occasion it to others, is their misfortune at our hands, however in integrity committed and in charity received. Life, also, is ever, to some extent, conditioned by adjacent life. What another life is, and *how* it is, is possible to be a large advantage or disadvantage to it; which would, under a general state of rational intelligence, unavoidably result in enactments of arbitrary dispensations from the higher, and finally the *highest*, for the lower.

While conformity to law of this character, to whatever details it might extend, might well be spontaneous, drifting independently after casual impulses, without regard to their mature and fit condition, and hence justification, would be greatly inconsistent with the requirements of such a state as would be characterized true intelligence. Companionships, then, might result not alone from a disposition to follow social tastes, but from the desire of obedience to needful regulations,—to satisfy the claims of sympathy and justice; the realization of which might often be as helpful in the progress of self as would be the exhilarating companionship of equals in attainments. Quite nearly as strong attachments as those existing between the more attained parent and the less attained child, and from similar facts of life, could exist between the more attained and the less attained, as teacher and pupil, in that future state. There is entertainment of the highest order in the scene of life unfolding from its beginnings; and to remove the obstructions would be correspondingly a work of pleasure, not only to the sense of generosity, but to intelligence; and this, together with the fact that feebleness is ever looking toward strength and rejoicing in its superiors on account of their helpfulness, would, also, suggest a bond of companionship.

The sexual element, the most prominent distinction in human life, and one of the most powerful social incentives, has been regarded as primarily an appointment to serve the need of reproduction. This superficial view discovers but a small part of its purpose. It is chiefly important as a nourishment to the two equal lives. First of all, it pertains to *mind* and all the essential *self*, and *next*, to the person. Reciprocally, the qualities of the one nature refer to a want in the other, to establish a requisite fullness and completeness of being. Hence the distinction could not be referred to temporary causes. Social life is nowhere complete in the one element of either; while the elements in proper union, ever result in a sense of social satisfaction and contentment. But from the best results arising out of the most intimate reciprocities, special claims and concessions, as to individual unions, would seem to be always required; resulting in companionships, which, in instances of greatest compatibility, would be long enduring, and for aught that now appears, might be eternal.

In respect to the continuance of companionships established in this life, ordinarily, none would be more probable than those of the family, where more of the conditions of sympathy and affection are present, and where so many of the strongest obligations have been created. Here the facts of life are so deeply and intimately interwoven in all directions, as that the several bonds might be safely supposed to be of long continuance. The facts of parent and child, of common parentage, of joined parentage, of husband and wife, and of common family vicissitudes, could be a matter of memory, interest, and preference, through vast measures of time, and in some respects, eternal time.

EDUCATION.

That wonderful element of the human mind, above

all else, craves attainment,—not alone of facts and the better use of the faculties of thought, but the greater perfection of all the elements pertaining to self. Always the most *attained*, in respect to anything, and markedly so in respect to the attributes of life, is the most pleasing and the most satisfying. Hence, the ever eager pursuit of what lies still beyond—of *being* as well as of facts and principles. Of all surroundings, too, it is desired to have them at their best. The best animals of their kind, the best plants of their kind, the best minerals of their kind, the best achievements of the arts, and not the poorest of these, are the most highly valued. And so the interest of self calls equally for the labor of improvement to be bestowed upon the fellow life; and unendingly so. That this would be bestowed advantageously, by the use of appropriate devices whereby larger results could be secured than would accrue by casual contact, could not fail to be true where devising minds are concerned. The processes could not fail to be of *management* by conventional wisdom, and of the general character of institutions. The tendency in the higher attainments of mind is, without exception, *more*, instead of *less*, toward institutional means. Institutions are one of the salient marks that distinguish between mind in barbarism and in civilization. Not only is passive substance more commonly wrought into mechanisms, but the social forces are wrought into rules, laws, governments to secure harmony, and efficiency toward the ends desired.

Nature is all the time being placed more under

the dominion of mind, while, in its turn, the mind itself becomes the profited subject of its own legislation. And under association with fellow lives, life passes into subjection to conventional legislation,—is directed by its provisions and conformed to its own institutions; itself contributing to their creation as having a certain numerical value in the aggregation out of which the ruling sentiment is derived. As a rule, by its adaptations, it is directed to one or a class of those institutions, through which, by bestowing its labors there, it contributes its principal service to the world. And this can be no more true of rational mind in one world than in another. It is, also, necessarily as true of one world as of another, that where there is less attainment, from the less desire of attainment being coupled with weaker means for achieving it, but little progress, if any, may be made without the presence of arbitrary legislations and institutions, from superiors, and operated by superiors. Hence, dispensations and commissions from the higher states, and, finally, from the highest, must always be expected to descend to the lower states.

From these considerations, it is quite plain that the labor being bestowed upon fellow lives in the next world, partakes of the essential character of institutions of learning, analogous to those great systems found in our better society here,—with teachers, and classes, and seasons of work, of which, while the modes are unforeseeable, the elements are not alone of instruction in the abstract facts of being, but, also, in the education of self into the ever greater refinement and strength of every sense and passion pertaining to it. What in this world we see achieved in the most brilliant intelligence, the most exhilarating virtues, the most exquisite tastes, and in the most ardent affections, are but little more than our weak beginnings in these, which suggests to us, in part, what are the character and the ends of the labors that await us in the world of our next existence.

WORSHIP.

To have survived the ordeal of physical dissolution, alone would be, to the average life, an overwhelming fact, tending to move the whole consciousness to its greatest depths—to deepest reflections concerning the vastness and potency of the principle that must underlie such an event. It would hardly fail to induce an earnest self-questioning as to what this comprehensiveness and goodness of design must be owing, and to what embodiment these and the power of their execution must be finally ascribed. The same reflections, to be sure, are due from intelligences capable of estimating the facts of the present existence. But it may well be judged that to find one's self still living after the process of physical death has been fully accomplished, and that life is again surrounded with provisions suitable for subsistence and for enjoyment, and that these provisions are of a superior order, would very much aid in realizing that to a Being of incomprehensible superiority of mind and affection, of whatever mode of existence, such facts must be assigned. One could not, from such a standpoint, easily see all these facts, so taken together, to be matters of chance, nor indifferently set aside claims rising to view for grateful reverence and adoration, to be bestowed in the direction indicated by these tokens of interest and love.

The thoughts, too, pertaining to the now easily discernible fact of the endless continuance of this being, and of the adapting of supplies to its needs, however extreme the attainments that were being made, could not fail to still further strengthen the conviction of a living, infinite Being's presence and care in it all; while such regularity in punctually suiting these supplies to its ever varying wants, as would be apparent of the future, might make it strongly seen that these transpirings were mainly, if not wholly, for the sake of man.

Then, again, with increased general attainment must be included the sentiment of religion. And if the change of state should be more favorable to one sentiment of life than to another, it would by nature of the case be the religious. With such increased verifications of its claims to truth, not alone, but with so much more in the facts of that existence well calculated to immediately arouse and nourish it into power, would follow the devotion of a larger part of life to its exercises, its more extensive presence in all life's practices and affairs—giving more largely shape and character to all the manifold educational and social relations of that state.

We are, of course, unable to foresee the modes and rites employed in worship there. These we must leave to be made acquainted with on our arrival among the next scenes. But we always gain assurance and enthusiasm from the consciousness that others are employed from like motives to the same end. And when the views and the objective ends of worship are essentially the same, worship by one excites worship in another, as truly as the singing string excites the neighboring string to song. To a thinker the presence of thinking companions is an important aid. The work of thought, while it may require some measure of seclusion, goes on less efficiently without the consciousness of similar employment being engaged in by neighboring minds. Hence, thinkers are attracted to thinkers,—not alone to share the results of their labors, but by near proximity with them to have better results of their own minds. Human effort in no respect rises to its best when conscious of being wholly alone. One may be delighted and benefited greatly by pondering or mentally rehearsing a song—an oratorio—but only in hearing it rendered by a multitude of singers, does his musical mind come to a full waking in respect to it.

Then, too, in the seclusion of his thought, though one may pay very great and gratifying honors to the Supreme Being, and in that communion realize a very important aid to all his superior nature, the profounder sentiments of adoration and praise await the re-enforcing influence of the worshiping multitude—the assembly of worshipers in concert.

From this it would appear necessary that as in education, worship, too, in the respect in which it is a matter of mutual interest and for its best results depends upon mutual help, becomes, in the next world, the care of arbitrary law—of social legislation, emanating mainly or wholly from the more attained, who are ever more fully directed by the Divine Wisdom itself.

With the Deity omnipresent there as here, and as completely beyond all sensuous observation, no special great local altar upon which general attention would be directed, would be called for or practicable. But in its place might be seen the one common, essential faith, hope, and communion, upon the one vast altar of the outspread celestial universe.

CHAPTER XX.

Concluding Reflections and Parting Words.

HAVING now, substantially, completed the task undertaken in this work, I here submit a few parting words on taking leave of the reader. In the results of the investigations pursued in these chapters, it is not only ascertained that the individual human life is of endless continuance, but the coming state is foreseen to possess advantages and measures of happiness not found in this world, and that, all things considered, so far as human judgment can discover, entrance upon that state is a beneficent promotion. With that greatest of apostles, all may say, "To die is gain." Greater or total immunity from impurity of passions—from sinfulness or desire for unholy and rebellious life, seems a necessary good fortune of life in that world. That is, when taken in comparison with life in *this* world, the disparity in favor of that world would be thus great. Further than that, nothing we have discovered would justify a fixed conclusion. What alloys of *that state* might be objectionable to a state or to states yet further on than the one of our common immediate inheritance, is not brought into the discussion.

And yet not all could be paradise with all souls even in that fair world. There are foreseeable conditions in which many would partake, that might average far more sorrow and pain than happiness, perhaps for the long time coming. When in drunkenness—in the darkness of life occasioned from it—one inflicts an injury on another, *getting sober* does not make him a happier man. To reflect that he did it when, in the drunken paroxysms, he was beyond the command of himself, while it *may* under some circumstances cause some mitigation of pains, may, also, under others, render them even more intense. To have proved faithless in the proper charge over himself, still further injury is to be reckoned to his account, from the pain of which getting sober does not relieve him. So, likewise, to one having lived a life of injury—of sinning against man and God, entering upon a state of greater sensitiveness in respect to right and wrong, would not be the occasion of his happiness. Atonement by reparation, would seem to be the only way to relief. Full forgiveness, even by such in that world as would be immediate sufferers from those injuries, and forgiveness by the greatest in holiness, without an ordinance reversing, in this respect, the system of nature, could not avail to quench the burning pains so long as the consequences of the wrong were matters of distress. But, also, in a world freed from malice and given to universal friendship and affectionate help, and where the evidences of final release from all wrong conditions and evil effects, however long deferred, are so unmistakable none could be allowed to be the subject of unmixed suffering, and wholly without happifying impressions.

Among the pleasing considerations, already referred to, that would create longings for that world, are the reunions we are justified in expecting with those of special friendship and interest. These may not be the highest interest in heaven to be sometime attained to there, but to the people now living below, their dear and intimately related friends are the main attractions there, so long as its other excellencies are so little understood and appreciated. Many, too, must be the glad occasions in that many mansioned Father's home—that land of many home circles—constellations of spiritual happiness—to which Jesus so soothingly referred in his last hours of earth. Friends are being given back to friends; family members are being rejoined; mothers are having their babes replaced upon their bosoms; all with the circumstances and demonstrations of wild delight, praises and thanksgivings to God, such as are unknown in all below heaven. And from this cannot be separated the special familiar intercourse and rehearsals of the past, following on in due time; as when friends of special intimacy long separated meet again. It might be forgotten for the time that it really is the holy country spoken of, and seem to be the same old earth in a new dress and under a new sky.

Again, in the generally intensified life and increased activity of functions, will be the increased efficiency of the memory, to which reference has been made in cases of hypnotism, a state somewhat partaking of the nature of death, and as is frequently reported in cases of partial drowning. We also more commonly remember the right and appropriate experiences than the inappropriate. And among the things of interest in the life to come, it is probable that by a more clear mental recurrence, we shall be able to live over again the better and more agreeable part of our history—of our childhood, our youth, with every succeeding state of our advancing age, with their many dear associations. I say the *better* part, from the fact that the imperfect is the unadapted and finally rejected part. All growths are characterized by a conservative law, by which imperfections are caused to disappear, while that which is in harmony with the being's ends, assimilates and becomes identified with the being itself. So that the first that we would forget permanently would be the things that we would *least* care to remember. Then the right things—the harmonies—of *our* past lives, and not alone ours, but those of others, might often be food for happy contemplation there, and finally without the disturbing sensations of the evil parts therewith.

CONTEMPLATIONS OF DEATH.

As to death, whatever are seen to be the facts of the future, to many people it is associated with a sense of alarm and even terror; not from regrets as to parting with friends and cherished surroundings, the ordeal on its own account is looked upon with a suspicion of something dreadful. In part it may be owing to its so strongly seeming to be the final ending of all, and, also, in part from its not having been personally experienced. From whatever cause the sense is wholly illusory. Often persons must have felt all that one feels in dying and have afterward fully recovered. If complete death of the entire organism has not been experienced by any one now living in this world, many have undergone complete death of a considerable part thereof, in which all was illustrated. Amputations, woundings, convulsions—those terrifying spectacles—are not death, but only illustrations of disordered states of *life*, from which, indeed, death may be the result. Death follows after the vital forces have failed to maintain the organism. Their withdrawing is dying, denoted by a growing insensibility, and is realized as rest. Instead of being a matter of pain, death is a retiring from pain. Whoever has relaxed from severe exertion into profound sleep may be said to have undergone all the realizations of the dying. In cases of complete paralysis where all sensuous relation is discontinued, death is essentially illustrated. There are no intelligent reasons why death itself should be a subject of dread. To many heavily burdened lives, it might well be regarded as the pilgrim, wearied and bruised by the long fatiguing day, at nightfall regards the spread couch inviting him to rest. What pertains to life this side and the other side, could be to the informed the only matters to influence the choice as to dying. The indifferent to the requirements of duty—the laden with guilt, could not wish it,—would crave to first reform and make restitution. The good, conscious of having outlived all requirements of further service to the living, might well contemplate the event as one of signal blessing.

But that these facts, taken purely on their own merits in arriving at these conclusions, may accomplish the purpose intended in these labors, attention is recalled to the fact, which the good thinker will recognize as eminently just, that understanding them as true, and steadfastly believing in them—confiding in them, may not in all cases be the same thing. The truth would *seem* to be all that one could need. But this, after all, is not enough. The confiding power must be present before the truth can have its proper influence on the sentiments of life. The writer had an intimate friend of much more than ordinary accomplishment, and of special good judgment in matters pertaining to the exact sciences, who was, time after time, having what were to him very clear evidences of spirit intercourse. For the hour, nothing could be more satisfactory than those demonstrations. And yet this realization was at each time doomed to soon vanish away, leaving doubt as overmastering as before. Now though these evidences might not have been genuine, it was not because he had discovered any flaw in them that he so soon became doubting again, but there was a lack in the confiding power. What, therefore, this man needed was not more proof, having failed to dispose of what he had, but more strength in the believing department of his being,— especially in respect to the spiritual aspect of nature.

It is true that people sometimes have this too large

or too little qualified, and believe too soon and too much —without adequate inspection. But quite as often in our day the reverse exists; and people by doubting too much are liable to fail in receiving the benefits of truths that are mentally clear and well established. This is most liable to be the case in respect to truths of unusual import. Much of the evil arises from the acquired habit of negativing too promptly. Hence, too, the remedy is, in a large part, to be found in a change of this habit. Also, conforming to the habits of life maintained by people of more robust powers of belief, is of essential aid in strengthening this important element of rational being. Following submissively the mode of thought and of life known of those greatest minds and lives recorded in human history, as already referred to, Jesus and the apostles, this believing quality of mind could hardly fail to speedily enlarge into ample fullness for a just realization of this class of facts.

The facts of music, of mathematics, or of language will be apprehended with more difficulty by natures less adapted to these principles of being; and why not so of all other elements of knowledge? Then to yearn after evidences of the departed wisely, would, in most instances, require some of the self-discipline which would render the self-nature more available for the evidence; in accordance with the laws which universally apply to the acquisition of practical knowledge in any department of being.

But it is now become a matter of sincere congratulation that by due attention to the force of the facts of science as they are commonly received in this age of the world, the ordinary deficiencies in powers for discerning facts of a spiritual character, may be overcome by supplying proof from this source; proof of a future world not only, but of life's endlessness,—of that world's better adaptation to the higher wants of man, and of his endlessly attaining in that state. To essentially the same facts of a future world to which Christian teachings have for these centuries pointed the bereaved for comfort, the science of to-day coming forward, directs the suffering heart of man for consolation. It has raised man to an eminence of knowledge concerning the principles of being, from which the chasm of mortality is seen bridged and the passage of the dear ones to the common country and home beyond, safely accomplished; in seeing which, the paining mind drinks in the sweet relief.

In reverting to the deep past, at times one gets the living mass of those ages vividly on the field of his vision, and asks where are they now? One who is in love with the literature of the past, and has become intimate with the great lives whose benefits to mankind cease not descending to the generations rising along the course of time, asks with insuppressible solicitude, What has become of those great and precious energies—those vast mental and moral substances that for a brief time animated visible forms, then utterly disappeared from view? Science has substantially discovered them, and the world of their permanent abode.

INDEX.

	PAGE.
ABERCROMBIE, DR.—Important legal decision evolved in a dream	246
AGE, OLD, Abolished	409
ALGER, REV. MR.—Doctrine of the Greeks, concerning the soul!	48
ANIMAL—Being thereof inhering in animal ether	127–131
ANIMAL—Element thereof contrasted with that of the vegetable	131
ANIMAL—Lower forms less strong and differentiated and more easily confounded with the vegetable	242
ANIMAL—Wonderful Anatomic machinery thereof	136, 137
ANIMALS—Under man, probably not immortal	272, 373
APHASIA	333, 334
ARISTOTLE	47
ATHANASIAN Creed	216
ATOMS—They touch only by their atmospheres	297
BAAL	43
BABOONS—Cited by Dr. Darwin as examples of the presence of sympathy in brutes	174
BABOONS—Depredations of, cited by Brehm	174, 175
BAIN, PROF.—Double-faced unity theory of matter	210–213
BAIRD, MR.—His hypnotic subject sings with Jenny Lind	260
BEALE, DR. LIONEL S.—On nerve circuits	230, 231
BIGOTRY—Not limited to a class	83
BLUMENBACH, DR.—Experiments on brain action	253
BOILEAU, LIEUTENANT.—Witnesses self-mesmerization in India	308, 309
BRAIN—As an instrument comparatively simple	238
BRAIN—State of during sleep	257
BRAIN—The umbilical tie of self with the external world	265
BREHM—On the moral sense in birds	170
BUTLER, BP.—Assailed by Prof. Tyndall	196–200

INDEX.

	PAGE.
CARPENTER, PROF.—Acted dreams	247
CARPENTER, PROF.—Cited by Prof. Youmans on the employment of the mineral by the vital forces.	119, 120
CARPENTER, PROF.—Note on natural selection	90
CARPENTER, PROF.—On faith in a future life	192
CARPENTER, PROF.—Views on Mesmerism	301
CATALEPSY—A peculiar case of a young lady in Newark, N.J.	241
CHRISTIANS—Apostolic and modern compared	69
CHRISTISON, SIR ROB'T.—Paralyzation of the will faculty	332
CHURCH, THE—An important want of	34
CLOQUET, M.—Surgery performed under mesmerism	306
CONSCIOUSNESS—What is meant by a state of consciousness.	195
CREATION, SPECIAL—Difficult to set aside	225

DANA, PROF.—Definition of the term "mineral"	108, 109
DARWIN, DR.—Authority on Darwinism	166
DARWIN, DR.—Theory of the human intellect having ascended from the instinct, "well developed," in lower Animals	176
DEATH—Abolished, etc.	406, 407
DEATH—How generally contemplated	431
DEATH—The conditions which may effect a choice in respect to it	432
DEMOCRITUS	207
DENDY, DR.—Experiments on brain activity	253
DISTANCE—As applied to difference in measures of psychical capacities	96, 97
DREAMS AND SOMNAMBULISMS	242-252
DREAMS—Observations on	247, 248
DREAMS—Serial, etc.	250, 251
DURATION—Means of determining it of individual existences	267-270
DURHAM, MR.—Experiments by chloroform on the brain	256
DUTY—A distinct sense	163, 164
DUTY—Its relation with the moral sense	162

EDUCATION—In the spirit world	421-424
ELEPHANT—His sagacity, etc.	149-151
ENGINE, THE STEAM—In illustration of the reciprocal relation of body and mind	205, 206
ENVIRONMENT—Of life in the spirit world, and the results	393-397
EPIDENDRUM—Its subsistance from the atmosphere, etc.	122
ERAS OF SPECIAL ATTAINMENT	42

INDEX. 439

PAGE.

ESDAILE, DR.—His experiments in mesmerism in India. 306–308
ESQUIROL, DR.—Reports cases of insanity with homicidal
    promptings 327, 328
ETHER, VEGETABLE—Possible in the spiritual state......116–119
ETHER, VEGETABLE—Universally........................... 116
EXPECTANT ATTENTION—Case of the Jansenist Girl and the
    Holy Thorn.. 356
EXPECTANT ATTENTION—Its bruise of an ankle and of
    fingers 345, 346
EXPECTANT ATTENTION—Sir Humphrey Davy's experiments
    in, with the paralytic................................. 355
EXPECTANT ATTENTION——Utilized in mental intercourse.. 300

FERRIER, DR...................................... 235
    FIGUIER, PROF................................... 235
FORCES—Their universal presence and embodiment by
    substance 100
FRITCH, DR... 235

GENERATION, SPONTANEOUS—Not admissible, etc. 111–116
    GRAY, PROF.—Judges that the vegetable and animal
    kingdoms may unite in a loop below............ 143

HAECKEL, PROF.—His protogenes, etc................ 221
    HALLUCINATIONS—Of Herr Von Baczko by the spec-
    tral negro... 374
HALLUCINATIONS OF—Mrs. D. and her sister, related by R.
    Dale Owen......................................375–377
HALLUCINATIONS OF—The crew concerning the de-
    ceased cook... 379
HALLUCINATIONS OF—The Londoners concerning the
    Chimpanzee... 379
HALLUCINATION OF—The regiment concerning the spec-
    tral dog......................................380–382
HALLCINATION OF—Robert Dale Owen, concerning "Katie
    King"..384–387
HAMILTON, PROF.—Case of speaking unknown languages
    during fever delirium.........................262, 363
HAMILTON, PROF.—Respecting dreams.................. 249
HAMMOND, DR.—Account of the French speaking epileptic 261
HAMMOND, DR.—Experiment on brain in the lower ani-
    mals..253–256
HAMMOND, DR.—Suggests an explanation................ 247

INDEX.

	PAGE.
HAPPINESS—The state and conditions of, in the spirit world	428-431
HARRISON, FREDERIC	191
HAVEN, PROF.—The somnambulic painting girl, etc.	245
HITZIG, MR.	235
HOMER	47
HUXLEY, PROF.—Respect for the sentiment of faith in a future life	191
ICHNEUMONIDÆ	278
IMMORTALITY—As taught among the ancient Egyptians, Chaldeans and Hebrews	43-45
IMMORTALITY—Comparative value of the several ancient theories	46
IMMORTALITY.—Imperfectly stated prior to Christianity	40
IMMORTALITY—Man's proper, affirmed from the organic law of his being	267
IMMORTALITY—Right view of, an important need of the age	25-38
INSPIRATION—Law of	311-316
INSPIRATION—Peoples unequally available for its conditions	315, 320-324
INSTINCT AND REASON—The distinction	146-154
INTERCOURSE—Importance of it between the two worlds not always as great as supposed	339-340
INTERCOURSE, MENTAL—Mode of, and difficulties attending	293-319
INTERCOURSE—More difficult between the two worlds	337-338
INTERCOURSE—Necessity of, between worlds greater in early times	372, 387
INTERCOURSE—Special device for procuring intercourse with the spirit world attended with danger to mind and morals	364, 365
INTERCOURSE, SPIRIT—As found in the Bible	389, 391
JACKSON, DR. HUGHLINGS—Examination of the retina of the eye during sleep, etc	256, 257
JESUS—His allusions to the future life	56, 57, 65
JESUS—His Gospel	35
JESUS—His re-appearance after death	66
KNOCK	357
KNOWLEDGE	134, 135

INDEX. 441

PAGE.

LAVALETTE—His rapid mental movement in a dream in
    prison..258, 259
LEPIDOPTERA.. 280
LIEFDE, REV. JOHN DE—Cites a mathematical triumph
    wrought in sleep 244
LIFE IN THE SPIRIT WORLD................................. 392
LIFE—Origin of individual life............................. 271
LIND, JENNY—Sings with the hypnotized singing girl...... 260
LOBSTER—Its low order permits the renewal of lost parts.. 401
LOURDES 357
LUCRETIUS—His philosophy referred to...........196–198–200
LUCRETIUS—Terrified by insane promptings to lewdness,
    commits suicide....................................... 328, 329

MAN—His continuance beyond death.................. 188
    MARTINEAU, MISS H.—Cites the case of a congenital
    idiot... 243
MAUDSLEY, DR.—Statements concerning moral insanity 329, 330
MAUDSLEY, DR.—New brain routes used by mind.......... 335
MESMERISM—Example by Dr. Noble...................... 302
MESMERISM—Orientals more available for................ 305
MESMERISM—Self, by Indian Fakirs. 308, 309
METAMPSYCHOSIS...43–47–49
MILLER, HUGH—Observations on the flora of coal period 125, 126
MIMOSA—Its sensitiveness................................ 129
MIND—And body... 193
MIND—And organism..................................... 207
MIND—Forms its conceptions independently of brain..... 239
MIND—In the processes of insanity..................324–334
MIND—Rapid movement of, in dreams.................... 258
MIND—Soul and Spirit are substances, etc................ 144
MIND—The only element seizing upon and utilizing the
    aspects of nature..................................... 134
MINERAL, THE—Organized by the vegetable............109, 110
MINERALISM 208
MINERALISTIC—School unsatisfied....................... 227
MINERALISTIC—Theories of life........................... 218
MIVART, PROF.—Cited in mimicry in nature.............. 142
MORAL ELEMENT, THE—And the brute.................165, 166
MORAL ELEMENT, THE—A separate sense................. 160
MORAL ELEMENT, THE—Defined......................164, 165
MORAL ELEMENT, THE—State of.......................... 159

	PAGE
NERVES—Mode of their device	232
NERVES—Origin of—Theory by Mr. H. Spencer	225, 226
NEUROPTERA	282
NEWTON, SIR ISAAC—As an example of realizing powers	99
NOBLE—His experiments in mesmerism	302, 303

OLD AGE ABOLISHED	409
ORIENTALS—More available for mesmeric phenomena	305
OWEN, ROB'T D.—Cites the two sisters' impression of the spectral boy	375-377
OWEN, ROB'T D.—His relation in the "Katie King" affair	384-387
OXYGEN—Its discovery and prevalence	100

PAUL, ST.—His view of the future life	53
PIANO AND OPERATOR—Illustrating the brain operated by the Self	236, 237
PINEL, DR.—Reports an instance of insanity with promptings to suicide	326
PLANT, THE—Its modification by environment	114, 116
PLANT, THE—Its possible presence in the spiritual state	122-124
PLANT, THE—Not a mineral development	111
PLANT, THE—The most favored always attains to fruit	288
PLATO—His supposed sympathies with metempsychosis	50
PRESCIENCE—Evidence of	278
PRIESTLY—His discovery of Oxygen	100
PROTOPLASM—Present in all vital forms	113
PROTOPLASM—The term not of uniform meaning	293

REALIZATION—Not generally strong concerning the spirit world, and why	361, 362
REALIZING POWERS—Importance of	72-73
REALIZING POWERS—Development of	79
REASON—In lower animals not positively disclaimed	156
RECOGNITIONS in the spirit world	411-413
REUNIONS in the spirit world	413-416
ROME—Church of	53

SCIENCE—Tendency of, to confirm immortality	82-85
SELF—Characterized by drawing forces in reciprocity with selves	299
SELF—The physical senses lodge only on its environment	295
SELF—The realization thereof does not include the physical organism	229

INDEX.

	PAGE
SENSES, THE—Delusion of	80
SENSES, THE—Require supplementing by mind	81
SENTIENCE—The reasoning form requires successive enlargement of powers	275-277
SOCRATES	52
SPECTROSCOPE, THE	298
SPENCER, HERBERT—Definition of life	218-220
SPENCER, HEBERT—He abandons, temporarily, his theory of development by environment	225
SPENCER, HERBERT—Theory of psychological units	221-222
SPIRIT WORLD, THE—Location of	92, 93, 102-107
SPIRITS, EVIL—No evidence that departed mortals are such	387, 388
STANSBURY, CAPT.—Feeding of the blind pelican by its mates	170
STIGMATIZATION—Case of Louise Lateau	349, 350
SUBSTANCE AND MATTER—The terms how used	144
SUBSTANCE, MINERAL—Its ulterior oneness	106
SUBSTANCE—Origin of special forms of	106
SUBSTANCES—They do not impinge when their properties are unlike	93, 94
SUBSTANCES—When of the same properties they are mutually impenetrable—must be separate in space	95
SUBSTANCES—Universally present and resolvable into their insensuous states	100, 102
SWINDON, PROF. VON—A mathematical achievement in sleep	245
SYMPATHY—Definition of	172
SYMPATHY—The brute claimed to possess it	173, 174
TEMPORAL AID	31, 33
TENDENCY—The law of, is evidence of destiny	289, 291
THEODICY—Its conditions	23
TUKE, DR.—An instance of expectant attention	345
TYNDALL, PROF.—Matter, essence of life	209, 210
TYNDALL, PROF.—On the value of the realizing powers	98, 99
TYNDALL, PROF.—The Belfast address	204
TYNDALL, PROF.—Unable to follow the translation of light into consciousness	88, 89
UNITS—Mr. Spencer's of physiological units	221, 223
UNITS—The theory hopelessly involved	223, 224

INDEX.

	PAGE
VROCERATA	278

WADE, SIR CLAUDE H.—He witnesses the burial of the Fakir in India..................306, 308
WINCHELL, PROF.—Destined familiarity with the spirit world...... 91
WORLD, SPIRIT—Superior conditions of................402, 403
WORSHIP—How characterized in the Spirit World.....424, 427

YOUMANS, PROF.—Tendency of science toward the spiritual...........86, 88

ALSO BY THE SAME AUTHOR.

PROPHECY AND PROPHETS;
—— OR ——
The Laws of Inspiration and their Phenomena.

PRICE, $1.00.

This small work thoroughly discusses the subject of Prescience, Prediction and Inspiration, from the standpoint of science, and is of special value in the presence of modern agnosticism and materialistic unbelief.

From the table of contents the following are a few selections:

Prophecy, a Legitimate Subject for Science.
The Argument for Prophecy.—The Preliminary Conditions Stated.
Presciencing the Phenomena of the Future.—Knowledge of Future Events.—Prophecy the Communication of the Ends Rather than the Means of Discovery.—How Communicated.
Correspondence between Extremes of Mind.—Mode of the Higher with the Lower.
Intuition and Inspiration.—Their Relation.
Some Reasons why Prophetic Events are so rarely Met with in Profane History.
Principles to be Observed in Determining Prophetic Events.
Prophecy in Profane History.
The Phenomena in Sacred History.
History a Science.—Fossil Literature.—Ontological Outlook.

www.ingramcontent.com/pod-product-compliance
Lightning Source LLC
Chambersburg PA
CBHW022144300426
44115CB00006B/345